ABNORMAL BEHAVIOR
Perspectives in Conflict

RICHARD H. PRICE
Indiana University

HOLT, RINEHART AND WINSTON, INC.
New York • Chicago • San Francisco • Atlanta • Dallas
Montreal • Toronto • London • Sydney

To Mary

PREFACE

The purpose of this book is to describe a number of different approaches to understanding abnormal behavior. I do not feel that it is possible to make a choice between these competing points of view at this early stage in the development of the field. Rather, I will argue that these approaches see essentially the same set of events from different perspectives. Thus, my purpose has been to describe and critically examine each of these perspectives rather than to produce yet another polemic arguing for the superiority of some particular view.

I have found two things particularly striking in discussions of the relative merits of different approaches to understanding abnormal behavior. First, these discussions often lack the tentativeness and dispassionate treatment one might expect from behavioral scientists. I believe this is because the commitment to a particular point of view on the nature of abnormal behavior implies or even requires a commitment on the larger question of the nature of man. This is a volatile issue on which even behavioral scientists hold strong opinions.

A second aspect is the degree to which the participants tend to talk past each other. It is common to see disagreements arising over such basic questions as what evidence is relevant or even what assumptions, if any, can be held in common. I think we can understand why advocates of different points of view are often unable to agree, even on basic assumptions, if we examine how they have come to view the problem as they have. I have argued that the views discussed have evolved as a result of a common process of thought. This process shapes our perceptions of the events to be explained and has more in common with metaphor than it does with the more conventional "model." I have introduced a special meaning for the word "perspective" to emphasize the perceptual and organizing processes operating in these conceptualizations.

Both the emotional commitment and the disagreement over fundamental assumptions are hallmarks of what Thomas Kuhn has called the "paradigm clash" in his influential book, *The Structure of Scientific Revolutions*. Paradigm clashes occur in the history of a scientific field when the prevailing view of the problem is challenged by one or more new conceptual schemes. I believe that the field of abnormal psychology is currently experiencing a scientific revolution of this kind. At this point we can only guess which of the perspectives I have discussed, if any of them, will survive the conflict and dominate in the future.

As I suggested at the outset, I have attempted to avoid producing yet another polemic in favor of one view over another, but it should be clear that I am not immune to the influences that I have just described. Writing this book has been an exciting and rewarding task. I only hope that I have been able to communicate some of that excitement to the reader.

I have discovered in the process of writing this book that I have incurred many debts. A summer faculty fellowship from Indiana University in 1969 provided me with the time for writing free from teaching duties. Discussions with my colleagues, Leon H. Levy, Alexander M. Buchwald, Kenneth Heller and, especially, Bruce Denner, have been helpful in a number of important ways. Also, a number of people have read and commented on portions of this manuscript. I especially want to thank Lynn Bennett, Richard Hanish, Dennis Bouffard, Walter Keller and Roger Blashfield for their remarks and suggestions. Theodore Sarbin and Perry London read the entire manuscript and made a number of valuable suggestions. Each of these people has exerted an influence on my thinking and I think the final product is better as a result. The faults and errors that remain are, of course, my own responsibility. Also, I want to thank JoAnn Bradley, Nora Whaley, and Janet Peckinpaugh for their patience and accuracy in typing the several drafts of the manuscript. I owe the greatest debt to my wife, Mary. Not only has she contributed her support and encouragement throughout this task but her sound editorial judgment and critical skills have given this book whatever clarity of expression it may have.

RICHARD H. PRICE

Bloomington, Indiana
October 1971

CONTENTS

PART ONE
THINKING ABOUT ABNORMAL BEHAVIOR

CHAPTER 1

INTRODUCTION

Current State of the Field

Despite the fact that the literature concerned with the problem of abnormal behavior continues to increase at an enormous rate, no generally accepted view of the problem has yet emerged.

A common eventual result of increased attention to a scientific problem is that the number of conceptual alternatives which appear useful or reasonable is reduced. However, in the field of abnormal behavior there seems instead to be a proliferation of divergent viewpoints. The study of abnormal behavior appears to be undergoing what Kuhn (1962) has described as a "paradigm clash," in which a variety of fundamentally different viewpoints are competing for ascendency. Previously unquestioned assumptions are under attack from a variety of different sources. For example, Szasz (1961) asserts that "mental illness is a myth," while Ausubel (1961) asserts that "personality disorder *is* disease."

The purpose of this book is to describe a number of different perspectives on abnormal behavior. It is probably not possible to make a choice between these competing points of view at this early stage in the development of the field. Rather, it is argued that these approaches see essentially the same set of events from different perspectives. Thus, rather than produce another polemic arguing for the superiority of some particular view, we have chosen to describe these perspectives and to attempt to illustrate how each point of view transforms the "data" of abnormal behavior when it is used to construe a set of events in the life of a single individual.

Although this may seem to be a relatively nonpartisan undertaking, it is not without its dangers. If, as Kuhn (1962) suggests, advocates of particular perspectives often respond to critical accounts of their own view by asserting that they have been misunderstood, then our undertaking may be in jeopardy even at the outset. Nevertheless, our discussion is being undertaken in the hope that an explication of these points of view will enable others concerned with the problem of abnormal behavior to make their own choices and commitments.

The proliferation of competing viewpoints is apparently not unique to the field of abnormal psychology. In fact, there is some reason to believe that this state of affairs constitutes a distinct stage in the development of most or perhaps all scientific fields of inquiry. Kuhn (1962) argues that

> . . . the early developmental stages of most sciences have been characterized by continual competition between a number of distinct views of nature, each partially derived from, and all roughly compatible with, the dictates of scientific observation and method. What differentiated these various schools was not one or another failure of method —they were all "scientific"—but what we shall come to call their incommensurable ways of seeing the world and practicing science in it (p. 4).

Kuhn's remarks anticipate some themes that will recur in our discussion. Not only is the number of competing points of view increasing in the field of abnormal behavior, but the concerns are not "theoretical" in the usual sense. Most points of contention are pretheoretical, that is, they involve fundamentally different ways of viewing abnormal behavior rather than controversies within a particular point of view.

There are a number of reasons for the development of competing viewpoints in this field. Several views have taken as their point of departure an attack on the "mental illness" concept of abnormal behavior. Still other viewpoints have gained currency as a result of the increased emphasis upon interdisciplinary approaches to problems in the social and behavioral sciences. Even current concerns about alienation and social disruption have played a role. Each of these influences has added its voice to the growing controversy and each has brought its own insights to bear on the problem.

Understanding abnormal behavior is both a social and a scientific problem. In asserting this we do not wish to imply that it is always possible to distinguish between scientific and social influences upon current views. In fact, there is much evidence to the contrary. The demands of society and the needs of the scientist interact in complex ways which help to form the bases for our views. To cite only a single example, the current demands placed upon professionals for greater attention to current social conditions (The Conference Committee, 1966) have served as an impetus for a concerted attack on perhaps the most firmly established current view of abnormal behavior, the "illness" or "disease" approach (Szasz, 1961).

While it is true that social and scientific interests are inextricably intertwined in any attempt to understand the problem of abnormal behavior, this state of affairs has led to a number of problems. What passes for theory in the study of abnormal behavior is often mixed with large doses of ideology. Whether this is a beneficial effect is arguable. In any event, theory and ideology are often mistaken for one another, and it is sometimes unclear whether the intent of a particular viewpoint is descriptive or prescriptive.

Perhaps at this stage it is presumptuous of us to assert that social, political, and ideological considerations should be separated from the presumably more detached enterprise of examining these various perspectives on their own merit as conceptual systems. We may even find that it is not possible to do so. Nevertheless, for the purposes of our discussion the focus is on the perspectives themselves as ways of viewing the phenomena of abnormal behavior. Considerably less attention will be devoted to the social, political, and ideological problems and implications of these approaches. This latter problem is worthy of extended consideration and discussion in its own right, and even a cursory examination of the current professional literature in psychology and psychiatry would reveal that a lively debate is already underway.

Plan of the Book

In Part I we ask how advocates of different perspectives on abnormal behavior have come to view the problem as they have. It is argued that various views have evolved as the result of a common process of thought. This process has more in common with the use of metaphor than it does with the more conventional term "model." A special meaning for the term *perspective* is introduced to emphasize the influential perceptual and organizing processes operating in the conceptualizations to be discussed.

Part II discusses the psychoanalytic, learning, moral, humanistic, and social perspectives. Each of these chapters is divided into two major sections; the first section describes the perspective and the second provides a critical discussion and elaboration of the perspective. Part III provides an overview of the perspectives and considers factors that may influence the future of abnormal psychology.

A generalized case history also appears in Part III. It is then rewritten from the point of view of each of the perspectives discussed in the book.

The intention is to provide an illustration of how various perspectives on abnormal behavior mold and shape the raw data of abnormal behavior to fit their particular assumptions and basic metaphors.

In order to restrict our discussion we have attempted to select viewpoints that represent a relatively univocal and coherent approach to the phenomena and events usually associated with abnormal behavior. Thus, we were interested in discussing views that attempt to account for abnormal behavior as a general class of events. As a result, a number of viewpoints have been omitted that discuss only a particular symptom or behavior pattern.

Although there now exist in the field a relatively large number of competing approaches to the problem of abnormal behavior, we have made no attempt to discuss all of them. Instead, viewpoints which appear to be currently influential or show some promise of becoming influential have been selected.

References

AUSUBEL, D. P.   Personality disorder *is* disease. *American Psychologist,* 1961, *16,* 69–74.

THE CONFERENCE COMMITTEE   (C. C. Bennett, Chm.) *Community psychology, a report of the Boston Conference on the education of psychologists for community mental health.* Boston: Boston University Press, 1966.

KUHN, T. S.   *The structure of scientific revolutions.* Chicago: University of Chicago Press, 1962.

SZASZ, T. S.   *The myth of mental illness.* New York: Hoeber Medical Division, Harper & Row, 1961.

CHAPTER **2**

HOW DO WE THINK
ABOUT ABNORMAL BEHAVIOR?
Models, Metaphors, and Perspectives

"Not Theory-Using, but Theory-Finding"

How do advocates of various perspectives actually go about arriving at a particular view of abnormal behavior? In addressing ourselves to this question we will suggest that the different views discussed in this book are reached by a similar process or way of thinking about the problem. These similarities are presumed to exist regardless of the view that ultimately emerges. Thus our first task is to present an account of the thought process of the scientist himself.

It should be clear at the outset that we are not going to discuss the process of formal theory construction. Indeed, most of the approaches are quite tentative and lacking in detail and do not yet warrant treatment at the level of formal theorizing. In fact, most writers appear to recognize how modest our beginnings actually are; generally they avoid the term "theory" in characterizing what it is they are doing, favoring instead terms such as "model" to describe their view of abnormal behavior.

As we have suggested, we are interested in the prior question of describing the process by which a view of the problem of abnormal behavior is established and how it evolves. This is a process which occurs before the basic ideas of a particular view are elaborated and formalized to the point where what is being undertaken may be legitimately called theory construction.

In order to answer the questions we have posed, we must discuss the concepts of *model*, *metaphor*, and *perspective*. Each of these concepts involves a common process. In each case, a new, puzzling, or ambiguous situation or set of events is examined in terms of a more familiar concept. This process occurs before any formalized theory of abnormal behavior is possible. As Hanson puts it, "The issue is not theory-using, but theory-finding . . ." (Hanson, 1965, p. 3). We should note, too, that the psychological effects of the use of models, metaphors, and perspectives are as important for our understanding of the state of the field as are the more formal aspects of these approaches to theory-finding; we will consider these psychological effects as well.

Models

Perhaps the most popular term for describing the conceptualization of abnormal behavior is "model." Recent symposia (L'Abate, 1968; McKeachie, 1968) chose this term to characterize various views of abnormal behavior. At least one major text in the field (Maher, 1966) has also adopted this term. The term "model" has special appeal because of its scientific-sounding character. Perhaps its association with mathematical models has also added to its prestige, despite the fact that some authors (Mandler & Kessen, 1959) have argued that mathematical models are not models at all. In any case, it is fairly clear that most views of abnormal behavior are currently being characterized as models.

We shall examine briefly what is generally meant by this term, look at some examples of models, and discuss some of the functions which models seem to serve. Finally, we shall raise the question of whether the term model is appropriate to characterize various conceptualizations of abnormal behavior.

In general, a model may be described as any conceptual analogue which is used to initiate empirical research (Lachman, 1960). The basic character of the model is that it is an *analogy*. When we are confronted with a set of events or a structure we do not understand, we may attempt to give an account of the events or structure that relies upon analogy. Thus we may conceive of the brain *as if* it were a computer, or may think of the heart *as if* it were a pump. In each case we attempt to understand the puzzling events or structures that confront us by thinking of them as if they were other events or structures with which we are more familiar. Of course, we may use analogies to help us understand events that are much more broadly conceived or problems that are less well defined than our examples of the heart or brain. For example, we may think of abnormal or deviant behavior as if it were an illness or disease. In using illness as an analogue or model, we are attempting to understand a set of events and behaviors which are puzzling to us (that is, abnormal behavior) by assuming that it is analogous to events we understand in more detail (that is, disease or illness).

Models as we have described them have several functions. First, models help us to *select* certain events as relevant to our inquiry and reject other events as irrelevant. Thus, if we are using an illness model of abnormal behavior, we will select certain behaviors and regard them as "symptoms." Other events will be regarded as irrelevant and will not be regarded as symptoms. For example, other people's reactions to symptoms will not be regarded as directly relevant. These events are usually considered beyond the scope of the illness model.

A second function of models is to supply us with a *mode of representation*. Thus, within the context of an illness model, certain behaviors or patterns of thought or belief may be regarded as "symptomatic." Similarly, certain biological states of individuals regarded as ill will be represented as "etiological" factors.

Finally, models aid us in *organizing* the events in question. They help us to specify the relations between events or aspects of the situation that have been selected and represented. For example, if we are using an illness model of abnormal behavior, factors identified as etiological will presumably stand in causal relation to symptoms.

There are a number of difficulties in the use of models. An obvious one is that models invite generalization beyond the scope originally intended (Chapanis, 1961). When this happens models tend to lose their power to explicate the events in question. The very fact that models are merely analogies suggests this. For example, as Mandler and Kessen (1959) point out,

> . . . the theory of Oedipal conflict does not include the prediction that a son will be driven to blind himself or a mother to hang, regardless of the Sophoclean solution. Nor does the generalization about ontogeny recapitulating phylogeny entail the growth of feathers in children during the birdlike stage of their development (p. 274).

Furthermore, models are always incomplete representations. As a result, they seldom encompass all the events in the new or puzzling situation that we wish to have described and represented. Finally, models may specify relations between events that hold or are accurate in the original concept but are not accurate in the new situation we wish to understand.

In spite of these difficulties we have seen that the model is regarded as the conceptual tool most appropriate to describe how we think about abnormal behavior. It is questionable whether this is the case. Models have one characteristic that most views of abnormal behavior do not exhibit: they are tentative; they have an "as if" character. Models are in the subjunctive mood, whereas most views of abnormal behavior tend to be much more prescriptive and literal (Boring, 1957). For example, one seldom says abnormal behavior *may be viewed as if* it were an illness. Instead, one says that abnormal behavior *is* mental illness. Thus, although the concept of model does share certain characteristics with the way in which various views of abnormal behavior are formulated, it is not an accurate description of how these views are first established and are then developed. Instead, we would argue that various views of abnormal behavior much more closely resemble metaphors than they do analogies.

Metaphor

As we have said, the term "model" has become popular as a way of describing how we come to make puzzling events comprehensible. Metaphor, on the other hand, has been a much less popular term for describing the same process. However, some writers have discussed the concept of metaphor and its role in the emergence of new concepts. Cassirer (1946) has discussed what he calls the "radical metaphor," and some of his views have been elaborated and extended by Turbayne (1962), Schon (1963), and Mehrabian (1968). We will discuss the role of metaphor in the emergence of new concepts and attempt to examine how metaphors help to structure the new or strange.

There appears to be substantial historical reason for the lack of popularity of the concept of metaphor in discussing the process of scientific inquiry. Traditionally the use of metaphor has beeen regarded as principally a literary device and therefore "unscientific." There is a long rationalist tradition that has regarded the metaphor as an illegitimate device for aiding our understanding of phenomena. This tradition is apparent, for example, in Aristotle's discussion of metaphors in his *Poetics*. Aristotle views the metaphor as nothing more than a rhetorical device and a mere ornament of language (McKeon, 1941). Similarly, Hobbes in the *Leviathan* sees the metaphor as an inadmissible method of seeking truth (Burtt, 1939).

There has been much conflict between this rationalist view and the opposing view, which sees the metaphor as a way to establish the validity of certain forms of knowledge independent of the method of science. The latter position is taken by Langer in her *Philosophy in a New Key* (1957).

Schon (1963) argues that the rationalist–arationalist conflict has tended to oppose these two views when in fact metaphor may operate in the formation of concepts in general, whether the concepts in question are scientific or poetic in nature. He does not believe that this opposition is constructive and makes his point in saying

> In short, the conflict between partisans of scientific and metaphoric truth, with pressure for the dominance of one or for the complete separation of the two, has kept us from recognizing and examining the role of displacement of concepts in discovery, and in the formation of concepts generally (Schon, 1963, p. 44).

When we refer to the concept of metaphor as a means of arriving at an understanding of phenomena we view metaphor as a *process of thought*. Our view is similar to that of Schon (1963) and Cassirer (1946). This process of thought involves understanding new or puzzling events in terms of more familiar concepts. In this way, the function of metaphor is quite similar to that of models. But as we shall see, the concept of metaphor goes far beyond the idea of analogy or model. It has quite different effects on how we think about the problem of formulating a view of abnormal behavior—or of any problem for that matter.

Schon (1963) describes the metaphoric process of thought as the "displacement of concepts." He says that

> New concepts come through the shift of old concepts to new situations. In this process, the old concept is not applied to the new situation, as a concept to an instance, but is taken as a symbol or a metaphor for the new situation. The new concept grows out of the making, elaboration and correction of the metaphor. There is no one point at which it emerges since the process is continuous, like the emergence of a biological species, and its freezing at any one point is always arbitrary (Schon, 1963, p. 63).

In his description of the displacement of concepts, Schon identifies four phases. He makes it clear that these are not necessarily discrete events, and may not follow each other in a fixed order. Instead these phases may be thought of as different aspects of a complex process of thought.

The first phase is *transposition*. Transposition occurs when an old concept is shifted to a new situation and symbolic relations between the old situation and the new situation are first established. This is the making of the metaphor. For example, when we first identify odd and puzzling behavior in terms of illness we are transposing an old and familiar concept, that of illness, to a new situation. Transposition is not an all-or-none process, but instead involves a gradual transfer of clusters of concepts.

The second phase is *interpretation*. Interpretation involves assigning a term from the old and more familiar cluster of concepts to a specific aspect of the new situation. We may, for example, interpret a bizarre act or verbalization as a "symptom." Interpretation is distinguishable from transposition as a single "gesture" or act. Thus, when we transpose the concept of illness to the new situation of puzzling or odd behavior, we simultaneously transpose and interpret. Transposition and interpretation, then, are actually different aspects of the same act.

Once an old concept has been transposed and interpreted, it will not necessarily produce a good "fit." Both the new situation and the old concept require adjustment. For example, all the concepts that form the cluster of ideas we associate with "illness" may not apply in the new situation. As a result, they may be dropped in the application of the illness concept. This leads us to the third phase described by Schon, *correction*. Correction is a two-way process. That is, the old concept is not simply corrected in terms of the new situation nor is the new situation corrected only in terms of the old concept. Instead, there is a process of mutual adaptation. It should be noted at this point that as the old concept is elaborated and the new situation is structured in terms of the old concept, and as each modifies the other, we become less and less aware of the fact that we are using terms in a figurative sense only.

Schon calls the final phase in the displacement of concepts *spelling out the metaphor*. This phase involves examining areas of similarity and difference in the old concept and the new situation. At this point more elaboration of the metaphor occurs and a relatively complete description of the new situation is established in its terms.

Once the four phases of transposition, interpretation, correction and spelling out the metaphor have occurred, abnormal behavior *is* illness. The metaphor, too, is itself transformed. At this point formal theorizing may begin. As we have seen, the scientist has done a great deal of thinking before he can undertake formal theorizing. In fact, much of the conceptual work is already finished before formal theory construction has begun.

From this description of the process of metaphor in scientific thought, we should be able to abstract certain functions that the metaphor serves. In describing these functions we wish to indicate not only the abstract functions of metaphor but also to show how the use of metaphor affects our thinking about the problem of abnormal behavior. This aspect of metaphor has been largely ignored; yet, as we shall see, it has a profound effect on the nature of the views we ultimately adopt.

The metaphor as a process of thought shares some of its functions with analogy. Both metaphor and analogy aid us in selecting events as relevant. Also, both metaphor and analogy provide us with a mode of representation of the events in question. Finally, both metaphor and analogy help us in organizing these events; that is, they help us to specify the relations between the events identified by the metaphor or analogy.

We may identify, however, at least three other functions that are unique to the metaphor as a process of thought. First of all, when we use metaphor the original concept we apply to the new situation *is itself transformed*. There is an interplay between the old concept and the new situation, in a process of mutual adjustment to each other. Thus, in the case of metaphor the original concept is transformed, and we may say that a "new" concept emerges. For example, when we assert that abnormal behavior *is* mental illness, the behaviors in question are viewed differently. They come to be viewed as manifestations of illness. But the concept of illness itself is transformed. We no longer think of illness as physical illness. We do not regard physical illness and mental illness as identical. This transformation of the original concept occurs as it adjusts itself to the new events to which it is applied. In the case of the analogy the original concept is not altered but remains essentially the same as it was before being applied to the new situation. For example, our concept of computer is not altered by its application in analogy to the brain. Thus we see that metaphor and analogy differ in that with the former, an interplay between the old concept and the new situation transforms the old concept and, in effect, produces a new concept which is both similar to and different from the original.

A second function unique to metaphor is that it *fixes our view of the situation* in question. Once our view of the metaphor is established, further inquiry into the meaning of the events in question tends to stop. We tend not to look for new ways of construing the events in question. Once we have established that the behavior in question is mental illness we tend not to question this construction. In contrast, the tentativeness of analogy does not fix our view of the events as rigidly. Because analogy is in the subjunctive mood, we often continue to search for yet another analogy to describe the events in question.

A third unique function of the metaphor is that it *makes the new construction seem very real to us*. Once the events in question are identified by the metaphor and the process of the displacement of concepts is underway, the new construction begins to take on a reality of its own. Once the metaphor of mental illness is established, we do not doubt its reality. Similarly, the reality of symptoms as discrete entities is not questioned once the metaphor is established.

These three characteristics of metaphors have what we will call a "perceptual" aspect. This is the psychological effect of metaphor which we mentioned earlier. Once the metaphor is established and the displacement of concepts is underway we tend to "see" the events differently. Because of the unique functions of metaphor in transforming the original concept, making the events real, and fixing our view of the events, we now *see* abnormal behavior as mental illness.

A word of explanation is in order concerning what we mean when we say "see" the events in terms of the metaphor being used. Concepts and their application to new situations have a Gestalt character. When we view a relatively ambiguous set of events, our view of those events tends to be structured in terms of the concept we apply to those events. Our experience is structured by that concept.

Hanson (1965, p. 5) brings our point home forcibly when he poses the following situation:

> Let us consider Johannes Kepler: imagine him on a hill watching the dawn. With him is Tycho Brahe. Kepler regarded the sun as fixed:

it was the earth that moved. But Tycho followed Ptolemy and Aristotle in this much at least: the earth was fixed and all other celestial bodies moved around it. Do Kepler and Tycho see the same thing in the east at dawn?

Of course the answer to Hanson's question is no. Kepler and Tycho see the dawn in terms of their own conceptions of the nature of the universe. Similarly, we would argue that advocates of differing conceptions of abnormal behavior see the same events quite differently. Their perspectives are structured by the metaphor they use to construe the events in question. We tend to notice those aspects of the new situation that are identified in the displacement of the concept and we tend not to notice those aspects that are not identified by the concept.

To clarify this idea we can use the example of an ambiguous figure. Once we look at an ambiguous figure (for example, Figure 2.1) as a vase, our experience of the ambiguous structure tends to conform with our concept. If we are told, on the other hand, that what we are looking at is a picture of two faces in profile, we may shift our experience as a result of the introduction of this new concept. It is interesting to note, however, that no matter how hard we try, we cannot experience the ambiguous figures in both ways at the same time. It is either a vase or it is two faces in profile. We cannot experience it as both simultaneously. But what has changed? Nothing physical or optical has changed. It is the *organization* of what we see that has changed. The process of metaphor has a similar effect on our construction of events. We come to "see" the

Figure 2.1

events in terms of our concept, which becomes real for us and is very resistant to change.

A recent study by Chun and Sarbin (1970) illustrates nicely how metaphors may, although they begin as tentative formulations, take on a literal thing-like quality. The study presented experimental subjects with communications in the form of brief scientific reports. Both the titles and the contents were made to be either obscure or familiar. In each of the stories there appeared a number of statements containing "as if" qualifiers. Chun and Sarbin predicted that in the cases where either the title, the content or both were obscure the subjects would reproduce the stories with a higher frequency of "metaphor to myth transformations." That is, the carefully qualified "as if" statements would be transformed to literal statements in reproduction. The findings confirmed Chun and Sarbin's predictions both for immediate and delayed reproduction of the stories.

The views of abnormal behavior presented in this book share many of the characteristics of metaphor as we have described it. Most views of abnormal behavior at their current stage of development are attempts to structure ambiguous and puzzling events in terms of a fundamental concept or metaphor.

The Concept of Perspective

There is a feature of metaphor as we have described it that is particularly striking. This is the "perceptual" effect of metaphor discussed earlier. Because adherents of differing views of abnormal behavior seem to experience the same events in radically different ways and because they tend to see the behaviors and events in question in terms of their own metaphor, we wish to emphasize the perceptual effects of metaphor. Therefore in order to characterize the way in which investigators think about the problem of abnormal behavior, it is appropriate to use the term *perspective*.

Without denying the importance of the concept of metaphor in our thinking, we wish to use the term perspective to emphasize what we see as the perceptual and organizational aspects of this process of thought. We suggest that advocates of the various approaches to be discussed have literally a different perspective on the same events. These different perspectives transform the original concept; they fix the concept and they tend to make each construction real to the individual advocating his own perspective.

There are certain reasons for beginning with a description of the process by which particular views are formulated rather than immediately embarking on a discussion of various perspectives on abnormal behavior. First, our discussion should help to characterize the stage that most thinking about abnormal behavior seems to have reached at this point. Second, our discussion should help us to arrive at some answers to two puzzling but related questions.

The first question is, why do advocates of different perspectives have such difficulty in communicating with one another? Enthusiastic supporters of various perspectives have great difficulty going beyond polemics in their discussion. It is not hard to find evidence for this difficulty in communication. Often partisans of various views will assert that a different view has "missed the point," or that their opponents are not addressing themselves to the "real" issues. A typical reaction to criticism of one's preferred position is to argue that the criticism fails to "explain" the phenomena in question. The remarks of Wiest (1967) in defending a behavioral point of view provide a case in point.

> Examination of criticisms by Breger and McGaugh, Chomsky and others reveals that many of them contain errors of fact and interpretation, or stem from a confusion of observation and inference. *Providing pseudoexplanations by mere naming* is another phenomenon frequently found in mentalistic reformulations of behavior theory (p. 214, italics added).

Or note the opening remarks offered by Szasz (1961) in his attack on the concept of mental illness. "I submit that the traditional definition of psychiatry, which is still in vogue, places it alongside such things as alchemy and astrology, and commits it to the category of pseudo science" (p. 1).

These remarks suggest that even greater controversy rather than greater understanding is being generated by such discussions. This difficulty in communication is perplexing. But if one accepts the perceptual character of metaphor which we have described, it becomes clear that different advocates quite literally *see* the same problem differently. Each advocate sees the problem in terms of the central concepts of his perspective. In constructing reality in his way, he arrives at a view that is very resistant to competing viewpoints resulting from competing perspectives.

The second question is, why is it so difficult to choose on an empirical basis between differing views? The traditional means for solving scientific disputes involves making a differential prediction from competing theories or viewpoints. The predictions may then be tested by examining relevant evidence; the data serve to resolve the issue. This mode of resolution has seldom been used in attempts to choose between competing perspectives on abnormal behavior.

By now the answer to this question should be obvious. The same set of puzzling behaviors viewed from the two different perspectives may have little or no overlap in terms of the events which are considered by each perspective to be relevant. As a result differential predictions about the same events based on two different perspectives may be very difficult to formulate. The problem is a basic one: If two perspectives do not agree about what constitutes relevant data concerning the nature of abnormal behavior, settling the controversy by empirical methods is impossible.

Goals of Presentation

In examining a variety of perspectives on abnormal behavior we have several general goals in mind. First, we wish to present the basic assumptions, definitions, and language associated with each perspective. The perspectives we will examine consist of a concept and a cluster of related, subordinate concepts. We will describe these concepts and specify their relation to each other. Second, we wish to show how each perspective "works" when we apply it to a set of events and behaviors. In this way we can illustrate how each perspective deals with the phenomena of abnormal behavior and show how the perspective transforms the events to which it is applied. Third, we wish to examine the similarities and differences that exist among the perspectives under consideration. Finally, we wish to evaluate each perspective. Our method will be essentially opportunistic. We will be sensitive to the arguments of critics of particular perspectives when they are available. When they are not, we will fall back on our own analysis, citing research in cases where it seems appropriate.

None of these goals can be accomplished in the abstract. Without some concrete range of phenomena to which we might refer in our account, our discussion would be reduced to a mere listing of abstractions. As Kuhn (1962) suggests, new theories and concepts are never presented without a reference to a set of concrete phenomena.

> Scientists, it should already be clear, never learn concepts, laws and theories in the abstract and by themselves. Instead, these intellectual tools are from the start encountered in a historically and pedagogically prior unit *that displays them with and through their applications.* A new theory is always announced together with applications to some concrete range of phenomena; *without them it would not be even a candidate for acceptance* (p. 46, italics added).

Thus it seems reasonable to conclude that we will require "raw data" in some form if we are to do justice to the perspective we wish to discuss. The raw data we use should be at the level of concrete events that are accessible to observation and be of the sort familiar to the student of abnormal behavior. In addition the data should be capable of bringing the abstractions of various perspectives to life. We do not wish to examine perspectives as sterile abstractions devoid of their human referents.

The traditional device for illustration is the case history, a document that has the advantage of being familiar to students of abnormal behavior. On the other hand, the traditional case history format has disadvantages. It cannot really be considered "raw data," since it expresses a point of view either implicitly or explicitly. Hanson (1965) suggests that all observation is "theory laden," and this is certainly true of the clinical case history regardless of any disclaimers about objectivity or claims that only "facts" are being reported. There is a second, more serious, disadvantage associated with the use of the traditional case history. It is suspect because it may have been selected as a special case. That is, the case history presented to illustrate a particular perspective may have been chosen because it happened to illustrate the principal premise of a particular point of view or approach. Such a case history may effectively illustrate the language and concepts of a particular perspective, but it may still leave us with the uneasy feeling that it has been selected to "prove a point."

The ideal case history for our purposes should allow us *to examine the same events from each of the various perspectives we wish to discuss.* We could then observe how each perspective selects and construes the events described. This approach bears a great deal of resemblance to what Kelly (1963) has described as "constructive alternativism." He says, "We take the stand that there are always some alternative constructions available to choose among in dealing with the world" (p. 15).

A device that might allow us to view the same events from each perspective is what we shall call a *generalized case history*. The generalized case history should have certain special characteristics not necessarily possessed by the traditional case history. It should make an attempt to describe events with theoretical neutrality. Second, a generalized case history should be written as much as possible in everyday descriptive language. It should also have sufficient scope to allow for the selection of events by different perspectives and will therefore include more events than any single perspective would consider relevant.

In Chapter 10 a generalized case history is presented which has been rewritten from the point of view of each of the six perspectives discussed. The reader may find it useful to examine the relevant case history after reading about each perspective.

References

BERING, E. G. When is human behavior predetermined? *Scientific Monthly*, 1957, *84*, 189–196.

BURTT, E. A. (Ed.) *The English philosophers from Bacon to Mill.* New York: Modern Library, 1939.

CASSIRER, E. *Language and myth.* New York: Dover, 1946.

CHAPANIS, A. Men, machines and models. *American Psychologist*, 1961, *16*, 113–131.

CHUN, K. & SARBIN, T. R. An empirical study of "metaphor-to-myth transformation." *Philosophical Psychology*, 1970, *4*, 16–21.

HANSON, N. R. *Patterns of discovery.* New York: Cambridge University Press, 1965.

KELLY, G. A. *A theory of personality: The psychology of personal constructs.* New York: Norton, 1963.

KUHN, T. S. *The structure of scientific revolutions.* Chicago: University of Chicago Press, 1962.

L'ABATE, L. *The role of models in clinical psychology* (Symposium). Washington, D.C.: American Psychological Association, 1968.

LACHMAN, R. The model in theory construction. *Psychological Review*, 1960, *67*, 113–129.

LANGER, S. K. *Philosophy in a new key.* Cambridge: Harvard University Press, 1957.

MAHER, B. A. *Principles of psychopathology.* New York: McGraw-Hill, 1966.

MANDLER, G. & KESSEN, W. *The language of psychology.* New York: Wiley, 1959

McKEACHIE, W. *Psychology's dissolving commitment to the medical model* (Symposium). Washington, D.C.: American Psychological Association, 1968.

McKEON, R. (Ed.) *The basic works of Aristotle.* London: Oxford University Press; New York: Random House, 1941.

MEHRABIAN, A. *An analysis of personality theories.* Englewood Cliffs, N.J.: Prentice-Hall, 1968.

SCHON, D. A. *Displacement of concepts.* London: Tavistock, 1963.

SZASZ, T. S. *The myth of mental illness.* New York: Hoeber Medical Division, Harper & Row, 1961.

TURBAYNE, C. M. *The myth of metaphor.* New Haven: Yale University Press, 1962.

WIEST, W. M. Some recent criticisms of behaviorism and learning theory with special reference to Breger and McGaugh and to Chomsky. *Psychological Bulletin*, 1967, *67*, 214–225.

PART TWO
THE PERSPECTIVES

CHAPTER 3

THE PSYCHOANALYTIC PERSPECTIVE

The Perspective

An historical approach to the presentation of perspectives would suggest that we begin with the illness perspective rather than psychoanalysis. But in recent years psychoanalysis has been the more pervasive and influential view and thus seems to be the place to begin.

There is little question that the psychoanalytic perspective developed by Sigmund Freud stands today as one of the most influential approaches to the study of abnormal behavior. The intellectual daring and breadth of Freud's theories place him in the first rank of modern thinkers along with Einstein, Darwin, and Marx. His writings, over nearly the entire first half of the twentieth century, have radically altered the way Western man views himself.

The impact of Freud's thinking is not limited to professionals or academics. His ideas and language have become part of our culture. A great many people today have at least a rudimentary idea of Freud's fundamental concepts. Terms such as "Freudian slip," "ego," and "unconscious" are commonplace in our everyday language.

In addition Freud's thinking has had an impact on art, medicine, literature, child-rearing practices, and the social sciences. His insights have been used by social critics such as Herbert Marcuse (1955, 1964) and by historians such as E. R. Dodds (1951, 1965). The influence of Freudian thinking on the social scientist has recently been discussed in an excellent review by Hall and Lindzey (1968, pp. 245–319).

Despite, or perhaps because of, the enormous impact of Freud's thinking, the psychoanalytic perspective is now coming under heavy attack.

Both critics and leading psychoanalysts acknowledge the declining importance of psychoanalysis in psychiatric thinking. For example, Dr. Thomas Szasz has been quoted (Leo, 1968) as saying, "Psychoanalysis is vanishing. It's as moribund and irrelevant as the Liberal party in England." Similarly, Dr. Judd Marmor has stated (Leo, 1968) that psychoanalysis is in danger of "receding into an unimportant side street" of psychiatry. Virulent attacks on psychoanalysis have come from a number of different quarters. An excellent example of such an attack is Andrew Salter's book, *The Case against Psychoanalysis* (1963).

Within the field of abnormal psychology Freud's thinking has had at least two effects. First, a variety of theorists have explicated and extended Freud's original thinking in their own formulations concerning abnormal behavior. Two examples of such theorists are Fenichel, whose book *The Psychoanalytic Theory of Neurosis* (1945) is generally regarded as the single most authoritative account of a psychoanalytic view of neuroses, and Norman Cameron, who after a training analysis felt compelled to revise his views of abnormal behavior in the direction of psychoanalytic thinking. The result of this "conversion" is his text, *Personality Development and Psychopathology* (1963).

The psychoanalytic perspective has also had a heuristic impact of a different kind. Several proponents of newer perspectives on abnormal behavior have used Freud's ideas as a point of departure from which to launch their own competing ideas. We shall discuss this impact of Freud's thinking on other perspectives later in this chapter. Perhaps it is a tribute to Freud's influence that advocates of competing perspectives have found it necessary to attack his views in order to clarify and lend credence to their own.

Before beginning our discussion of the psychoanalytic perspective, a number of remarks are necessary. As Holzman (1970) has pointed out, psychoanalysis is not a single perspective but really a group of perspectives, focusing on three general areas. First, there is a group of ideas concerned with the nature of thinking and perception. Second, Freud formulated a series of propositions concerned with human development. And finally, a portion of Freud's thinking was devoted to the nature of psychopathology and its treatment. Our discussion will be limited to the last of these.

It is usually considered necessary for an adequate understanding of Freud's thinking to consider his work in historical perspective, since over the nearly fifty years of his work Freud's ideas underwent constant revision and evolution. But our description of the psychoanalytic perspective, while it will attempt a synthesis of his most important ideas concerning psychopathology, will be largely an ahistorical account. A number of excellent sources that examine the historical evolution of Freud's thinking are available. See, for example, Holzman's book *Psychoanalysis and Psychopathology* (1970). As a supplement to any historical analysis of Freud's thinking an understanding of Freud the man is also helpful. For this purpose unquestionably the finest source is Ernest Jones' three-volume biography of Freud (1953, 1955, 1957).

Basic Assumptions of the Psychoanalytic Perspective

The psychoanalytic perspective is based on a number of fundamental assumptions about human behavior. Several writers, including Munroe (1955), Rapaport and Gill (1967), and Holzman (1970) have summarized these assumptions. A number of these may appear commonplace to us today, but it is important to realize that although some of these ideas were not original with Freud, he was the first to bring them together to bear on the problem of abnormal behavior.

Holzman has described these basic assumptions as "metapsychological points of view" because no science of behavior has yet encompassed them all simultaneously. He suggests that for a complete psychoanalytic understanding of any behavior all of these metapsychological views are required.

Unconscious psychological processes

The concept of unconscious psychological processes was not new with Freud. Herbert and Helmholtz, among others, had suggested the existence of psychological processes which occur without the awareness of the individual. But two sorts of data especially convinced Freud of the need for a concept like the unconscious. His observations concerning post-hypnotic phenomena and the failures of many neurotic patients to recall crucial events in their lives both convinced him that psychological processes often occurred in individuals without being available to their awareness.

Freud was aware that unconscious processes could only be inferred from observable psychological phenomena, and that the unconscious itself could never be directly observed. Furthermore, he believed that unconscious ideas were subject to distortion and unlike conscious ideas often lacked a logical relation to one another. Unlike previous writers who had invoked the concept of unconscious processes, Freud was inclined to give them a primary role as determinants of behavior. Other writers had suggested that although unconscious processes might exist, they were of secondary importance in the psychological life of the individual. Freud, on the other hand, perhaps because of his unique experiences with hypnosis and neurotic patients, was convinced that unconscious processes played a dominant role in determining behavior.

Behavior is motivated, purposive, and goal-directed

For Freud, all behavior, both neurotic and normal, was seen as motivated or caused. Freud's causal statements about behavior attempted to describe both the present purposes of the behavior and its earlier determinants. Thus, symptoms did not simply appear but served a purpose. Often the purpose of symptoms as Freud saw them was to avoid painful memories or thoughts.

The conflict of motives or drives

For Freud man was continually struggling with conflicts within himself. Freud saw these conflicts as occurring between opposing motives or drives. For example, he was particularly impressed with the fact that his patients often experienced conflicts between sexual drives and the constraints of reality. Once opposing drives were in conflict they seemed not to be openly expressed; nevertheless Freud saw the drives as remaining in force although blocked and out of awareness. Furthermore, the form that conflicts took within an individual changed as the person developed from childhood into adulthood. During development these conflicts became entirely internalized. Thus the conflicts which Freud's patients experienced were intrapsychic and existed totally within the individual.

The developmental nature of man

As Holzman (1970) puts it, for every man the "past persists into the present." Thus, a psychoanalytic understanding of any behavior or symptom requires the tracing of its history. The behavior or symptom under consideration is understandable only in terms of the behavior or previous events from which it has developed. In addition, previous solutions or compromises of an intrapsychic conflict were thought to continue from the past into the present life of the individual. Some motives, aims, or drives may be "frozen" or fixated at infantile levels of development and may persist in their relatively undifferentiated form in the adult life of the individual. Freud believed that an understanding of such fixations is only possible when one looks at human behavior from a developmental point of view.

The quantitative aspects of behavior

Freud assumed that drives or needs may differ in their intensity or quantity. The variations in the apparent intensity of suffering among his patients and the marked differences in their concern with themselves or the world around them led Freud to postulate this quantitative aspect of behavior.

For Freud this was a crucial assumption since he regarded "abnormal" behavior as only quantitatively different from normal behavior. Thus, the distinction between what we call abnormal and normal behavior was a matter of degree, not kind.

Man's behavior as an adaptation to his world

Despite the fact that the psychoanalytic perspective is to a very large degree intrapsychic, Freud did not ignore the influence of man's external environment on his behavior. Instead, he argued that the behavior of man must be understood as a response to the demands placed on the person by both the physical and the social environment. This principle has been described by Rapaport and Gill (1967) as the "adaptative point of view."

These basic principles or assumptions about human behavior lay the groundwork for the psychoanalytic perspective. They comprise Freud's most fundamental ideas about the nature of man. These themes will recur repeatedly as we examine the psychoanalytic perspective and its unique view of the character and genesis of abnormal behavior.

Language of the Psychoanalytic Perspective

The terms described below are offered only to give the reader a feeling for psychoanalytic concepts. They are explained in detail in the context in which they appear in the chapter.

Id   The reservoir of instinctual drives in the psychological structure of the individual. It is the most primitive and most inaccessible structure of the personality.

Ego   That part of the psychological structure which is usually described as the "self." It is the aspect of the personality that mediates between the needs of the id and reality.

Superego   That structure of the personality which is concerned with ethical and moral feelings and attitudes. The superego is usually identified with the "conscience."

Defense mechanism   A reaction designed to maintain the individual's feelings of adequacy and to reduce anxiety. Defense mechanisms operate at an unconscious level and tend to distort reality.

Repression   One of the fundamental defense mechanisms. Repression removes psychologically painful ideas from the individual's awareness.

Dangerous desires or intolerable memories are kept out of consciousness by this mechanism as well.

Cathexis   A cathexis is the investment of an idea or an action with special significance or affect for the person.

Unconscious   The portion of the psychological structure of the individual where repressed or forgotten memories or desires reside. These memories or desires are not directly available to consciousness but can be made available through psychoanalysis or hypnosis.

Libido   The instinctual drives of the id. The energy of the sexual drive.

Fixation   Occurs when aspects of the earlier development of the individual acquire a primary role in later development. Typically fixation is thought to represent a cathexis of earlier development and earlier ways of dealing with id–ego conflicts which persist in later behavior.

Primary process   Usually refers to modes of thinking that are primitive, illogical, and perceptually vivid. Primary process may also refer to drive energy which is mobile and can be displaced onto other objects.

Secondary process   Usually refers to thinking that is logical or rational. It is also used to refer to drive or drive energy that is bound or cathected to specific objects or ideas.

The Stages of Psychosexual Development

Consistent with his basic assumption concerning the importance of psychological development, Freud postulated a series of developmental stages usually called the psychosexual stages of development. The term "sexual" as it is used by Freud has a much broader meaning than the term usually connotes. It refers not only to the stimulation of the genital area but also of other erogenous zones. The principal erogenous zones were thought to be the mouth, the anus, and the genital organs.

Freud believed that the erogenous zones were important for the development of personality because they are the first sources of excitation with which the child must contend. In addition, actions that the child undertakes involving the erogenous zones may lead to parental censure. The child must deal with the resulting frustration and anxiety that may occur, and these initial modes of coping are of great importance in later development. Thus, the parents' concerns with the child's eating, elimination, and genital manipulation are assumed to have great impact on how the child comes to cope with problems later in life.

Freud differentiated three pregenital stages of development: the *oral stage*, the *anal stage*, and the *phallic stage*. Following the phallic stage, a period of 5 or 6 years (called the period of *latency*) occurs, when the dynamics of development are more or less stabilized. Following the latency period comes the final stage of development, the *genital stage*, during adolescence.

The oral stage

During the first year of life the predominant erogenous zone is the mouth. The child gratifies his hunger through sucking and often incorporates objects into his mouth for the pleasurable tactile stimulation it provides. Later, as the child develops teeth, biting also becomes an important function in the oral stage. As Munroe (1955) points out, the Freudian perspective argues that most modes of relating to objects are derived from the oral stage of development.

The two basic modes of oral activity, incorporation and biting, may become "prototypes" for later character traits. Thus, the child who is fixated on an incorporative mode of development may later develop an "oral incorporative" personality. For example, he may be gullible and therefore "swallow" almost anything he is told. On the other hand, if the child is fixated in the biting mode, oral aggression may become the dominant character trait. He later may become a person who indulges in argumentativeness or verbal hostility. Since the child is almost entirely dependent on his mother for protection and sustenance, the oral stage of development also may have important effects on later adult feelings of dependency.

The anal stage

In the second and third year of development the child begins to focus on the pressure upon the anal sphincter as a source of discomfort. The natural mode of relieving this discomfort is defecation. However, coincidently toilet training is initiated by the parents. This usually represents the first instance in which the child must learn to regulate an instinctual impulse; consequently one of the important conflicts between the parents and child occurs.

As toilet training proceeds, the crucial issue is the nature of the relationship between the parents and the child. If the parents are extremely strict and harsh in their methods, the child may hold back his feces and this mode of handling anal elimination becomes a prototype for later behavior. The child may develop a retentive character in later life, or on the other hand he may, because of his frustration and anger at repressive toilet training methods, develop what has been called an "anal expulsive" character organization, as an extension of having expelled his feces at inappropriate times during the anal stage. Freud also believed that if the parents praise the child for his production of feces the child will come to believe that this is an important activity and the product a valuable one. The effect of this mode of parental training in the character of the individual may become the basis for creativity or productivity.

The phallic stage

During the fourth and fifth years of the child's development, the genital organs become the principal source of satisfaction for the child. He begins to engage in masturbation and autoerotic activity. The phallic stage is the stage in which the Oedipus complex develops. In general, the Oedipus complex involves the sexual attraction to the parent of the opposite sex and anger or hostility toward the parent of the same sex. Thus, the boy wishes to possess his mother and displace his father, whereas the girl wishes to possess her father and displace her mother. For Freud the Oedipus complex was a crucial determiner of later adult attitudes toward the opposite sex and toward people in authority.

In the case of the boy, he imagines that his father is a rival who may harm him for his desire of his mother. Since the genital organs are the major focus of this period, the child associates sensations from his genital organs with his affectionate feeling for his mother. He also fears that his father will remove the offending organs. This Freud described as "castration anxiety." Because of his fear of castration, the boy comes to repress his sexual desire for his mother and to identify with his father.

For the girl, the Oedipus complex has a somewhat different sequence of development. As she discovers that a boy possesses an exterior sexual organ while she possesses none, she holds her mother responsible for her castrated condition. Furthermore, she comes to view her father as a love object because he has the valued organ she wishes to have herself. She also is envious of her father and all other males because they have something she does not. This envy Freud called "penis envy." The Oedipus complex of the girl does not undergo repression as it did for the boy. Instead, it undergoes some slight modification during this period because of the realistic constraints against sexual relations with her father.

The Oedipus complex both for the boy and the girl during the fourth and fifth years of life were seen by Freud as major landmarks in the development of the child. Furthermore, as we have suggested, the resolution of the Oedipus complex and the modes of relationship that develop from it produce a variety of important modes of adaptation that persist in the later relationships of both males and females to members of their own and the opposite sex.

The genital stage

Following the period of latency there is a final active stage of psychosexual development in the child. This usually occurs during adolescence, when the narcissistic or self-oriented concerns of the pregenital stages are replaced to a large degree by realistic object choices in the real world. During the genital stage the child is transformed from a narcissistic self-oriented infant into a socialized adult. He becomes concerned with vocational choice, socialization, and peer relationships.

It should be noted, however, that the effects of the pregenital stages of development do not entirely disappear but remain "fused" with the later effects of the genital stage. Thus the final personality organization of the individual is not a product of the genital stage alone but of the residue of each of the stages of development as they persist in the adult character of the individual.

Psychological Structure

The psychoanalytic perspective that Freud developed took on a much more explicit metaphorical character with the publication of "The Ego and the Id" (Freud, 1923, 1961, pp. 3–66). In this paper he laid the groundwork for a psychological structure of man that delineated the three major provinces of the mind. For Freud, these three provinces were the major functional units of mental life. These units were called the *id*, the *ego*, and the *superego* and became the basic building blocks on which the dynamics of behavior were based. Later we shall examine the interaction among these three structures since their interaction is fundamental to the dynamics of behavior.

The id

The id is the most primitive province of the personality structure. It contains the instincts and is the source of psychic energy in man. The function of the id is to discharge energy released in the organism either by internal or external stimulation and to keep the level of tension in the organism as low as possible. Thus the id seeks to gratify instinctual drives immediately and is said to operate according to the *pleasure principle*.

The id is the biological substratum of man's personality. It does not develop over time but remains unchanged and unaltered by external reality. For Freud the id is unorganized, "a chaos, a cauldron of seething excitement" (Freud, 1933, pp. 103–104).

The id may seek gratification and the discharge of tension directly through a motor reflex or through the *primary process*, which operates in the following way. If immediate gratification of a wish or drive is impossible, then the memory traces of the individual are activated and an image of the desired object may be produced to gratify the need for tension reduction. This is known as *wish fulfillment*. It is important to realize that the id does not distinguish between the image of the object and the object itself. It makes no distinction between objective reality and subjective reality. Thus the primary process may produce hallucinations or dreams in order to gratify id instincts or drives. For example, the hungry sleeper may dream of food. The image of the food then serves as the object for tension reduction for the id.

In order to survive in the harsh realities of man's external environment, however, the id will not suffice. Thus a second structure of mind develops from the id, and the basic function of this structure is to deal with external reality.

The ego

As the contraints of the external world impinge upon the organism, a part of the id develops and becomes more differentiated. This new structure is called the ego. The role of the ego is to pursue gratification but at the same time to take account of the demands of external reality. Thus the ego is said to operate according to the *reality principle*.

The ego acts as a mediator between id impulses and reality; however, as Freud points out (1911, 1949, pp. 13–21), it does not actually displace id impulses but acts to assure the gratification of these impulses. For example, the ego may function to delay a short term gratification only to assure a more enduring form of gratification that may occur at a later time.

The mode of operation by which this "executive function" is carried out is called the *secondary process*. Unlike the primary process of the id, the secondary process differentiates between subjective and objective reality. The secondary process relies on past experience and the evaluation of this experience to make judgments about the most appropriate means of obtaining gratification. In order to carry out this task the ego must be a highly organized and differentiated structure. It is a structure in contact with both the conscious perceptions of the external world and the incessant demands of the id. The psychological functions of action, thought, memory, and perception are all used by the ego in order to evaluate the experience and to provide realistic gratification. Freud (1940, 1949) described the functions of the ego in the following way:

> Its constructive function consists in interposing between the demand made by an instinct and the action that satisfies it, an intellective

activity which, after considering the present state of things and weighing up earlier experiences, endeavors by means of experimental actions to calculate the consequences of the proposed line of conduct. In this way the ego comes to a decision whether the attempt to obtain satisfaction is to be carried out or postponed or whether it may not be necessary for the demand of the instinct to be altogether suppressed as being dangerous (p. 110).

Thus we see that the ego functions to maintain the organism in the face of "three harsh masters," (a) the id's demands of total fulfillment of biological impulses, (b) the persistent demands of external reality, and (c) the injunctions of the superego.

The superego

Just as the ego develops out of a portion of the id, so the superego develops from a portion of the ego. As the child grows he is influenced by his parents through reward and punishment. In this way he learns his values from his parents, and as the child identifies himself with his parents, he internalizes or *introjects* these values.

Thus a portion of the ego, the superego, comes to evaluate acts according to moral standards and the child learns to judge himself using these standards. He comes to react with shame or pride when evaluating his own actions.

The superego is usually identified with the idea of *conscience*. In addition, however, a second system is associated with the superego, that of the *ego ideal*. The ego ideal is a composite of the values the child has learned. The ego ideal becomes important for the growing child as an image of the sort of person he should strive to become. Usually parents are the source of this ego ideal in children and become the person with whom the child identifies. But later, particularly in adolescence, the child may come to identify with other figures as the ego ideal.

Both the ego ideal and the conscience aspects of the superego play a crucial role in the socialization of the child. The dictates and values of society are transmitted through the parents to the child and the parents become the first representations of the society with which the child must ultimately cope.

We have noted that the three provinces of mind we have just described were offered by Freud originally as organizational principles to give order and form to the enormous complexity of human behavior. But from their initially tentative nature in his earliest writings these structures began to take on a life and a reality of their own. We noted in the chapter on models, metaphors, and perspectives that one of the functions of metaphorical constructions is to make the new construction seem very real to us. So it is with these three metaphorical structures of personality. The id, the ego, and the superego may have originally been only convenient concepts to organize the data of man's behavior, but they soon came to be viewed as real entities. Later psychoanalytic writers and Freud himself tended to reify the concepts of id, ego, and superego, and they were thus assured a permanent place in the psychoanalytic perspective.

We can see that these three structures represent potentially conflicting motives and goals for the individual. Although the ego may attempt to mediate these conflicts, situations in the life of the individual will continually arise in which conflict is inevitable. It should be somewhat clearer to the reader at this point why Freud made the existence of intrapsychic conflict one of his basic assumptions about the nature of man's psychological life. Next, we shall discuss the nature of this conflict and its relationship to anxiety.

Anxiety and Conflict

Still another important concept for the psychoanalytic perspective is that of anxiety. Anxiety plays a role not only in the understanding of abnormal behavior but also in the normal development of the personality. In one of his best-known works, *The Problem of Anxiety* (1926), Freud described anxiety as an unpleasant feeling which is associated with the excitation of the autonomic nervous system.

For Freud the birth trauma is the prototypical anxiety experience. The neonate experiences intense stimulation for the first time at birth. His first exposure to the world around him produces an "emergency reaction" in his physiological system. This mobilization of his physiological system is an adaptive reaction but anxiety is far from a pleasant experience, and the developing organism attempts to devise ways of reducing or removing anxiety.

Anxiety functions as a signal to the ego and, as we shall see, the ego may institute measures to deal with the anxiety. Thus, anxiety also serves the function of alerting the person to the presence of existing or potential internal or external threats.

Freud differentiated three types of anxiety: (a) reality or objective anxiety, (b) neurotic anxiety, and (c) moral anxiety. In all three types, the ego is threatened with being overwhelmed by internal or external forces. In addition, with each of these three types of anxiety ego mechanisms are instituted that come into conflict with external or internal forces. Reality, neurotic, and moral anxiety do not differ in quality. All three forms of anxiety are experienced as fear by the ego, but, as we shall see, they do differ in the source of threat.

Reality anxiety

Reality anxiety is an unpleasant emotional experience resulting from the perception of danger or threat from the external environment. Reality anxiety may be learned through experience. For example, we learn the realistic fears associated with touching a hot object through experience. Or, reality anxiety may be a reflex reaction such as the organism's reaction to sudden physical stimulation, loud noises, or pain.

It is the ego that experiences the threat of reality anxiety. As the organism develops and accumulates experience, the ego learns methods of coping with reality anxicty by avoiding the threatening situation or feeling.

Figure 3.1 is a diagrammatic portrayal of reality anxiety. This diagram suggests that the coping mechanisms of the ego and the forces of the external threat come into conflict. The product of that conflict is reality anxiety. It should also be noted that the ego learns to feel reality anxiety not only in the actual physical presence of danger but also in the expectation of danger or threat from the external world.

Neurotic anxiety

The ego is threatened not only by external forces but by internal forces as well. The second major type of anxiety postulated by Freud is neurotic anxiety. In the case of neurotic anxiety the ego is aroused by its perception of the possibility of being overwhelmed by the instincts of the id.

Again the basic paradigm is one of conflict. In this case the conflict exists between the incessant instinctual demands of the id for some object (object cathexis) and the attempts of the ego to counteract the object cathexis, thus protecting itself from being overwhelmed (anti-cathexis). Figure 3.2 shows the nature of the id–ego conflict and the resulting neurotic anxiety.

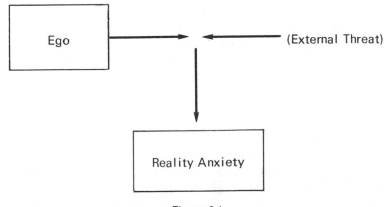

Figure 3.1

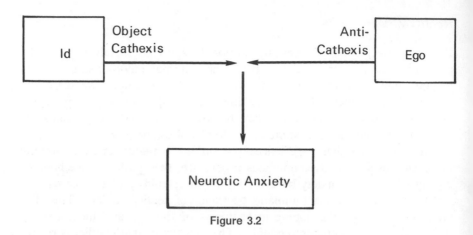

Figure 3.2

Neurotic anxiety is a danger signal to the ego that the instinctual demands of the id are striving for expression and that the ego is struggling to avoid being overwhelmed, seized, and made helpless.

Neurotic anxiety may be expressed clinically in at least three different ways. These are free-floating anxiety, phobia, and panic reaction. In the case of free-floating anxiety the person appears always to be apprehensive or fearful that something dreadful will happen to him. Often this free-floating anxiety will attach itself to almost any convenient environmental event and the person will attribute his fear to that event. As Hall (1954) says, "We might better say that he is afraid of his own id. What he is actually afraid of is that the id which is constantly exerting pressure upon the ego will seize control of the ego and reduce it to a state of helplessness" (p. 65).

The person experiencing phobic anxiety is one for whom neurotic anxiety is manifested as an intense irrational fear. The fear is irrational in that it is out of proportion to the actual physical danger presented by the feared object. For example, an individual experiencing phobic anxiety may experience it as an intense terror of high places, crowds, or snakes. The object of the fear in phobic anxiety is thought to be a symbolic representation of a temptation to instinctual gratification. Thus, behind the phobic fear there is actually a primitive wish of the id for the object or something which the object may represent. An example of a phobic fear is the following offered by Hall (1954):

A young woman was deathly afraid of touching anything made of rubber. She did not know why she had this fear; she only knew that she had had it as long as she could remember. Analysis brought out the following facts. When she was a little girl, her father had brought home two balloons, one for her and one for her younger sister. In a fit of temper, she broke her sister's balloon, for which she was severely punished by her father. Moreover, she had to give her sister her balloon. Upon further analysis, it was learned that she had been very jealous of her younger sister, so much so that she had secretly wished that her sister might die and leave her the sole object of her father's devotion. The breaking of her sister's balloon signified a destructive act against her sister. The ensuing punishment and her own guilt feeling became associated with the rubber balloon. Whenever she came into contact with rubber, the old fear of the wish to destroy her sister made her shrink away (pp. 65–66).

Yet another example of phobic anxiety is the famous case of "Little Hans."

The most famous case of zoophobia is also the first one ever to be studied dynamically, the case of Little Hans. This boy of five years refused to go out into the street because he was afraid of horses, actually feared being bitten by them. In the course of therapy it turned out that the horses symbolized the hated and feared aspect of his father. The little patient harbored hostile aggression against his only male rival for his mother's love, but at the same time he also loved his father dearly.

Reduced to its simplest terms the phobic solution was about as follows. The love this boy bore his mother was repressed, it disappeared. The love for his father was retained, while the hatred for him was displaced on the horses. This had the added advantage that the horse could easily be avoided, whereas his father could not. In the usual role reversal of fantasies and dreams, the boy expected primitive retaliation from his father for the primitive hostility he himself felt. This expectation likewise was displaced. It became the regressive oral fear that horses would bite him.

The whole displacement in the case of Little Hans was made easy by certain other partial identities. (a) The father had often played "horsie" with Hans; (b) the horses' bridles reminded Hans fearfully of his father's dark moustache; (c) therapy also brought out his wishes that his father might fall and hurt himself, as the boy had seen horses fall, and as his playmate with whom he also played "horsie" had fallen and hurt himself. As a result of therapy this patient recovered from his phobia. It is interesting that, years later when Hans chanced upon the account of his illness and its treatment, all memory of the once vivid phobia had been completely repressed. Some of the incidental comments about his parents made him wonder if he could have been this famous little patient, and led him to visit Freud where he found out that he was (Cameron, 1963, pp. 294–295).

A third form which neurotic anxiety may take is that of panic reaction. The panic reaction is characterized by the sudden appearance of intense, debilitating fear with no apparent reason. Usually the individual experiencing a panic reaction is at a loss to explain it. Panic reactions may also be associated with sudden, impulsive antisocial behavior. In this case the panic reaction is a reaction to the discharge or breaking through of id impulses. The behavior is an attempt to rid the person of painful anxiety by doing that which the id demands.

Despite the fact that id–ego conflicts often result in "neurotic" anxiety we should realize that normal individuals also experience neurotic anxiety. Neurotic anxieties are not the sole possession of the clinically diagnosed neurotic individual. Here Freud's quantitative principle is again being invoked. The difference between the "neurotic" and normal individual is the degree to which the person's life is controlled by the anxiety.

Finally, in the case of neurotic anxiety we should recognize that the conflict is genuinely *intrapsychic*. That is, the conflict exists between two of the major provinces of the personality. Intrapsychic conflicts are difficult for the individual to identify or cope with since they exist within the person. Because neurotic anxieties are exclusively intrapsychic, they are always with us and cannot be handled by mere escape or avoidance as is the case with many types of reality anxiety.

Moral anxiety

The third major form of anxiety which Freud differentiated was moral anxiety. Moral anxiety is the result of a conflict between id impulses and the superego or conscience. The individual experiencing moral anxiety often will feel intense shame or guilt. The diagrammatic paradigm for moral anxiety is shown in Figure 3.3. We can see that when an instinctual

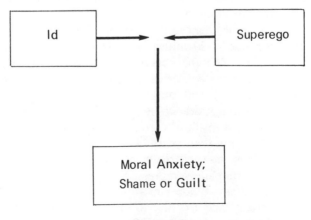

Figure 3.3

object choice of the id seeks expression in the form of an act or even in the form of the thought of an act, the superego or conscience is threatened. Thus the superego, the internalized agent of parental authority, will block the id impulse. Although the id impulse is blocked, the conflict remains in force; the product of that conflict is moral anxiety, often, as we have said, in the form of shame or guilt. For example, the id may express an instinctual sexual impulse or object cathexis toward some sexually attractive person. The superego, however, may react to this impulse as wrong or immoral, producing an anti-cathexis.

Our brief review of the three types of anxiety Freud described should make it clear that anxiety is a result of the conflict between the various provinces of the personality. Conflict inevitably results in anxiety experienced by the ego. Anxiety is a danger signal indicating to the ego either that it is being threatened by some event in the external world or that the id is seeking expression and is being blocked by either an ego or superego anti-cathexis.

Our discussion of the various forms of anxiety should leave us with some appreciation of how the various provinces of the personality interact with one another dynamically. As we proceed through our discussion of defenses and their relation to conflict and anxiety, the fundamental structural metaphor of the psychoanalytic perspective and its dynamics will become clearer.

The Defense Mechanisms

How does the ego cope with the problem of painful anxiety? Freud suggested that the ego may engage either in realistic problem-solving (as is often the case in dealing with reality anxiety), or it may resort to irrational methods which distort or deny reality. These irrational methods of dealing with anxiety were grouped under the general classification of defense mechanisms.

Freud, earlier in his thinking (1894, 1962, pp. 43–61), used the term "defense" purely to refer to attempts by the person to protect himself from dangerous instinctual demands through repression. However, as his thinking progressed and as his clinical experience became more extensive, Freud decided to use the concept of defense in a much more general way. Thus in 1926 in his monograph, *The Problem of Anxiety*, he wrote:

> I now think that it confers a distinct advantage to readopt the old
> concept of defense if in doing so it is laid down that this shall be
> the general designation for all techniques of which the ego makes use

in the conflict which could potentially lead to neurosis, while repression is the term reserved for one particular method of defense, one which because of the direction that our investigations took was the first with which we became acquainted (Freud, 1936, p. 144).

We will not attempt to describe the defense mechanisms in detail, nor will we provide an extensive list. Our description will serve only the purpose of providing the reader with the general idea of the nature of defense mechanisms. In the course of our discussion certain things will become apparent, namely, that defense mechanisms are operations of the ego, and that the defense mechanisms will exhibit two features in common: (a) the denial or distortion of reality, and (b) operation at an unconscious level.

Repression

Repression is the mechanism by which dangerous instinctual impulses derived from the id and in conflict with the ego or superego are dismissed from consciousness. These instinctual choices, when they are kept from consciousness, are unable to evoke anxiety. Repression may operate in a number of different ways. It may distort what we see or hear, thus protecting the ego from the perception of objects it may regard as dangerous, or it may operate on the memory. Memories that have been associated with traumatic experiences or which remind us of threatening events may be repressed and simply made unavailable to awareness. In either case, the purpose of repression is to deal with moral, neurotic, or reality anxiety by removing from consciousness the internal or external threat to the ego.

As an example, recall that in the case of "Little Hans" the memory of his once vivid phobia of horses had been completely repressed. Only a chance remark about his parents in the case history led him to discover that he was the subject of one of Freud's most famous cases.

Although repression is actually accomplished by the ego in order to remove threatening id impulses from our awareness, it may be initiated by the superego. Thus a wish that appears wrong to the superego and is derived from the id may be repressed (removed from consciousness) by the ego, yet the initiator of the repression is the superego.

Many psychoanalytic thinkers believe that a number of psychosomatic disturbances, such as ulcers, asthma, and arthritis stem from repression. Although the anxiety-provoking id impulse may be kept out of awareness, it will express itself through some physiological system such as the musculature, the pulmonary system, or the digestive system. Furthermore, repressed ideas or impulses, although they remain out of awareness, may continue to develop in the unconscious.

Reaction formation

In some cases the ego will deal with an instinctual demand by the expression of its opposite. Thus feelings of hate and anger may be transformed into exaggerated expressions of love. Similarly, intense sexual impulses may be transformed into extreme feelings of disgust at the thought of sexual contact. The mechanism by which an instinctual impulse is hidden from awareness by its opposite is usually called reaction formation. One of the cardinal characteristics of reaction formation is its exaggeration. That is, we can usually distinguish between a real impulse and a reaction formation in that the reaction formation is considerably more extreme than we might expect. The individual "protests too much" and the id impulse is kept out of awareness by the strong development of an impulse in the opposite direction. However, in many cases the direct expression of the id impulse and the reaction formation may exist side by side in the personality of an individual. For example, he may appear to love and hate the same object or he may appear to desire sexual contact and at the same time be repulsed by it.

A fairly typical example of reaction formation is given by Cameron (1963). The subject here was deeply resentful of the attentions of her parents for her younger brother.

> After Billy was born everything got worse. He was clearly the favorite of her father no less than of her mother. All through the rest of her childhood she felt herself compared unfavorably with him. At first she used to say to her father, "Put him down! Take your own baby!" She remembered brooding over this preference for her brother, feeling terribly jealous of him and resentful toward her parents.
>
> In time, however, Sally gave up expressing hatred toward Billy. She adopted instead a protective attitude toward him of tender loving care. This change was a product of *reaction formation*. The hate was still there not far from the surface; for whenever Billy teased her, she responded with violent temper outbursts (Cameron, p. 389).

Projection

Another mechanism by which id impulses may be denied is to attribute them to some object or person in the external world. Thus, the individual who experiences sexual impulses toward another but who cannot tolerate this feeling will project the impulses onto the other person. Instead of saying "I love him," he may say, "he loves me." When the ego resorts to projection, it is as if neurotic anxiety is transformed into "objective" anxiety. That is, it places the object of threat in the external world. This is not surprising if we understand that developmentally the individual has learned that it is much easier to cope with threats in the external world than it is to cope with threats from the id. Moreover, projection may do a good deal more than simply remove anxiety. It provides the individual with an opportunity to express his real feelings, but now his feelings are projected onto an external object. For example, the individual who hates another may say "he hates me" (the projected impulse) and therefore "I hate him." The original impulse is allowed expression by its external provocation.

An example of the development of projective defense is offered by Shapiro (1965).

A very intelligent thirty-three-year-old college professor, stiff and self-conscious but also quite ambitious and sometimes rather arrogant, had always been sensitive to any rebuff or slight to his dignity, to being "forced" or ordered to do anything arbitrarily, or otherwise treated, as it seemed to him, like a "kid." In this instance, he had recently taken a new job with a different institution and had become interested, although ashamed to admit it, in impressing an important senior professor, obviously with the hope of becoming a protegé of his and probably also with the idea of ultimately outstripping him. At any rate, he was initially quite impressed with this man, and, consequently, he was quite nervous in his presence and concerned with what the older man might think of him. Sometimes, he was concerned that he might be thought "weak" while, at other times, too self-aggrandizing. He watched for signs of both reactions.

So far, this intensification of defensive tension, including the intensified sense of vulnerability and defensive concern, may still be regarded as preprojective. However, it soon became clear that this defensive tension and intensified sense of vulnerability was gradually giving rise to an intensification of rigidity and an increasingly antagonistic defensive stiffening. Thus, he not only watched for signs of rebuff or disapproval, but also increasingly anticipated them and, accordingly, braced himself with each hesitant overture. He remembered now that he despised fawning yes-men, and, therefore, he now approached the older man only in a determinedly dignified and equalitarian way.

In the course of some weeks, apparently marked mostly by indifference on the side of the older man, this defensive stiffening progressed further. He watched the older man closely now, no longer with concern, but with suspicion. He angrily seized on some quite ambiguous evidence of disparaging slights and arbitrary commanding attitudes on the senior man's part. He would not "take it," and he frequently became not merely equalitarian, but defensively arrogant in the relationship. Thus, he refused "menial" department assignments. Once angry and suspicious, he began to watch the colleague, in the way such people do, like a small boy playing cops and robbers around an unconcerned father, only with more intensity and seriousness, interpreting each movement according to the game—now he is pretending not to notice me, now he is getting ready to shoot, and so on. From this angry, suspicious, and, by now, defensively quite haughty view, he discovered clues that showed him that he had been right; the older man resented his independence, wanted only a mediocre yes-man in the department, and was trying to reduce him to that status. He declared that the situation between them had come to a "contest of wills" (pp. 90–91).

Denial

Denial is a relatively primitive defense mechanism, often observed in children. Typically denial is used when the conflict is between an id impulse and some reality frustration in the external world. When circumstances of reality frustrate an impulse, denial acts in such a way as to deny the existence of the realistic situation that confronts the person.

Denial should not be confused with repression. In the case of repression, the conflict is between id impulses and either the ego or the superego, but in the case of denial, the conflict is between id impulses and realistic circumstances in the external world.

Regression

Once an individual has reached a certain stage of development, if he is threatened by id impulses, he may retreat to an earlier stage of development in his behavior. This retreat is called regression. Regression allows the expression of id impulses in a way that would not be possible at higher levels of development and is yet another way of dealing with the instinctual impulses of the id.

Kisker (1964) offers the following clinical example of regression.

Ora J. is a 17-year-old high school girl who was admitted to the psychiatric hospital as a result of an episode in which she seemed suddenly to regress to her early childhood. She sat on the floor and played with her younger sister's dolls, and appeared not to recognize any of her other brothers and sisters. The difficulty began approximately eight weeks earlier when the patient received her report card at school. Her grades were not high enough for her to obtain a college scholarship, and she became extremely upset. She withdrew from her family and friends, did not want to go to school, and spent most of her time sleeping (p. 293).

Psychoanalysts interpret a wide variety of different behaviors as regressive, particularly when they appear in adults. Hall (1954) includes among them the tendency to talk baby talk, destroy property, masturbate, have temper tantrums, dress like a child, fight, and even the tendency to take naps.

When Is Behavior Abnormal?

Our discussion of the stages of psychosexual development, anxiety, conflict, and defense gives us a reasonably clear idea of the psychoanalytic view of the genesis of abnormal behavior, but it does not answer the question of when behavior is considered abnormal. When does a defense become "pathological"? Freud readily acknowledged that anxiety and defenses are a part of every person's psychological life and, indeed, in *The Psychopathology of Everyday Life* (1901, 1960) he suggests and illustrates this explicitly.

But when does a defense become a symptom? When does a particular behavior become neurotic? Does the presence of conflict or defense or anxiety indicate that a person is abnormal? Freud's answer is derived from the quantitative metapsychological point of view we discussed earlier. Munroe describes his position:

> Freud repeatedly emphasized the idea that the trends and conflicts he discovered were not the specific "cause" of neurosis. Neurosis results from the *quantitative distribution of energies*, not from the mere existence of conflict. . . . Pathology develops as one or another aspect of the problem becomes quantitatively unmanageable by the techniques that the personality has established (p. 281).

Behavior is pathological when it becomes unmanageable and interferes with the day-to-day functioning of the individual. The implication is clear that the criterion for deciding when a given behavior is or is not abnormal is fundamentally quantitative.

In making this point, we should not overlook a related idea concerning the function of pathology which qualifies the quantitative view. Freud also held that symptoms may function as *adaptive* mechanisms, that is, represent ways of dealing with conflict and the resulting anxiety. Thus, although a symptom may be adaptive in that it "copes" with underlying conflict, it may also—if the quantitative distribution of energies is intense enough—interfere with the daily functioning of the individual and be abnormal or pathological.

Thus, from the psychoanalytic perspective, a defense is seen as "adaptive" when it deals with psychic energies and conflicts. It is considered abnormal only when it comes to interfere with the daily life of the individual.

Summary

The psychoanalytic perspective makes a number of assumptions about the nature of man and his behavior. It posits the existence of unconscious psychological processes, the idea that behavior is motivated, that drives or motives may conflict with each other, that man's behavior is a result of development, that the perspective has a quantitative aspect, and that man is an adapting organism.

From the psychoanalytic point of view, all men go through a series of dynamically differentiated stages of psychosexual development: the anal, the oral, the phallic, and the genital stages. Each of these stages represents a different period of interaction between the child and the socializing forces that impinge upon him, principally his parents, and each stage leaves its residue in the final adult character of the individual.

Freud described the adult personality as consisting of three basic structures: the id, which is the reservoir of instinctual impulses; the ego, which deals with external reality; and the superego, which is the conscience of the individual. The motives associated with each of these psychological structures inevitably come into conflict, and one product of this conflict is anxiety. In order to deal with the anxiety, defense mechanisms arise that operate at an unconscious level and deny or distort reality. Everyone uses defense mechanisms to deal with anxiety at one time or another; by themselves, the existence of defenses do not constitute the crucial criterion of abnormal behavior. Instead, behavior is considered abnormal from a psychoanalytic point of view only when it begins to interfere in an individual's effective functioning.

Commentary

Is Psychoanalysis a Scientific Theory?

One of the most frequent charges made against psychoanalysis is that it is a vague, speculative, and loosely formulated set of ideas rather than a scientific theory (Lehrman, 1960). Despite the frequency with which these charges are made, critics seldom describe explicit criteria against which the scientific merit of psychoanalysis can be assessed. One author, however, has offered such criteria. Nagel (1959) describes three basic requirements he believes any theory must satisfy if it is to be capable of empirical validation.

First, it must be possible to identify explicit consequences that will arise from the assumptions made by the theory. This is necessary in order to judge the meaning of any empirical data for the assumption we are examining. Nagel argues that unless a theory meets this basic requirement it has no definite content and the validity of the assumption can only be decided by "privileged authority or arbitrary caprice" (p. 40).

Nagel offers an example of the inability of psychoanalytic theory to meet this requirement. In doing so he examines several of Freud's theoretical assumptions as they are described by Hartmann (1959):

> Dr. Hartmann has stated for us the four classes of assumptions that constitute metapsychology; and among the energic principles he mentions the following two: "the drives (in particular 'sexuality' and 'aggression') are the main sources of energy in the mental apparatus"; and, secondly, "the regulation of energies in the mental apparatus follows the pleasure principle ('the tendency to immediate discharge'), the reality principle (i.e., 'considerations of reality') derived from it under the influence of ego-development, and a tendency to keep the level of excitation constant, or at a minimum." Now is it really possible to deduce from these assumptions, even when they are conjoined with the remaining ones, any determinate conclusions in the familiar sense of "deduce"? For example, can one conclude anything even as to the general conditions under which the sexual drive will discharge its "energy," rather than (to use Freud's own locution) combine with the aggressive drive to form a "compromise" or have its "level of excitation" raised because of "considerations of reality"? (pp. 40–41).

Second, Nagel suggests that even if many or most theoretical assumptions are not explicitly defined by empirical procedures, at least some of them must be given definite and unambiguous specifications in terms of some rules of procedure. Often these rules of procedure are called "coordinating definitions" or "operational definitions." Nagel finds the attempts by psychoanalysts to provide operational definitions for their concepts to be wanting as well. For example, he notes that the operational referents of id, ego, and superego are extremely vague, as are the attempts to specify the interrelations between them.

Nagel offers a third requirement which theories must meet in order to qualify as scientific. This third requirement is related to the second. It is that a theory must not only be capable of confirmation, but also must be capable of being disconfirmed. Thus a theory cannot be formulated in such a way as to be able to be manipulated in order to fit the evidence at hand, no matter what that evidence might be.

Sidney Hook (1959) regards the criterion of disconfirmability as extremely important in deciding whether a theory is "scientific" or not. Hook describes a question he posed to a group of psychoanalysts and that he feels speaks to the question of disconfirmability for Freudian theory.

> It was in order to pinpoint the discussion on the possibility of falsifying one of the central doctrines of psychoanalysis that I asked psychoanalysts present to describe what kind of evidence they were prepared to accept which would lead them to declare in any specific case that a child did not have an Oedipus complex. . . .
>
> In asking this question I was *not* assuming that an Oedipus complex can be seen or touched or directly observed any more than intelligence can be seen or touched or directly observed. I was not even assuming that it was an observable. All I was asking for was the evidence on the basis of which one could legitimately deny its presence. This is not a tricky question but one often asked to specify the meaning of terms, the statements that contain them, and the conditions under which the statements are warranted. For example, we hear that someone is "intelligent" or "friendly." Many types of behavior can be cited as evidence for the presence of "intelligence" or "friendliness." But unless we are also told what we would have to observe to conclude that an individual is not intelligent or friendly, the terms could be applied to anyone in all situations (pp. 214–215).

It was not surprising that Hook could not find any psychoanalysts who were able to provide him with adequate evidence which would lead them to conclude that the Oedipus complex did not exist in a particular case. In fact, there is little question that the psychoanalytic perspective has great difficulty in meeting this requirement described by Nagel and Hook for status as a scientific theory.

The requirements we have described are widely accepted ways of judging the qualifications of a particular set of ideas for status as a scientific theory. They are not idiosyncratic or unduly rigid, but we may ask whether psychoanalysis or any of the other perspectives we discuss in this book could qualify as a scientific theory using such criteria. The answer is that it is unlikely.

Perspectives are by their very nature metaphors which are prescientific and pretheoretical in nature. That is, they represent fundamental reorganizations of data based on a set of often vaguely defined concepts. Perspectives are conceptual tools that scientists may use when they begin to examine phenomena and before they engage in the painstaking task of making their definitions explicit, attempting predictions based on their assumptions, and specifying the rules of evidence and the data on which their theory may be tested.

The Use of Clinical Evidence in Validating Psychoanalytic Principles

The psychoanalytic interview and the clinical data derived from it have been used as both a source of psychoanalytic hypotheses and a source of data for the validation of those hypotheses. As we might anticipate from the preceding discussion, a number of difficulties arise when one uses clinical evidence from the psychoanalytic interview as a means of validating the assumptions of the psychoanalytic perspective. We shall examine some of Nagel's (1959) criticisms of the use of evidence drawn from clinical interviews.

In the psychoanalytic interview the analyst seeks to discover the cause of the patient's present condition. Generally speaking, he assumes that the patient's difficulties are a result of internal conflicts which have in turn been produced by repressed wishes. The principal technique the analyst uses is to interpret the free associations of the patient. The question is, what are the difficulties inherent in the psychoanalytic interview which render questionable the evidence he takes as appropriate to validate his hypotheses?

The problem of standardized and public observation

In the psychoanalytic interview the analyst is presumably a passive observer of the "free" associations of the patient. How free these associations actually are, of course, is questionable. It is certainly likely that associative material produced by the patient is often directed and influenced in subtle ways by the therapist.

Furthermore, no matter how objective the therapist tries to be, the material of the analytic interview is private. Thus the analyst is the sole reporter of the nature of his interventions or the lack of them as they occur in the consulting room. The validation of hypotheses and the pursuit of objectivity can only be achieved through independent examination of publicly accessible information by independent observers. Unfortunately, this is seldom the case in the presentation of clinical evidence. Regardless of how much the analyst strives for standardized and objective observations, we cannot know anything about the usefulness of the evidence he presents from clinical interviews unless this evidence is available to public scrutiny.

Is coherence enough?

Psychoanalysts often argue that an interpretation is likely to be valid if it is consistent with all the other material disclosed by the patient. Thus the coherence of the psychoanalyst's interpretation becomes the criterion for the acceptance of its validity. We may ask, is the interpretation coherent with all information or only with selected portions of it? If, as is likely, it is coherent or consistent only with selected portions of the material, we must ask how these portions have been selected. Unfortunately, such information is seldom available.

In addition, it is possible that alternative interpretation of a very different kind might be offered on the basis of other selections of the material which are equally "coherent." This problem calls into question the usefulness of coherence as a criterion for validating analytic propositions in the clinical interview.

The assertion that "predictable" reactions are elicited
by valid interpretations

Another argument often offered by psychoanalysts is that the analyst may choose between alternative interpretations on the basis of whether the patient states that the interpretation has given him "insight" into his difficulties. Often the analyst attributes insight to the patient when the interpretation elicits the sudden recollection of past experiences that the patient previously could not remember. But why should the patient's assertion that he now "understands" the nature of his difficulties be taken as competent evidence that the interpretation the analyst offered is correct?

Another "predictable" reaction which analysts often take as evidence for the validity of their interpretation is symptom change. When an interpretation is followed by a symptom change, the analyst may attribute the change in the patient's behavior to the interpretation. This is acceptable only if it can be shown that the interpretation and only the interpretation —rather than some other aspect of the interview situation or the patient's life—produced the change in the symptom picture. Naturally this is virtually impossible in the relatively uncontrolled circumstances of the clinical interview. Thus, use of the criterion of symptom change as an index of interpretative validity may be questioned.

The laws of developmental psychology as a source
of valid interpretations

The psychoanalyst may argue that different neurotic syndromes are the result of different types of childhood experiences. As we pointed out in our discussion of the psychosexual stages of development, the regularities that are observed in the current patterns of the patient's neurotic behavior may elicit interpretations concerning previous childhood events in his life.

But, we may ask, are these relationships between particular symptom patterns and the patient's *allegations* of childhood experiences, or between the symptom patterns and his actual experience? Of course, it is virtually impossible to collect evidence on this point. The systematic biases and distortions in the patient's reports of his past experiences are now almost universally recognized as important sources of error in the use of retrospective information. Besides, we may still ask, because some event (real or imagined) occurred in childhood, must it necessarily lead to the production of a particular symptom pattern? How do we know that there are not large numbers of people with similar childhood experiences who have never developed the predicted symptom patterns?

Nagel clarifies this point when he says:

> Thus, the fact that many men who have certain kinds of traumatic experiences in childhood develop into neurotic adults does not establish a causal relation between the two, if there is about the same proportion of men who undergo similar childhood experiences but develop into reasonably normal adults. In short, data must be analyzed so as to make possible comparisons on the basis of some *control* group, if they are to constitute cogent evidence for a causal inference. The introduction of such controls is the *minimum* requirement for reliable interpretation and use of empirical data (p. 53).

The lack of standardized and public observation procedures, the questionable use of the coherence criterion, the capricious use of interpretation, and the uncritical acceptance of postulated relationships between developmental experiences and current behavior all pose problems for the use of clinical evidence for the validation of psychoanalytic hypotheses. Thus we may conclude that psychoanalytic interpretation of therapeutic events clearly is not the appropriate source of evidence for the validation of psychoanalytic hypotheses. However, as Levy (1963) points out, this does not mean that interpretation itself is an illegitimate enterprise, or that interpretation does not have predictable effects upon the patient–therapist relationship and the subsequent behavior of the patient. In an original and thorough examination of the process of psychological interpretation, Levy (1963) has described some of these effects and has offered a theory of interpretation in psychotherapy.

Research Derived from the Psychoanalytic Perspective

The tone of the preceding sections might suggest that few attempts have been made to provide empirical evidence for psychoanalytic propositions.

Just the opposite is true; one indication of the impact of psychoanalysis has been the large volume of research it has stimulated. For example, the work of Sears, Maccoby, and Levin (1957) on patterns of child rearing, Sarnoff and Corwin (1959) on castration anxiety, and Blum and Miller (1952) on the oral character were all stimulated to a large degree by psychoanalytic thinking. A recent brief review of experimental work on psychoanalytic propositions has been offered by Hilgard (1968, pp. 37–45).

We will examine here two different lines of research that use very different methods. The first, on perceptual defense, uses controlled laboratory techniques and has today nearly run its course. It does, however, provide us with an example of how a psychoanalytic hypothesis was translated into operational terms and tested. The second line of research concerns the genesis of symptoms in the psychiatric interview setting. Unlike the research on perceptual defense, this line of research is relatively recent and represents a new departure in the testing of psychoanalytic propositions. Although a review of both these research programs is instructive, it is not intended to provide a comprehensive discussion of research in this area.

Perceptual defense

We have noted that defense mechanisms such as repression or denial are hypothesized to involve the perceptual distortion of threatening material. Thus it is not surprising that researchers have attempted to study the effects of potentially ego-threatening material on perceptual processes. We will briefly examine some of this research since it provides an excellent example of experimental attempts to test psychoanalytic hypotheses and since it represents a line of research which, although now relatively inactive, was at one point the subject of considerable controversy in the field.

An example of early work in this area is a study conducted by McGinnies (1949). He studied the perceptual recognition threshold and galvanic skin response (GSR) of persons when they were exposed to brief visual presentations of both "taboo" and neutral words. Essentially, the perceptual recognition threshold reflects the amount of time required for an individual to recognize correctly a word presented to him for a very short time. The galvanic skin response is a measure of autonomic activity and is therefore presumed to be an indication of the relative level of anxiety experienced by an individual.

McGinnies found that higher recognition thresholds were obtained for taboo words than for neutral words. Furthermore, he found higher galvanic skin responses on the prerecognition trials (the trials before the subject correctly identified the word) for taboo words than for neutral words. He interpreted the recognition threshold result as evidence for an active inhibition of conscious detection of taboo words. The GSR findings were interpreted as "unconscious" detection of threatening material and a manifestation of anxiety associated with the presentation of the taboo words.

However, shortly thereafter, Howes and Solomon (1950) attacked this research on two grounds. The first basis on which the McGinnies research was attacked is summarized by Eriksen (1963).

> Consider the typical undergraduate brought into the experimental situation by a professor. The subject is exposed to fragmentary perception through tachistoscopic exposure. Let us assume that the word "house" is projected and the subject sees what looks like a medium-length word with an "H" at the beginning and what looks like an "S" toward the end. Let us say that he tried to think of some word that will fit these partial cues and comes up with "house." The next word exposed is "whore." He may pick up a fragmentary perception of something resembling a "W" and maybe an "H" and he guesses "whom." On the next occurrence of this stimulus word he actually says to himself, "My God, that looks like whore, but it couldn't be. The professor wouldn't show a word like that." And so he waits for a longer duration before hazarding a guess, or overtly he says "whom" again. Of course, one would expect a very sizeable GSR to accompany this rather startling subjective experience. On the subsequent exposure he may be even more certain that the word is "whore" but he is not going to risk saying "whore" and being incorrect. After all, what would the experimenter think of somebody who would say a word like that when it really wasn't the word that was being shown? This possibility of deliberate response suppression is sufficient to account not only for the longer durations required for recognition of the "taboo words" but also for the greater GSRs accompanying the prerecognition response to these words (p. 38).

The second basis on which Howes and Solomon (1950) criticized McGinnies' experiment was that the "taboo" and neutral words differed in their familiarity and thus the non-taboo words were relatively easier to recognize than were the taboo words. Both of these criticisms led investigators to remain skeptical about the phenomenon of perceptual defense.

However, Eriksen (1963) pointed out that most experiments on perceptual defense had failed to meet two conditions necessary for the demonstration of perceptual defense. These conditions were (a) that independent operations must exist to show that the stimulus which was expected to produce perceptual defense is in fact anxiety-producing for that particular subject and (b) that independent criteria were required to demonstrate that the subject does in fact use avoidance defenses rather than other possible defensive reactions in the situation. In a series of ingenious and carefully designed experiments Eriksen (1951a, 1951b, 1952) did meet these criteria and demonstrated that it is in fact true that higher recognition thresholds can be obtained for emotionally threatening words.

However, Eriksen does not explain the perceptual defense demonstrated in recognition experiments as a process by which the unconscious detection of threatening material leads to repression, as analytic supporters of the hypothesis might suggest. Instead, he points out that we must distinguish between perceptual processes and the responses from which they are inferred. He suggests further that the perceptual defense studies (including his own) have only demonstrated the effect of threatening words on the observer's responses. He suggests that taboo words have been punished more than non-taboo words in the experience of most people, and therefore "we are in a position to account for perceptual defense effects in terms of nothing more mysterious than the empirically established effects of punishment on the probability of occurrence of responses" (p. 54).

This line of research provides an example of how competing explanations from another perspective—in this case the learning perspective— have supplanted earlier psychoanalytic hypotheses. It also demonstrates how advances in methodology, in particular the distinction between perceptual processes and the responses from which they are inferred, have clarified the general problem of the relation between perception and personality (Price, 1966).

Examining the Context of Symptoms in Psychoanalysis

Although a number of lines of research based on psychoanalytic views have ceased to be productive, there are new lines of research being developed which have psychoanalytic assumptions as important features of their conceptual base.

One notable example is the work of Luborsky and his colleagues (Luborsky, 1964, 1967, pp. 175–217, 1970), who are interested in the formation of symptoms by patients during the psychoanalytic hour. He notes that one of the problems of previous research on symptom formation is that the research is retrospective. That is, patients describe symptoms after they have appeared and then discuss the circumstances surrounding the symptom formation. As we noted earlier, evidence of this kind—because of the possibility of systematic distortion—is of limited value in understanding the genesis of the symptom.

Thus Luborsky and his colleagues have developed a method to find crucial points in the psychoanalytic hour when symptoms occur and then

to examine the context of thoughts which surround the symptom formation. They call their method the *symptom-context* method.

The symptom-context method has been used to test a specific hypothesis offered by Freud (1926b, 1953). The hypothesis states that the neurotic symptom is an attempted solution to a situation or event that the
person evaluates as being dangerous and in the face of which he experiences feelings of helplessness. An example Luborsky (1970) offers should
help clarify this hypothesis.

> For example, each time Mr. H, the patient to be described, had a
> memory dysfunction (momentary forgetting), it was preceded by a
> trend of associations which brought him to recall a situation he evalu-
> ated as dangerous: his impulse to feel affection or sexuality for a girl.
> Our method should tell us whether the patient's language in treatment
> would regularly reveal specific verbal contents corresponding to the
> "latent meanings" of the symptom, as specified in Freud's hypotheses,
> and whether the specific contents appear more frequently before a
> symptom than at other times. No one knows, furthermore, whether all
> symptoms would have similar psychological preconditions, or whether
> some, such as headache, palpitation, or other physical symptoms,
> would have fewer of them than the psychological one, such as obses-
> sional thoughts about being killed in an auto accident (p. 661).

As the above example suggests, Luborsky sees momentary forgetting
as a prime example of symptom formation. He examined the verbal pro-
ductions of 19 patients during a total of 2079 psychoanalytic sessions.
Fifteen of the 19 patients produced at least one example of momentary
forgetting. The total number of instances of momentary forgetting was 69,
a surprisingly low figure. The 550 words preceding and the 550 words
following each instance of momentary forgetting were examined and compared to control passages that did not include instances of momentary
forgetting. These passages were rated for the degree of cognitive disturbance they reflected and the type of thematic material that preceded and
followed the instance of momentary forgetting.

Luborsky and his colleagues found a gradual increase in the amount
of cognitive disturbance before the forgetting and then a gradual disappear-
ance shortly after the instance of forgetting. They also found a significant
increase in the number of direct references to the therapist in the time
immediately preceding the momentary forgetting. These references were
ones which were judged to be threatening to the patient and Luborsky
believes that they may reflect an increasing and immediate involvement in
those aspects of the therapeutic relationship that are of particular significance to the patient.

These investigators have extended their symptom-content method to examine other symptoms including stomach pain, migraine headaches, and petit mal epilepsy. Among their general findings were the following: First, they found consistent differences within a given patient between control passages and passages that contained instances of a symptom. Second, they found that thematic differences between symptom and control passages tend to be more similar within than between patients. Third, they found that the thematic material they found for somatic symptoms differed from that for instances of forgetting. For example, the theme of helplessness was central for the occurrence of somatic symptoms. Luborsky sees this as a confirmation of Freud's hypothesis concerning the genesis of neurotic symptomatology.

This is an interesting new line of research and, as the authors point out, it is a method more appropriate for generating hypotheses than for testing them. Despite this caveat, we may ask about the relative importance of the phenomenon that Luborsky and his colleagues are investigating, especially in the light of the fact that only 69 instances of symptom formation were found in over two thousand psychoanalytic sessions. We might wonder, too, how many instances of the appropriate thematic content (for example, "feelings of helplessness") occur *without* the occurrence of the predicted somatic symptoms. Luborsky offers no evidence on this crucial point.

The symptom-context method used by Luborsky remains essentially retrospective despite the fact that it is relatively free of the usual distortions of retrospective report. A study using prospective methods would seek to identify antecedent thematic material and examine the probability of symptom occurrence. Knowing how likely a symptom is to occur given the appropriate thematic content is as important as knowing the likelihood of the occurrence of the predicted thematic content when the symptom has occurred. Nevertheless, the work of Luborsky and his colleagues represents a new direction in research drawn from the psychoanalytic perspective and one that ultimately may yield support for certain psychoanalytic hypotheses.

Psychoanalysis and Other Perspectives on Abnormal Behavior

We have suggested in the introduction to this chapter that psychoanalysis stands in special relation to other perspectives on abnormal behavior in at least two ways. First, many of the basic assumptions of psychoanalysis —for example, the idea of psychological determinism, the developmental point of view, and the idea of behavior as goal directed—appear in slightly different forms in other perspectives. Second, we suggested that a number of the other perspectives have used psychoanalysis as a sort of intellectual springboard in which one or another of the fundamental assumptions of the psychoanalytic point of view have become a point of contention for competing perspectives.

We are now in a position to examine this second effect of psychoanalysis on other perspectives in more detail. For some perspectives, an attack on psychoanalysis is fundamental to the argument advanced—this is true of Mowrer's moral point of view. For other perspectives, the difference is less dramatic but equally real. Let us examine what appears to be the fundamental point of conflict for each of the perspectives that we will consider in the following chapters.

Although Freud himself was a physician and borrowed many terms from medical usage for his formulations, his view represents a distinct departure from the illness perspective (e.g., Meehl, 1962) with its organic orientation. For Freud, many symptoms of psychological disturbance did not have exclusively organic origins but were instead psychologically determined. Freud acknowledged that all behavior had a constitutional basis and in fact he never doubted that the organic and structural basis of behavior would ultimately be discovered. Nevertheless, the crucial point is that his idea of psychological determinism of symptoms stands in contrast to the more organically oriented position of the illness perspective.

For the *learning perspective* the principal point of controversy concerns the nature and etiology of symptoms. Learning theorists such as Eysenck and Rachman (1965) assert that the symptom *is* the disorder. That is, symptoms are viewed as behavior or habits which have been acquired as a result of the application of certain reinforcements. To quote Eysenck and Rachman,

> Freudian theory regards neurotic symptoms as adaptive mechanisms which are evidence of repression; they are the "visible upshot of unconscious causes." Learning theory does not postulate any such "unconscious" causes, but regards neurotic symptoms as simply learned habits; there is no neurosis underlying the symptom, but merely the symptom itself (p. 10).

A corollary of this point is the issue of "symptom substitution" as discussed by Ullman and Krasner (1969). They argue that the Freudian view suggests that the removal of symptoms will leave the underlying dynamics of the individual unaffected, and therefore that a new symptom will replace the previous one if it is removed by the application of reinforcement techniques. Ullman and Krasner devote considerable effort to refuting the symptom substitution position since the existence of symptom subsititution would undermine their fundamental argument that symptoms are simply learned behaviors.

Although the *moral perspective* as presented by Mowrer (1961) leans heavily on an attack on the Freudian view throughout, one point appears central. The issue that divides Mowrer and Freud most decisively is the question of the effects of socialization on the person. Freud suggests in *Civilization and Its Discontents* (1930, 1961) that much of the socializing influence on the individual leads to dangerous repression. Mowrer on the other hand argues that wholehearted acceptance of this view has led to dangerous permissiveness which has minimized the importance of individual responsibility for one's actions. This lack of responsibility for one's own actions and the consequent weakening of the superego Mowrer vehemently opposes; for him it constitutes the source of much symptomatology.

The *humanistic perspective* finds yet another point of issue with the psychoanalytic view. The crucial issue for Rogers, in particular, concerns a basic assumption about the nature of man. For Rogers and other advocates of the humanistic perspective man is potentially good. He has the capacity for growth and self-transcendence. The humanistic perspective holds an essentially optimistic view of man, whereas Freud held a basically pessimistic view. For example, Freud's conception of the id as a reservoir of seething, bestial, instinctual impulses that can only be controlled by ego mechanisms suggests his pessimistic view of man's perfectibility.

Rogers (1959) points out this fundamental discrepancy when he says:

> Very briefly stated, the Freudian group, on the basis of its experience, tends to see the individual as "innately destructive" (to use Karl Menninger's words) and hence in need of control. . . . In very much related fashion, the theory which Gordon and others have formulated regarding group behavior and group leadership is almost diametrically opposed to the Freudian theory in this respect. Freud's statements that "groups have never thirsted after truth" and that "a group is an obedient herd which could never live without a master" suggests something of the deep discrepancy which exists between the two views (p. 248).

Finally, the *social perspective* takes issue with psychoanalysis on still different grounds. Scheff (1966) suggests that the difficulty with the psychoanalytic view is its fundamental narrowness.

> The objection to psychoanalytic theory that is made here is not that it posits neurotic behavior as part of a closed system, but that the system that it formulates is too narrow, in that it leaves out aspects of the social contacts that are vital for understanding mental disorder (p. 14).

For Scheff, then, the appropriate level of analysis for understanding abnormal behavior is at issue. He believes that psychoanalysis, because it is basically an intrapsychic view, cannot come to terms with aspects of the social order and the person's role in the social order which are necessary for a full understanding of the nature and genesis of abnormal behavior.

Thus, each of the perspectives on abnormal behavior which we will discuss in the following chapters find themselves in conflict with some aspect of the psychoanalytic perspective. This brief discussion provides us with an opportunity to anticipate some of the central features of other perspectives to be examined later. It is perhaps a tribute to the impact of the psychoanalytic perspective that advocates of such diverse approaches have found it necessary to criticize psychoanalysis in order to add credibility to their own views.

Summary

We have seen that psychoanalysis, as judged by contemporary standards, fails to meet the criteria necessary for status as a scientific theory. In particular, many of the propositions of psychoanalysis fail to meet the basic criterion of disconfirmability. We have tried to point out, however, that few if any of the perspectives discussed in this book would meet such rigorous standards and that perhaps psychoanalysis is best viewed as a perspective or group of related metaphors which are essentially pretheoretical in nature.

In addition, clinical evidence offered to support the psychoanalytic view has been criticized on a number of grounds. Several lines of research, including that on the issue of perceptual defense, have either failed to support the psychoanalytic view or have substantially modified earlier conceptions. Nevertheless, new approaches such as that of Luborsky and his colleagues continue to evolve; these hold promise that solid empirical evidence will emerge on some psychoanalytic hypotheses.

Finally, psychoanalysis stands in special relation to the other perspectives on abnormal behavior which we will discuss. Each of them, although indebted to the ideas originated by Freud, object to some fundamental aspect of the psychoanalytic perspective.

In the last analysis we must agree with Holzman that psychoanalysis represents an influential view of human nature and of man himself.

It is more than the conception of multiple determined factors and behavior, or the idea of unconscious processes that continuously influence our experience and our behavior, or the importance accorded the experiences within our patients, or the recognition of drive motivation. The psychoanalytic epic regards man as the shaper of his own fate, the forger of his own history, a being who is born to struggle against and ally himself with his inner nature and his surrounding world. In this epic, psychopathology is to be regarded not as a thing that plunders the person but as an expression of man's struggles with love and hate, life and death (p. 177).

References

BLUM, G. S., & MILLER, D. R.   Exploring the psychoanalytic theory of the "oral character." *Journal of Personality*, 1952, *20*, 287–304.

CAMERON, N.   *Personality development and psychopathology: A dynamic approach.* Boston: Houghton Mifflin, 1963.

DODDS, E. R.   *The Greeks and the irrational.* Berkeley: University of California Press, 1951.

DODDS, E. R.   *Pagan and Christian in an age of anxiety.* New York: Cambridge University Press, 1965.

ERIKSEN, C. W.   Perceptual defense as a function of unacceptable needs. *Journal of Abnormal and Social Psychology*, 1951, *46*, 557–564. (a)

ERIKSEN, C. W.   Some implications for TAT interpretation arising from need and perception experiments. *Journal of Personality*, 1951, *19*, 283–288. (b)

ERIKSEN, C. W.   Defense against ego-threat in memory and perception. *Journal of Abnormal and Social Psychology*, 1952, *27*, 430–435.

ERIKSEN, C. W.   Discrimination and learning without awareness: A methodological survey and evaluation. *Psychological Review*, 1960, *67*, 279–300.

ERIKSEN, C. W.   Perception and personality. In J. M. Wepman & R. W. Heine (Eds.), *Concepts of personality.* Chicago: Aldine, 1963.

EYSENCK, H. J., & RACHMAN, S.   *The causes and cures of neurosis.* London: Routledge & Kegan Paul, 1965.

FENICHEL, O.   *The psychoanalytic theory of neurosis.* New York: Norton, 1945.

FREUD, S. (1894)   The neuropsychoses of defense. *The standard edition of the complete psychological works.* J. Strachey (Ed.) Vol. 3. London: Hogarth, 1962.

FREUD, S. (1901)   Psychopathology of everyday life. *Standard edition*, Vol. 6. London: Hogarth, 1960.

FREUD, S. (1911)   Formulations on the two principles of mental functioning. In *Collected papers of Sigmund Freud.* Vol. IV. London: Hogarth, 1949.

FREUD, S. (1923)   The ego and the id. *Standard edition*, Vol. 19. London: Hogarth, 1961.

FREUD, S. (1926a)   *The problem of anxiety.* New York: Norton, 1936.
FREUD, S. (1926b)   Inhibitions, symptoms and anxiety. *Standard edition,* Vol. 20. London: Hogarth, 1953, pp. 77–175.
FREUD, S. (1930)   Civilization and its discontents. *Standard edition,* Vol. 21. London: Hogarth, 1961.
FREUD, S. (1933)   *New introductory lectures on psychoanalysis.* New York: Norton, 1933.
FREUD, S. (1940) *An outline of psychoanalysis.* New York: Norton, 1949.
HALL, C. S.   *A primer of Freudian psychology.* New York: New American Library, 1954.
HALL, C. S., & LINDZEY, G.   The relevance of Freudian psychology and related viewpoints for the social sciences. In G. Lindzey & E. Aronson (Eds.), *Handbook of social psychology.* Vol. 1. Cambridge: Addison-Wesley, 1968.
HARTMANN, H.   Psychoanalysis as a scientific theory. In S. Hood (Ed.), *Psychoanalysis, scientific method, and philosophy.* New York: New York University Press, 1959.
HILGARD, E. R.   Psychoanalysis: Experimental studies. In D. L. Sills (Ed.), *International Encyclopedia of the Social Sciences.* Vol. 13. New York: Macmillan, 1968.
HOLZMAN, P. S.   *Psychoanalysis and psychopathology.* New York: McGraw-Hill, 1970.
HOOK, S.   Science and mythology in psychoanalysis. In S. Hook (Ed.), *Psychoanalysis, scientific method, and philosophy.* New York: New York University Press, 1959.
HOWES, D., & SOLOMON, R. L.   A note on McGinnies' emotionality and perceptual defense. *Psychological Review,* 1950, *57,* 229–234.
JONES, E.   *The life and work of Sigmund Freud.* New York: Basic Books, Vol. 1, 1953; Vol. 2, 1955; Vol. 3, 1957.
KISKER, G. W.   *The disorganized personality.* New York: McGraw-Hill, 1964.
LEHRMAN, N. S.   Precision in psychoanalysis. *American Journal of Psychiatry,* 1960, *116,* 1097–1103.
LEO, J.   Psychoanalysis reaches a crossroad. *New York Times,* Aug. 4, 1968, pp. 1, 56.
LEVY, L.   *Psychological interpretation.* New York: Holt, Rinehart and Winston, 1963.
LUBORSKY, L.   A psychoanalytic research on momentary forgetting during free association. *Bulletin of the Philadelphia Association for Psychoanalysis,* 1964, *14,* 119–137.
LUBORSKY, L.   Momentary forgetting during psychotherapy and psychoanalysis: A theory and research method. In R. R. Holt (Ed.), *Motives and thought: Contributions to a psychoanalytic theory of behavior.* New York: International Universities, 1967.

LUBORSKY, L.   New directions in research on neurotic and psychosomatic symptoms. *American Scientist*, 1970, *58*, 661–668.

MARCUSE, H.   *Eros and civilization*. Boston: Beacon Press, 1955.

MARCUSE, H.   *One dimensional man*. Boston: Beacon Press, 1964.

MCGINNIES, E.   Emotionality and perceptual defense. *Psychological Review*, 1949, *56*, 244–251.

MEEHL, P.   Schizotaxia, schizotypy, schizophrenia. *American Psychologist*, 1962, *17*, 211–221.

MOWRER, O. H.   *The crisis in psychiatry and religion*. Princeton, N. J.: Van Nostrand, 1961.

MUNROE, R. L.   *Schools of psychoanalytic thought*. New York: Holt, Rinehart and Winston, 1955,

NAGEL, E.   Methodological issues in psychoanalytic theory. In S. Hook (Ed.), *Psychoanalysis, scientific method, and philosophy*. New York: New York University Press, 1959.

PRICE, R. H.   Signal-detection methods in personality and perception. *Psychological Bulletin*, 1966, *66*, 55–62.

RAPAPORT, D., & GILL, M. M.   The points of view and assumptions of metapsychology. In Merton M. Gill (Ed.), *Collected papers of David Rapaport*. New York: Basic Books, 1967.

ROGERS, C. R.   A theory of therapy, personality, and interpersonal relationships, as developed in the client-centered framework. In S. Koch (Ed.), *Psychology: A study of a science*. Vol. 3. New York: McGraw-Hill, 1959.

SALTER, A.   *The case against psychoanalysis*. New York: Citadel, 1963.

SARNOFF, I., & CORWIN, S. M.   Castration anxiety and the fear of death. *Journal of Personality*, 1959, *27*, 374–385.

SCHEFF, T. J.   *Being mentally ill: A sociological theory*. Chicago: Aldine, 1966.

SEARS, R. R., MACCOBY, E. E., & LEVIN, H.   *Patterns of child rearing*. Evanston, Ill.: Row, Peterson, 1957.

SHAPIRO, D.   *Neurotic styles*. New York: Basic Books, 1965.

ULLMAN, L. P., & KRASNER, L.   *A psychological approach to abnormal behavior*. Englewood Cliffs, N. J.: Prentice-Hall, 1969.

CHAPTER 4
THE ILLNESS PERSPECTIVE

The Perspective

The mental illness perspective is unquestionably the most widely held view of abnormal behavior. In discussing abnormal behavior, we use the language and concepts of physical medicine as a matter of course. Seldom, however, do we consider the source of these concepts. As Maher (1966) puts it,

> Society currently uses the model of physical illness as a basis for the terms and concepts to be applied to deviant behavior. Such behavior is termed *pathological* and is classified on the basis of *symptoms,* classification being called *diagnosis*. Processes designed to change behavior are called *therapies* and are applied to *patients* in mental *hospitals*. If the deviant behavior ceases, the patient is described as *cured* (pp. 21–22).

Similarly, our major social and governmental institutions concerned with the problem of abnormal behavior identify themselves in ways which suggest that they are concerned with the problem of health and illness (e.g. National Institute of Mental Health, Mental Health Administration). Some authors (Cumming & Cumming, 1957; Schroder & Ehrlich, 1968; Schwartz, 1957) have distinguished between the public's normative view of abnormal behavior and the psychiatric view held by mental health professionals. Nevertheless, many professionals and the public at large retain the idea that deviant behavior *is* mental illness.

Milton and Wahler (1969) illustrate this point nicely by quoting from pamphlets designed to educate the public about abnormal behavior:

The most important thing for your patient's chances of recovery and for your own peace of mind is to realize that mental illnesses are illnesses like any others. (Stern, 1957)

If everyone would just realize that mental illness is no different from any other prolonged disease and that a heart attack victim differs only from a mental victim in the localization of the affliction, the psychiatrist-therapist's job would be greatly simplified. (*Mind Over Matter*, 1962)

While the signs of a neurosis frequently first appear in the late teens or in early adult life, the disease may have a background in events of early infancy. (*The Mind*, 1954)

People with either mental or emotional illness need help from a medical specialist, just the same as people with pneumonia, or ptomaine. (*Some Things You Should Know About Mental and Emotional Illness*)

At least 50% of all the millions of medical and surgical cases treated by private doctors and hospitals have a mental illness complication. (*Facts About Mental Illness*, 1963) (p. 8)

It should be made very clear that these assertions about abnormal behavior refer to the *functional disorders*; that is, disordered behavior which does not have known physiological or organic correlates. Even the most strident critics of the illness perspective do not argue that general paresis or Korsakoff's syndrome, for example, are not illnesses. Rather the disputed territory involves those disorders which have not yet been shown to have organic etiologies.

Some Initial Distinctions

Varieties of "medical models"

Recently a great deal more has been written in criticism of the medical or illness perspective on abnormal behavior than has been written in support of it. The so-called medical model is under attack from a number of different quarters (Sarbin, 1967; Szasz, 1961; Ullmann & Krasner, 1965).

Critics of the illness perspective often confuse several different but important issues. Sarason and Ganzer (1968) suggest that there are actually several different models which have been called the "medical model." For example, Ullmann and Krasner (1965) have included two distinguishably different approaches to abnormal behavior under this rubric. These two points of view are (a) a formulation of abnormal behavior which assumes that the determinants are organic, and (b) approaches to abnormal behavior which assume that the determinants are psychodynamic.

Sarason and Ganzer (1968) suggest that these two versions of the medical or illness perspective should be distinguished from one another.

> Current dynamic formulations of maladaptive behavior are not necessarily based on the assumption of physical pathology and are therefore not strictly medical. It is inappropriate to criticize psychological approaches to deviant behavior as invalid because they are based on a medical model when the only basic similarities they bear to medicine are the assumption of underlying cause and some borrowed terminology (e.g., symptom, prognosis) (p. 507).

We agree with Sarason and Ganzer on this point. In our description of the illness perspective, we will restrict our discussion to formulations that are fundamentally organic or physiological in what they assume about the determinants of abnormal behavior.

The confusion between organic and psychodynamic formulations may be partly a result of the fact that medical professionals and particularly psychiatrists may advocate both dynamic and organic approaches. However, this fact in itself should not constitute grounds for treating both the dynamic and the organic approach to abnormal behavior as parts of the same model or perspective.

There is one real similarity between the psychodynamic and the organic approaches, however, which should not be ignored. Wolfer (1969) calls it the "symptom-underlying-illness paradigm." According to Wolfer, the symptom-underlying-illness paradigm assumes that the determinants of abnormal behavior are agents or processes residing in the organism. The abnormal behavior is thought to be symptomatic of the underlying illness. According to this view, symptoms will remain until the underlying cause is discovered and corrected.

Intellectual versus value issues

Sarason and Ganzer (1968) make a second distinction well worth mentioning. On the one hand, there is the question of what professional group should be responsible for the management and care of those designated as mentally ill. This is fundamentally a professional and value issue. On the other hand, there is an intellectual issue that has been discussed much less. This involves the question of the suitability of the illness perspective as a theoretical framework and classification scheme.

It is the intellectual issue that we will consider for the most part in the discussion that follows. However, it is not always possible in practice to separate value issues from intellectual issues. For example, in one sense, the issues are related, as Wolfer (1969) points out: "Acceptance of this model may have provided some tacit justification for institutionalized medical control of the training for and delivery of therapeutic services" (p. 607).

But the distinction between intellectual and value issues is still a useful one, even if it can be made only in principle. It should allow us to examine the intellectual issue (the assertion that abnormal behavior is mental illness) while, on the issue of value, still recognize that the illness perspective has profound social and professional implications which deserve separate and detailed treatment in their own right.

The Beginnings of the Illness Perspective

Although Hippocrates (460–357 B.C.) certainly may be credited with one of the earliest discussions of abnormal behavior as a product of illness, it was probably Johann Weyer (1515–1588) who made the first modern use of the illness perspective. In 1563, Weyer declared that most individuals accused of and punished for their practices of witchcraft were actually mentally ill.

Weyer may have been one of the earliest spokesmen for the illness perspective, but it was Philippe Pinel who was instrumental in popularizing this view. As chief physician in the Bicetre in Paris, Pinel was responsible for the removal of chains and other restraints that had been routinely used to control the behavior of deviant individuals. Pinel's desire for humanitarian reform in the treatment of deviant individuals led him to his conclusion that these were sick people who deserved all the consideration that sick people require.

With Kraepelin's comprehensive, descriptive work, the illness perspective began to be elaborated, drawing increasingly upon the concepts of physical medicine. Diefendorf (1921) quotes Kraepelin as saying that

> Judging from our experience in internal medicine, it is a fair assumption that similar disease processes will produce identical symptom pictures, identical pathological anatomy, and identical etiology. If, therefore, we possessed a comprehensive knowledge of any one of these three fields—pathological anatomy, symptomatology, or etiology —we would at once have a uniform and standard classification of mental diseases. A similar comprehensive knowledge of either of the two fields would give not only just as uniform and standard classifications, but all these classifications would exactly coincide. Cases of

mental disease originating in the same cause must also present the same symptoms and the same pathological findings (p. 200).

Kraepelin is quite clearly adapting the concepts of physical medicine to the problems of deviant behavior. Despite the fact that his formulation is now considered entirely too naïve and simplistic to account for the observed findings, it was a statement based on the belief that deviant behavior could be understood in precisely the same way as other organic illnesses. As Sarason and Ganzer (1968) point out:

> The system represented the first cohesive classification of diseases and is credited with being among the first comprehensive medical models of deviant behavior. It was a true medical analogy in the strict sense: the etiology was organic (a central nervous system disease or disorder), and the prognosis was believed definite. From a Kraepelinian standpoint, it was necessary to describe and classify as accurately as possible a given set of symptoms in order that appropriate therapy might be applied (p. 508).

Thus, by the end of the nineteenth and the beginning of the twentieth centuries, the illness perspective had developed considerably. No longer merely a slogan used in the name of humanitarian reform, it had become a fully elaborated metaphor embodying specific assumptions about the nature of abnormal behavior which served as a conceptual framework for psychiatry.

Current Structure of the Illness Perspective

Today the illness perspective occupies a central position in psychiatric thinking. As we have suggested in the introduction to this chapter, many of the concepts and much of the language of the illness perspective are used so frequently in the discussion of abnormal behavior that we often forget the origin of these terms in physical medicine. Let us examine briefly some of the basic concepts of the illness perspective.

Nosology   Naming and classification of diseases.
Etiology   Causation; the systematic study of the causes of disorders.
Symptom   A physical or behavioral manifestation of illness or emotional disturbance.
Syndrome   Patterns or constellations of symptoms that are typical of a disorder.
Disorder   One or more syndromes with common etiological factors.
Acute disorder   Disorder with a sudden onset and of short duration. Acute disorders are usually considered reversible.

Chronic disorder   Disorder that is long lasting and tends to be irreversible.

Diagnosis   The determination of the nature of a disease or abnormality based on symptoms displayed.

Therapy   The application of various treatment techniques either to affect symptoms or to affect etiological factors.

Prognosis   Statement concerning the likely course and outcome of a disorder.

These definitions may aid us in our understanding of the illness perspective, but we should also have at least a rudimentary understanding of the relations between these various concepts. Figure 4.1 shows the relationships between etiological factors, symptoms, syndromes, and disorders. It also shows the points at which diagnosis or therapy may occur in relation to the disorder. The role of research activities is also shown, both in terms of attempts to identify syndromes from the examination of symptom clusters (nosological research) and attempts to discover the etiology of syndromes that have already been described (etiological research).

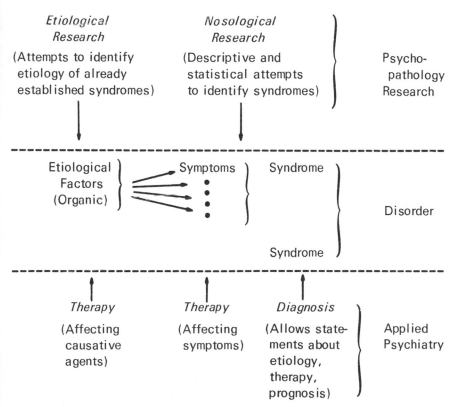

Figure 4.1

Diagnosis

Diagnosis is of great importance in the illness perspective. Putting patients into diagnostic categories serves at least three functions. First, treatment decisions are most often based upon diagnosis. For example, a patient who is diagnosed as depressed is likely to receive electroconvulsive therapy or antidepressant drugs, while a patient diagnosed as schizophrenic is more likely to receive tranquilizing drugs as his major form of treatment. Second, identifying the syndrome a patient displays is usually thought to be a necessary prerequisite for the discovery of causal factors or etiology of the illness. As Cattell (1940) puts it, "nosology necessarily precedes etiology." Similarly, Marzolf (1945) indicates that the "establishment of syndromes is preliminary to the discovery of etiologies." Third, diagnosis of illness provides the diagnostician with information concerning the prognosis—the probable course and outcome of the illness.

Typically in diagnosis the patient is examined to determine the syndrome or symptom cluster which he has developed. The syndrome identified in the examination is then taken as an indication of the disorder from which the patient suffers. Eysenck (1960) notes that similarity between diagnostic practice in psychopathology and physical medicine when he says:

> Traditionally, classification in the field of abnormal psychology has been by means of specific diseases or syndromes; we speak of hysteria, or schizophrenia, or manic-depressive psychosis in much the same way as we speak of tuberculosis, or neurosyphilis, or cancer (p. 1).

The diagnostic examination involves a number of different procedures. The patient may undergo a series of laboratory tests to assess his current physiological status. In addition, psychological tests may be administered. Finally, the patient will often be given a mental status interview to evaluate his affect, memory, judgment, and orientation, and his insight into the nature of his illness. The diagnostician combines and evaluates all of this information and uses it as the basis for his final diagnostic decision.

In medicine, as Eysenck (1960) suggests, diagnosis may be made in terms of the agent that is designated the "cause" of the disease or on the basis of the symptom syndrome which is regarded as characteristic of the disease; in some cases both types of information may be presented at the same time. In psychiatry, diagnosis is almost never based upon causal factors since they are seldom known. Thus the diagnosis of abnormal behavior is done almost exclusively on the basis of symptoms or syndromes.

In the United States the standard reference for diagnosis is the *Diagnostic and Statistical Manual of Mental Disorders* (*DSM II*) (1968).

Interestingly, in the Foreword to the most recent edition of the Manual, Gruenberg (1968, pp. vii–x) states that this revision has been constructed to conform closely with the International Classification of Diseases. Gruenberg indicates that "The rapid integration of psychiatry also helped to create a need to have psychiatric nomenclature and classification closely integrated with those of other medical practitioners" (p. vii). The intention of those producing the official nosology of the American Psychiatric Association was to retain an explicitly medical orientation. This most recent revision of the nomenclature (*DSM II*) contains the ten following major diagnostic subgroupings.

I. Mental Retardation
II. Organic Brain Syndromes
III. Psychoses Not Attributed to Physical Conditions Listed Previously
IV. Neuroses
V. Personality Disorders and Certain Other Non-Psychotic Mental Disorders
VI. Psychophysiological Disorders
VII. Special Symptoms
VIII. Transient Situational Disturbances
IX. Behavior Disorders of Childhood and Adolescence
X. Conditions Without Manifest Psychiatric Disorder and Non-Specific Conditions

This revision is a product of compromise, as Kramer (1968) points out. Variations in the orientation of consultants with differing points of view have been reconciled by finding a middle ground acceptable to all those involved in the task rather than by recourse to empirical methods.

Although considerable skepticism has been voiced recently concerning the effectiveness of diagnostic practice, Meehl (1966) remains convinced of its usefulness:

> The fundamental argument for the utility of formal diagnosis can be put either causally or statistically, but it amounts to the same kind of thing one would say in defending formal diagnosis in organic medicine. One holds that there is a sufficient amount of aetiological and prognostic homogeneity among patients belonging to a given diagnostic group, so that the assignment of a patient to this group has probability implications which it is clinically unsound to ignore (p. 9).

Meehl's language is certainly more sophisticated and more cautious than Kraepelin's remarks quoted earlier, but we can see certain similarities in their views.

Diagnosis, then, plays a vital role in the identification of symptom syndromes, whether the problem is in organic medicine or abnormal behavior. Furthermore, once the patient is identified as a member of a particular nosological group, it is assumed that we can make inferences about etiology and statements about prognosis. Such statements are possible because members of the same nosological group are assumed to be suffering from the same illness.

Etiology

One accompaniment of the illness perspective on abnormal behavior is what Maher (1966) calls the "organic orientation." Once one assumes that deviant or abnormal behavior is a consequence of illness, then it follows that research into organic causes will be undertaken as a matter of course.

We should not find it surprising that considerable effort has been devoted to biochemical (Kety, 1959) and genetic (Kallman, 1953; Rosenthal, 1970) research with various diagnostic groups. The goal of such investigations is to identify organic factors that may have etiological significance for particular syndromes.

As we have suggested, Kraepelin's original notions of etiology are considered today to be much too simplistic to account for our observations concerning the nature of abnormal behavior. However, the illness perspective still retains a strong set of assumptions about the determinants of abnormal behavior.

In his now-famous paper describing his theory of schizophrenia, Meehl (1962) describes one such set of causal assumptions. Drawing directly upon nonpsychiatric medicine he suggests that we consider the concept of *specific etiology*. Briefly, this concept refers to that causal condition which is necessary but not sufficient for the illness to occur. Thus, the causal factor which is designated as the specific etiology must be present for the illness to occur but this causal factor may not by itself produce the illness. The specific etiology is the *sine qua non* or essential condition for the occurrence of the illness.

Meehl uses the analogy of a "color psychosis" to illustrate the concept of specific etiology. He points out that the specific etiology of color-blindness is known to involve a mutated gene on the X chromosome. If an individual who possessed this specific etiology and who therefore was colorblind grew up in a society which was entirely oriented around making fine color discriminations, he might develop a "color psychosis." Cultural and social factors would inevitably play a role in the development of his illness. Nevertheless, if we ask "what is basically the matter with the patient?" the answer must be, according to Meehl, that the mutated gene on the X chromosome is the specific etiology of the "color psychosis."

Meehl is careful to point out, however, that when the concept of specific etiology is applied to a disorder such as schizophrenia a number of misunderstandings may arise. In particular, he points to five misunderstandings concerning the concept of specific etiology: (1) The presence of the etiological factor does not necessarily produce the clinically observed disorder; (2) The form and content of the clinically observed disorder is not necessarily understandable or derivable from the specific etiology alone; (3) The course of the disorder is not treatable only by procedures which are directed against the specific etiology itself; (4) People who share the specific etiology will not necessarily have the same or closely similar histories and symptoms; and (5) The largest source of variance in symptoms is not necessarily the specific etiology.

These disclaimers make it clear that the notion of specific etiology does not imply a simple cause-effect relationship between etiological factors and symptoms. In fact there may be a large number of links in the causal chain between the specific etiology and the symptoms ultimately displayed by the patient.

One important reason that different symptom patterns may arise with the same specific etiology is that some of the behavior displayed by the patient may be compensatory in nature. That is, two patients with the same specific etiology or organic defect may behave quite differently in response to that defect. One patient may respond with lethargy and withdrawal while the other might engage in a series of energetic attempts to overcome the difficulty. The result, of course, will be two quite different symptom pictures associated with the same specific etiological factor.

Summary

We have seen that the illness perspective views abnormal behavior as the product of disease or illness. The discipline of physical medicine provides the principal source of concepts for the perspective. Thus mental illness is manifested by symptoms that are grouped into syndromes and have an organic etiology. Furthermore, various nosological entities or diseases are assumed to have similar prognoses. The determinants of abnormal or symptomatic behavior are presumed to be either (1) the organic etiology itself, (2) compensatory reactions to the basic organic defect, or (3) some combination of these. In any case, the organic etiology plays the crucial role in understanding the illness.

The displacement of these concepts from physical medicine to the problem of abnormal behavior and the resulting mutual adaptation of events is apparent in several ways. First, abnormal behavior is often assumed to be the product of illness even when there is no known organic etiology that would properly qualify the disorder as a disease. Second, the concept of illness is significantly broadened in its application to deviant behavior. Behavior patterns such as psychopathy, or even homosexuality, are sometimes considered illnesses, thus significantly extending what is meant by the term "illness." Both the original concepts from physical medicine and the phenomena to which they are applied are changed and restructured in the process.

Commentary

Mental Illness: Myth or Disease?

The controversy over the usefulness of the concept of mental illness is one of the best known and most heated debates to have taken place recently in the field of abnormal psychology. At this point we should remind ourselves that the controversy we are about to describe revolves around the status of the functional disorders. Both critics and defenders of the illness perspective are concerned with the question of whether or not deviant behavior for which there are currently no known physiological correlates should be seen as disease. Unquestionably the single most vocal leader of the "anti-mental illness" movement is Thomas Szasz (1960, 1967). Although a psychiatrist himself, Szasz has been one of the profession's severest critics.

Mental illness as myth

Szasz begins his attack by asserting that mental illness is a myth. He argues that most behavior deviations may be more usefully thought of simply as problems in living. Problems in living were historically conceived first in terms of demonology and possession. Then, with the advent of humanitarian reform, problems in living were viewed as the products of medical disease and called mental illness. At the time, this shift in perspective constituted a sweeping conceptual revolution and marked a great step forward in the humane treatment of deviant individuals. Today, however, the concept of mental illness has outlived its usefulness.

Szasz is convinced that the concept of mental illness cannot withstand logical scrutiny. For example, he argues that although mental illness is a medical term it is defined not by medical but by social criteria. More specifically, the defining criteria of mental illness tend to be ethical, psychosocial, and legal. And if this were not inconsistent enough, we use social criteria to define this medical term "mental illness," and at the same time we assume that medical actions will correct the disorder. Thus the mental illness concept is subject to the double inconsistency of being a medical term defined by nonmedical criteria but nevertheless treated by medical means.

We have suggested that the illness perspective implies an organic orientation to possible causal factors in abnormal behavior. Szasz (1960) is in essential agreement with this point and notes that

> "Mental illnesses" are thus regarded as basically no different than all other diseases (that is, of the body). The only difference, in this view, between mental and bodily diseases is that the former, affecting the brain, manifest themselves by means of mental symptoms; whereas the latter, affecting other organ systems (for example, the skin, liver, etc.), manifest themselves by means of symptoms referrable to those parts of the body (p. 113).

In Szasz's view, this set of assumptions contains two fundamental errors. First, if an illness is the result of neurological defects, then it is in fact a disease of the nervous system, and not a problem in living. As such, it should be described as a neurological disease, and not as "mental illness."

The second error is epistemological and involves a fundamental dualism between physical and mental events. Physical symptoms are a manifestation of physical disturbances, whereas mental symptoms refer to the way in which a patient communicates about himself and others and the world around him. Thus the dualism implied in the term mental illness is a confusion of anatomical and social contexts.

From this point of view, the phenomena to which we refer when we use the term mental illness are actually communications which express unacceptable ideas often framed in an unusual idiom. In addition, these communications are judged within a value context. Both the values of the patient and those of the examining physician are involved in the use of the concept of mental illness.

Furthermore, Szasz argues, the responsibility both of the patient and of the psychiatrist are obscured when problems in living are seen as products of mental illness. In particular, the patient is relieved of responsibility for his actions when he is able to view his behavior as mental illness—a condition over which he has no control. Similarly, the psychiatrist by implication is absolved of his responsibility to take action on the behavior of the individual who has problems in living, since he views the behavior as mental illness for which there is no known cure.

Szasz (1960) summarizes his argument in the following way:

Our adversaries are not demons, witches, fate, or mental illness. We have no enemy whom we can fight, exorcise, or dispel by "cure." What we do have are problems in living—whether these be biologic, economic, political, or socio-psychological. In this essay I was concerned only with problems belonging in this last mentioned category, and within this group mainly with those pertaining to moral values. The field to which modern psychiatry addresses itself is that, and I made no effort to encompass it all. My argument was limited to the proposition that mental illness is a myth, whose function it is to distinguish and thus render more palatable a bitter pill of moral conflict in human relations (p. 118).

Personality disorder as disease

Szasz's criticisms of the mental illness concept have not gone unchallenged. Ausubel (1961) has examined Szasz's argument and concludes that the assertion that mental illness is a myth is based upon four "unsubstantiated and logically untenable propositions" (p. 70).

Ausubel begins by questioning Szasz's argument that only symptoms from demonstrable physical lesions are legitimately considered as manifestations of disease, and that therefore mental symptoms that do not involve physical lesions may not qualify as examples of illness. Ausubel points out that the somatic view of illness supports the idea that anatomic or physiological integrity has an effect upon behavior only in a general fashion. He goes on to point out that even if we accept Szasz's notion that brain pathology does not account for personality disorders, we still do not have to accept the idea that a disease must have physical symptoms in order to qualify as such.

Adoption of such a criterion would be arbitrary and inconsistent both with medical and lay connotations of the term "disease," which in current usage is generally regarded as including any marked deviation, physical, mental, or behavioral, from normally desirable standards of structural and functional integrity (p. 71).

The second of Szasz's propositions with which Ausubel takes issue is the dichotomy between mental and physical symptoms. He argues that this distinction is not as clearcut as Szasz would suggest. Nearly all symptoms of bodily disease involve some subjective judgment, either on the part of the examining physician or on the part of the patient. For example, pain may be a response to real physical damage, but it is a subjective state as well. Similarly, almost all patients will react psychologically to physical illness, thus requiring subjective decisions by the examining physician. Even if it were possible to distinguish between mental and physical symptoms, Ausubel suggests that this does not mean that physical treatment is unwarranted for mental symptoms.

Another of Szasz's arguments with which Ausubel disagrees is that mental symptoms are simply problems in living and therefore cannot be regarded as a result of some pathological condition. It is possible, Ausubel points out, that a particular symptom may be a reflection of problems in living *and* a manifestation of disease.

> It is quite true, as Szasz points out, that "human relations are inherently fraught with difficulties" (p. 117), and that most people manage to cope with such difficulties without becoming mentally ill. But conceding this fact hardly precludes the possibility that some individuals, either because of the magnitude of the stress involved, or because of genetically or environmentally induced susceptibility to ordinary degrees of stress, respond to the problems of living with behavior that is either seriously distorted or sufficiently unadaptive to prevent normal interpersonal relations and vocational functioning. The latter outcome—gross deviation from a designated range of desirable behavioral variability—conforms to the generally understood meaning of mental illness (p. 72).

Finally, Ausubel questions the proposition that personality disorders are a product of moral conflict and ethical choice. While he admits that Szasz may be correct in saying that the mental health profession has underemphasized the ethical and moral bases of human behavior, Ausubel feels that it is usually possible to distinguish between ordinary cases of immoral behavior and mental illness.

Physiological and psychological disease

The Szasz–Ausubel exchange provides us with an opportunity to consider the usefulness of the disease concept as a way of characterizing abnormal behavior. The basic issue confronting us here involves the question of what we mean by "disease" in a general sense, and what we mean by disease when we refer specifically to abnormal behavior. Szasz wishes to distinguish between "mental disease," which he assumes affects an individual's neurological system and results in "mental symptoms," and "bodily disease," which affects other organ systems of the body and results in "bodily symptoms." Ausubel, on the other hand, suggests that such a distinction is unnecessary; he regards disease as "any marked deviation, physical, mental, or behavioral, from normally desirable standards of structural and functional integrity."

Neither of these definitions is entirely satisfactory. Ausubel's definition of disease is so broad and inclusive that it is difficult to imagine any difficulty that an individual might encounter which would not qualify as a "disease" or as "mental illness." Also, this definition is so general that it begs the question of what we mean when we use these terms. Furthermore, since any deviation from "normally desirable standards" can qualify as disease, the possibility exists that even the "ordinary cases of immorality" which he wishes to distinguish from personality disorders could also be legitimately described as examples of disease. Thus, Ausubel's definition of disease has been stripped of much of the explanatory power it might have had by its extreme generality.

One implication of Szasz's distinction between mental and bodily illness is that there is in fact a real difference between physiological disease and what has been called "mental illness." In particular, Szasz would argue that physiological diseases have known organic etiologies, whereas mental illness is a misuse of medical terminology to characterize human problems in living which are essentially ethical, legal, or social in nature.

An earlier discussion by Marzolf (1947) seems to have anticipated Szasz in making a distinction between physiological and psychological disease. Marzolf discussed the disease concept in psychology in considerable detail and made a number of interesting comparisons between the concepts of physiological and psychological disease. He uses three points of comparison: (1) phenomena that exemplify each, (2) bases for differentiating diseased from normal states, and (3) factors that bring them about.

Phenomena that exemplify physiological disease include pain, discomfort, structural changes in tissue, and loss of physiological efficiency. Phenomena that exemplify psychological or mental disease are typically psychological discomfort, loss of contact with reality, lack of insight, and changes in behavior toward others.

Marzolf argues that it is not necessary to distinguish between physiological disease and normal physiological functioning. "In disease we have the manifestation of general principles of chemical, cellular, tissue, or organ function under special contingent circumstances" (p. 211). Mental disease, on the other hand, is usually distinguished from normal functioning because the behavior in question cannot be explained by any known motives, and the individual is therefore presumed not responsible for his acts, as in "pathological lying." Additionally, the factors which bring about physiological disease are considered to be inherited, nutritive, exogenous chemical agents, physical forces, or the vital activity of invading organisms (Marzolf, 1947), while mental illness is presumed to be brought about by psychological factors such as conflict.

Marzolf concludes that physiological and mental illness are not analogous concepts and he goes on to say that, "In fact there is no need for the term 'mental disease.' Disease is not an important concept in physiology; syndromes of dysfunction is a fully adequate expression. 'Syndromes of dysfunction' is adequate for psychology, too" (p. 219).

Social Utility of the Illness Perspective

We have indicated that the illness perspective is unquestionably the dominant public perspective for understanding abnormal behavior. A number of writers have been concerned recently about the social utility of the illness perspective. Do individuals whose behavior is considered abnormal benefit from being called mentally ill? Or, on the other hand, does this designation derogate and stigmatize them? A recent exchange between Ellis (1967) and Sarbin (1967) provides an excellent review of this problem and the arguments on both sides.

After reviewing literature which suggests that people labeled as mentally ill may suffer social discrimination (Davidson, 1958; Menninger, 1965), self-denigration, and interference with their treatment, Ellis (1967) nevertheless remains convinced that at least some people should be so labeled. He believes that the term mental illness can be used as a sort of shorthand for more elaborate operational definitions and in this way can be appropriately applied to certain individuals without necessarily having negative consequences.

> Thus, instead of saying, "He is mentally ill," we could say, "He is a human being who at the present time is behaving in a self-defeating and/or needlessly antisocial manner and who will most probably continue to do so in the future, and, although he is partially creating or causing (and in this sense is responsible for) his aberrant behavior, he is still not to be condemned for creating it but is to be helped to overcome it." This second statement is more precise, accurate, and helpful than the first one, but it is often impractical to spell it out in this detail. It is, therefore, legitimate to use the first statement, "He is mentally ill," as long as we clearly understand that it means the longer version (p. 445).

Sarbin (1967) strongly disagrees with this argument and suggests that Ellis is guilty of accepting the premise which he has set out to prove. He feels that Ellis' arguments

> represent not so much a lack of attention to the rules of evidence . . . as the acceptance of an entrenched and unwarranted belief that operates as a major premise. When operative, the premise may be stated: The label "mental illness" reliably denotes certain forms of conduct that are discriminable from forms of conduct that may be reliably denoted as "not mentally ill" (p. 447).

Sarbin argues that retaining the mental illness label leads Ellis and others so disposed to accept a number of tacit but fundamentally wrong assumptions concerning the nature of people so labeled. Not only are these assumptions incorrect or misleading, but they tend to restrict our descriptions of the conduct we are trying to understand. That is, once the conduct called mental illness has been identified as such, we view the person displaying that conduct quite differently. Finally, Sarbin would argue that once our perceptions of the individual have been restricted, alternative actions toward that person have been restricted as well. When we see the person as mentally ill, we behave toward him in highly predictable ways. For example, since he is mentally ill we may incorrectly conclude that he requires hospitalization for his illness.

Sarbin's conclusions flow from a linguistic and historical analysis of the concepts of "illness" and "mind." Illness, according to Sarbin, was first used as a metaphor and later transformed into a myth by dropping the qualifying "as if," as in, "he acts *as if* he were ill."

> "Illness," as in mental illness, is an illicit transformation of a metaphorical concept to a literal one. To save unfortunate people from being labeled witches, it was humane to treat persons who exhibited misconduct of certain kinds as if they were ill. The Galenic model facilitated the eliding of the hypothetical phrase, the "as if," and the concept of illness was thus deformed to include events that did not meet the orginal conjunctive criteria for illness. A second transformation assured the validity of the Galenic model. The mystifying behaviors could be treated as if they were symptoms equivalent to somatic symptoms. By dropping the "as if" modifier, observed behavior could be interpreted as symptomatic of underlying internal pathology (p. 449).

It is not only illness that is reified in the dual metaphor "mental illness." Mental states are also seen as real, palpable objects.

> Thus mental states—the objects of interest and study for the diagnostician of "mental illness"—were postulated to fill gaps in early knowledge. Through historical and linguistic processes, the construct was reified. Contemporary users of the mental-illness concept are guilty of illicitly shifting from metaphor to myth. Instead of maintaining the metaphorical rhetoric "it is as if there were states of mind," and "it is as if some 'states of mind' could be characterized as sickness," the contemporary mentalist conducts much of his work as if he believes that minds are "real" entities and that, like bodies, they can be sick or healthy (p. 450).

These linguistic and historical developments in the case of the mental illness label have led us to regard people who carry that label as different from those who do not. According to Sarbin's argument, however, there is no set of behaviors which can reliably distinguish those people we regard as mentally ill from those we do not.

From Sarbin's point of view, the solution lies in omitting the label "mental illness" from our vocabulary, since there is no evidence that societal problems can be ameliorated by diagnosing deviant individuals as "ill." In place of the mental illness metaphor Sarbin suggests that we refer to "the transformation of social identity." This term captures the antecedent and concurrent events associated with becoming a *norm violator* (Sarbin, 1967).

The Scientific Utility of the Illness Perspective

Although some of the original assumptions Kraepelin made in elaborating the illness perspectives are now thought to lack strong empirical support, Kraepelin still has advocates. Among the most forthright of these is Meehl whose work we have already mentioned. In a paper entitled "Some Ruminations on the Validation of Clinical Procedures" (1966) Meehl makes his position quite clear regarding Kraepelin's assumptions and the concept of schizophrenia as a disease.

> I consider that there are such things as disease entities in functional psychiatry, and I do not think that Kraepelin was as mistaken as some of my psychological contemporaries seem to think. It is my belief, for example, that there is a *disease* schizophrenia, fundamentally of an organic nature, and probably of largely constitutional aetiology. I would explain the viability of the Kraepelinean nomenclature by the hypothesis that there is a considerable amount of truth contained in the system; and that, therefore, the practical implications associated with these labels are still sufficiently great, especially when compared with the predictive power of competing concepts, that even the most anti-nosological clinician finds himself worrying about whether a patient whom he has been treating as an obsessional character "is really a schizophrenic" (p. 9).

Several things are worth noting about Meehl's formulation. He appears to mean by disease something quite similar to what we have outlined in our description of the illness perspective. It is interesting to note that his position is a clearcut example of the displacement of concepts: the concept of disease is applied to a new and puzzling situation, i.e., schizophrenia, applied not by analogy but as a literal statement.

Meehl appears to believe that calling schizophrenia a disease has scientific utility. Specifically, he believes that the use of the disease concept will yield superior *predictions* concerning future behavior than will alternative concepts. Although he does not elaborate what he means by this, we may infer that he means reasoning something like the following:

1. Given a cluster of symptoms or syndrome diagnosed as schizophrenia,
2. And given that the disease entity schizophrenia has certain reliable properties,
3. We may predict:
   a. the etiology of the disorder when discovered will be organic and perhaps genetic.
   b. the outcome of the disorder in terms of prognosis.

Of course, such a set of statements has clearcut empirical implications. The utility of asserting that schizophrenia is a disease can be judged by the degree to which these predictions can be empirically verified.

For some disorders these assumptions have produced promising preliminary results. For example, the work of Coppen (1967) and of Reich, Clayton, and Winokur (1969) on affective disorders suggests that mania is a disorder of genetic origin with biochemical and metabolic correlates. An excellent review of genetic theory and abnormal behavior is also now available (Rosenthal, 1970).

Perhaps the single most outstanding issue raised by our commentary is the question of whether mental illness should be viewed as myth or disease. Both Sarbin and Szasz strongly suggest that mental illness is essentially mythical in nature, a label without reliably observable behavioral referents. Ellis and Meehl, on the other hand, believe there is a substantive, real thing called mental illness which results in ineffective social behavior and which can be studied scientifically like any other disease.

It is unlikely that any reconciliation of these views would please all of these authors. Yet we may be able to integrate their views in a way that is consistent with our position, namely, that approaches to psychopathology are essentially metaphors which serve to provide the psychopathologist with a way of viewing human behavior.

In another connection, Sarbin suggests there is a common tendency to transform metaphors to myths. By myth he means ". . . a literal statement, unsupported by empirical evidence, used as a guide to action" (Sarbin, 1968, p. 414). Given the current state of knowledge concerning most forms of abnormal behavior, the assertion that abnormal behavior is mental illness certainly seems to qualify as a myth as Sarbin describes it.

There is a real danger in concepts that have attained the status of myth. They may lose the tentativeness of scientific hypotheses and become, instead, dogmatically espoused guides to action. We would suggest that, in this sense at least, Sarbin and Szasz are justified in attacking the concept of mental illness.

On the other hand, we have also suggested earlier that metaphors, whether they have become myths or not, have other important functions. To review briefly, the metaphor aids us in selecting events as relevant, provides a mode of representation of the events in question, and allows us to specify the relations between events. These are important functions that lay the groundwork for systematic inquiry.

We would suggest that when Meehl says that there are disease entities in functional psychiatry, he is in effect proposing a systematic framework and mode of attack on the problem of abnormal behavior. In general, treating one set of events (abnormal behavior) as if they were another set of events (disease) is just such a proposal. This proposal has as one of its products a set of testable hypotheses concerning the events in question. For example, to assert that "schizophrenia is a disease" implies that there are discoverable organic etiological factors involved. Similar hypotheses have invited and will continue to invite empirical test. The future of the illness perspective will depend upon the outcome of these tests.

Summary

The controversy over the usefulness of the illness perspective centers on the question of whether abnormal behavior may be legitimately considered a disease or not. We noted that Szasz has asserted that mental illness is not a disease but a myth and that behaviors now classified as mental illness are more usefully considered to be simply problems in living. Such a designation would, according to Szasz, serve to emphasize the fact that most abnormal behavior involves moral and ethical conflict.

Ausubel has criticized Szasz's argument on a number of grounds and has asserted that a particular symptom may be both a problem in living and a manifestation of disease. But we noted that Ausubel defines disease so broadly that he weakens the potential persuasiveness of his argument considerably.

We also suggested that the term "mental illness" is not strictly analogous to the concept of physiological disease. It is interesting to note that this may in part reflect the fact that metaphors tend to undergo a process of mutual adaptation when they are taken from one field of inquiry and applied to a new and puzzling problem. The original meaning of the concept of disease has, it appears, been altered in its application to the problem of abnormal behavior.

We have also considered the social usefulness of the concept of mental illness. Ellis suggests that we may use the term mental illness as a kind of shorthand to designate certain persons as being in need of psychological help without necessarily producing negative social consequences for the person so labeled. Sarbin, on the other hand, has provided a linguistic and historical analysis of the concept of mental illness and suggests that it functions as a reified metaphor. That is, mental illness is a metaphor which is now uncritically accepted as a real, palpable entity. Sarbin goes on to assert that we cannot identify a set of behaviors which reliably distinguishes those people who are mentally ill from those people who are not.

We concluded that the scientific usefulness of the illness perspective will depend heavily on whether it is used as a source of testable hypotheses or merely accepted as an established fact. If it is taken as a broad assumption suggesting a series of conceptually related and testable hypotheses, then there remains at least the possibility of empirical test of the assumption. If, on the other hand, it is taken uncritically as a dogmatically espoused guide to action, then it is likely to impede both scientific and social progress.

References

AMERICAN PSYCHIATRIC ASSOCIATION   *Diagnostic and statistical manual: Mental disorders (DSM-I).* Washington: American Psychiatric Association, 1952.

AMERICAN PSYCHIATRIC ASSOCIATION   *Diagnostic and statistical manual of mental disorders (DSM-II).* (2nd ed.) Washington: American Psychiatric Association, 1968.

AUSUBEL, D. P.   Personality disorder *is* disease. *American Psychologist,* 1961, *16*, 69–74.

CATTELL, R. B.   The description of personality. I. Foundations as trait measurement. *Psychological Review,* 1940, *50*, 559–594.

COPPEN, A.   The biochemistry of affective disorders. *British Journal Psychiatry,* 1967, *113*, 1237–1264.

CUMMING, J., & CUMMING, E.   *Closed ranks: An experiment in mental health education.* Cambridge: Harvard University Press, 1957.

DAVIDSON, H.   Dr. Whatsisname. *Mental Hospitals,* 1958, *9*, 8.

DIEFENDORF, A. R.   *Clinical psychiatry.* New York: Macmillan, 1921.

ELLIS, A.   Should some people be labeled mentally ill? *Journal of Consulting Psychology,* 1967, *31*, 435–446.

EYSENCK, H. J.   Classification and the problem of diagnosis. In H. J. Eysenck (Ed.), *Handbook of abnormal psychology.* London: Pitman, 1960.

GRUENBERG, E. M.   Foreword. In *DSM-II.* Washington: American Psychiatric Association, 1968.

JOHN HANCOCK MUTUAL LIFE INSURANCE COMPANY. *The Mind.* Pamphlet, 1954, p. 15.

KALLMAN, F. J. *Heredity in mental health and disorder.* New York: Norton, 1953.

KETY, S. Biochemical theories of schizophrenia. *Science,* 1959, *129,* 1520, 1590, 3362.

KRAMER, M. Introduction: The historical background of ICD-8 (International Classification of Diseases-8). In *DSM-II.* Washington: American Psychiatric Association, 1968.

MAHER, B. A. *Principles of psychopathology.* New York: Mc-Graw-Hill, 1966.

MARZOLF, S. S. Symptom and syndrome statistically interpreted. *Psychological Bulletin,* 1945, *42,* 162–176.

MARZOLF, S. S. The disease concept in psychology. *Psychological Review,* 1947, *54,* 211–221.

MEEHL, P. E. Schizotaxia, schizotypy, schizophrenia. *American Psychologist,* 1962, *17,* 827–838.

MEEHL, P. Some ruminations on the validation of clinical procedures. In E. Megargee (Ed.), *Research in clinical assessment.* New York: Harper & Row, 1966.

MENNINGER, K. *The vital balance.* New York: Viking, 1965.

MILTON, O., & WAHLER, R. G. Perspectives and trends. In Milton, O., & Wahler, R. G. (Eds.), *Behavior disorders: Perspectives and trends.* (2nd ed.) New York: Lippincott, 1969.

NATIONAL ASSOCIATION FOR MENTAL HEALTH. *Facts about mental illness, fact sheet.* 1963.

NATIONAL ASSOCIATION FOR MENTAL HEALTH. *Some things you should know about mental and emotional illness.* Leaflet (no date).

REICH, T., CLAYTON, P. J., & WINOKUR, G. Family history studies: V. The genetics of mania. *American Journal of Psychiatry,* 1969, *125,* 64–75.

ROSENTHAL, D. *Genetic theory and abnormal behavior.* New York: Mc-Graw-Hill, 1970.

SARASON, I. G., & GANZER, V. J. Concerning the medical model. *American Psychologist,* 1968, *23,* 507–510.

SARBIN, T. R. On the futility of the proposition that some people be labeled "mentally ill." *Journal of Consulting Psychology,* 1967, *31,* 447–453.

SARBIN, T. R. Ontology recapitulates philology. The mythic nature of anxiety. *American Psychologist,* 1968, *23,* 411–418.

SCHRODER, D., & EHRLICH, D. Rejection by mental health professionals: A possible consequence of not seeking appropriate help for emotional disorders. *Journal of Health and Social Behavior,* 1968, *9,* 222–232.

SCHWARTZ, C. G.   Perspective on deviance—wives' definitions of their husbands' mental illness. *Psychiatry*, 1957, *20*, 275–291.

STERN, EDITH.   *Mental illness: A guide for the family*. National Association for Mental Health, 1957, p. 1.

SZASZ, T. S.   The myth of mental illness. *American Psychologist*, 1960, *15*, 113–118.

SZASZ, T. S.   *The myth of mental illness*. New York: Dell, 1967.

TENNESSEE DEPARTMENT OF MENTAL HEALTH.   *Mind Over Matter*, Vol. 7, No. 4, 1962.

ULLMANN, L. P., & KRASNER, L.   *Case studies in behavior modification*. New York: Holt, Rinehart and Winston, 1965.

ULLMANN, L. P., & KRASNER, L.   *A psychological approach to abnormal behavior*. Englewood Cliffs, N. J.: Prentice-Hall, 1969.

WOLFER, J. A.   Concerning the concern over the medical model. *American Psychologist*, 1969, *24*, 606–607.

CHAPTER 5

THE LEARNING PERSPECTIVE

The Perspective

Introduction

The learning perspective is currently one of the most rapidly growing approaches to the study of abnormal behavior. Part of its appeal is undoubtedly, as Breger and McGaugh (1965) suggest, because the perspective carries with it a quality of scientific respectability. Adherents of the approach (e.g., Ullmann & Krasner, 1969) usually take pains to point out that its basis is modern learning theory. As such, the learning perspective draws upon basic concepts from learning theory as well as a sizeable body of empirical information.

Another reason for its appeal is the fact that the learning perspective offers not only a formulation of abnormal behavior, but also a relatively well defined program of treatment based upon the same principles. Thus, typically, the formulation of a particular case within the learning framework suggests at the same time a means of changing the behavior in question.

The history of the current learning movement can certainly be traced as far back as John Locke's (1632–1704) doctrine of man as a *tabula rasa*. However, the recent history of the perspective as it is applied to abnormal behavior is perhaps more informative in understanding the current state of the field.

In 1950 Dollard and Miller published *Personality and Psychotherapy* in which they attempted to reexamine some traditional psychoanalytic principles of psychotherapy in light of learning concepts. Although theirs was an impressive attempt, the reaction of fellow professionals, after an initial burst of enthusiasm, was to view the book as little more than a translation of one set of principles into another with the addition of little that was new or innovative.

Shortly thereafter, in 1953, Skinner published *Science and Human Behavior*, an attempt to apply the principles of operant conditioning to a wide variety of human behaviors. Its strength was and remains Skinner's ability to convince us of the power of his approach with his striking examples. Skinner's work was considered impressive by many, but it did not deal in detail with the problem of abnormal behavior and thus did not have great impact on those specifically concerned with this problem.

It remained for Wolpe's *Psychotherapy by Reciprocal Inhibition* (1958) to produce this impact. In this volume Wolpe described his laboratory work on the conditioning of anxiety in animals and the therapeutic technique of systematic desensitization of fear responses which developed out of this work. From this point on, acceptance of the learning perspective increased rapidly. The journal *Behavior Research and Therapy* was established in 1963, to be devoted to theoretical and empirical contributions to the learning approach to abnormal behavior.

Early in the 1960's two distinguishably different orientations within the learning perspective began to emerge. One approach was based largely upon the principles of classical conditioning as described by Wolpe (1958) and Eysenck (1960). The other approach was Skinnerian in orientation and relied much more heavily upon the principles of operant conditioning. The work of Ullmann and Krasner (1965) was greatly influenced by the Skinnerian orientation, and, although it was based largely upon operant principles, it also extended the learning perspective to encompass a much broader range of social phenomena associated with abnormal behavior. Most recently, their work has resulted in a text (Ullmann & Krasner, 1969) written from what they described as a "socio-psychological" point of view.

These two approaches exist today side by side as the major streams of thought in the learning perspective. They do not represent mutually exclusive approaches but instead overlap and complement each other. Both take as their point of departure the assumption that abnormal behavior is *learned* behavior. We shall have occasion to refer to both of these approaches in our description of the learning perspective.

Basic Concepts from the Field of Learning

Before we can begin to appreciate the learning perspective on abnormal behavior it is necessary to examine briefly some of the most fundamental concepts of learning theory as Hilgard (1962) describes them.

Stimulus   A stimulus is any objectively defined situation or event that is the occasion for an organism's response.

Response   A response is the behavioral result of stimulation in the form of a movement or glandular secretion.

Reinforcement   The process which increases the strength of conditioning (i.e., the probability of a response) as a result of either classical conditioning or operant conditioning.

Classical conditioning   The process whereby an originally neutral conditioned stimulus, through continuous pairing with an unconditioned stimulus, acquires the ability to elicit a response originally given to the unconditioned stimulus. Figure 5.1 describes the standard classical conditioning paradigm.

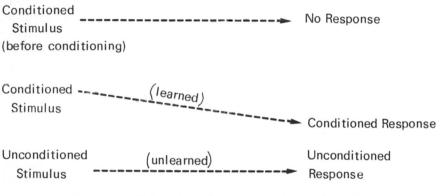

Figure 5.1   Classical conditioning paradigm (after Hilgard, 1962, p. 255)

Operant conditioning   Operant conditioning involves the strengthening of an operant response (one which is emitted rather than elicited) by the presentation of a reinforcing stimulus if, and only if, the operant response occure. The paradigm is outlined in Figure 5.2.

Learning   Both classical and operant conditioning arrangements are

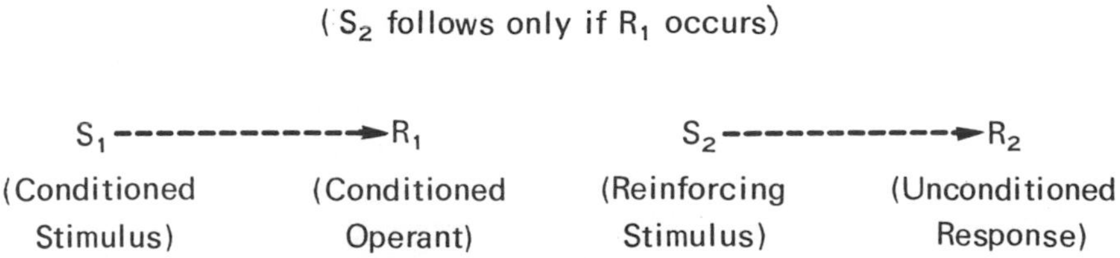

(S_2 follows only if R_1 occurs)

S_1 -----------► R_1 S_2 -----------► R_2

(Conditioned   (Conditioned   (Reinforcing   (Unconditioned
Stimulus)   Operant)   Stimulus)   Response)

Figure 5.2   Operant conditioning paradigm (after Hilgard, 1962, p. 255)

said to result in learning. Learning may simply be defined as a functional connection or association between a stimulus and a response.

Extinction   When either the unconditioned stimulus in the case of classical conditioning or the reinforcing stimulus in the case of operant conditioning is omitted, the acquired response will gradually diminish. This is the process of extinction.

Discrimination   Discrimination is said to occur when a response to a particular stimulus is selectively reinforced and that response is not reinforced when it is made to other stimuli.

Generalization   Once a conditioned response is established in the presence of a particular stimulus, it will also be elicited by other stimuli, particularly stimuli which are similar to the original conditioned stimulus.

With these basic learning concepts in mind, we may now examine their application to the phenomena of abnormal behavior. As we shall see, the learning perspective on abnormal behavior uses these as well as some additional concepts such as "adaptation" and "role" in defining abnormal behavior.

Abnormal Behavior as Learned Maladaptive Behavior

Both Eysenck and his coworkers (Eysenck, 1960) and Ullmann and Krasner (1965) offer similar definitions of abnormal behavior. Ullmann and Krasner begin by asserting that abnormal behavior is maladaptive behavior. Such behavior has several characteristics or attributes. First, it is not assumed to differ from any other presumably normal behavior either in terms of its development or maintenance. Since there is presumed to be no discontinuity between adaptive and maladaptive behavior, the decision to call any particular behavior pathological must depend to a large extent upon social factors. Specifically, Ullmann and Krasner (1965) assume in their account that all societies prescribe certain roles which have a particular range of reinforcement associated with them. These roles are then maintained by reinforcement.

Thus, for Ullmann and Krasner, maladaptive behavior has two identifying characteristics. First, it is considered inappropriate by those individuals in a particular person's life who control the reinforcers or reinforcing events for that person. Second, maladaptive behavior tends in general to lead to a reduction or decrease in the amount of positive reinforcement given to the individual who engages in that behavior.

Eysenck and Rachman (1965) are in general agreement with the Ullmann and Krasner view of abnormal behavior as both learned and maladaptive. They also wish to distinguish learned abnormal behavior from innate or instinctive behavior on the one hand, and behavior due to organic lesions on the other. Eysenck further clarifies what he means by the term "maladaptive," particularly in the case of neurotic behavior:

> As nearly all human behavior may be said to be learned, how do we distinguish neurotic behavior from other types of behavior? The answer must be that neurotic behavior is maladaptive; the individual who adopts a neurotic behavior pattern fails to achieve what he is trying to do and succeeds in doing what in fact is highly disadvantageous to him. Mowrer (1950) refers to this as the "neurotic paradox." (p. 3)

For Eysenck and Rachman, then, abnormal behavior is learned and maladaptive in the sense that it is self-defeating for the individual engaging in it.

Types of Maladaptive Behavior

It is only a short step from postulating different learning mechanisms to account for different types of maladaptive behavior to developing a rudimentary taxonomy of abnormal behavior based upon a learning perspective. Ullmann and Krasner suggest this in their discussion of the development of maladaptive behavior but do not make it as explicit as do Eysenck and Rachman.

Eysenck and Rachman distinguish between "disorders of the first kind" (i.e., *dysthymic*) and "disorders of the second kind." Disorders of the first kind include phobic phenomena, anxiety reactions, and obsessive-compulsive disorders. These disorders are explained in the following way:

> . . . Our general hypothesis is that they are caused by conditioned autonomic fear responses and the reactions, skeletal, muscular and hormonal, of the organism to these conditioned responses. (p. 6)

An example of the conditioning view of phobic behavior is provided by Eysenck and Rachman as well as an explanation cast in learning terms.

> The classical demonstration of the development of a phobia was provided by Watson and Rayner in 1920. Having first ascertained that it was a neutral object, the authors presented an 11-month-old boy, Albert, with a white rat to play with. Whenever he reached for the animal the experimenters made a loud noise behind him. After only five trials Albert began showing signs of fear in the presence of the white rat. This fear then generalized to similar stimuli such as furry objects, cotton wool, white rabbits. The phobic reactions were still present when Albert was tested four months later.

The process involved in this demonstration provides a striking illustration of the manner in which phobias develop, and may be represented in this way:

1. Neutral stimulus (rat)_____Approach R

2. Painful noise stimulus (UCS)_____Fear (UCR)

3. Rats (CS) + noise (UCS)_____Fear

4. Rats (CS)_____Fear (CR)

5. Rabbit (GS^1)_____Fear (GR)

6. Cotton wool (GS^2)_____Fear (GCR)

The essentials of the theory may be summarized in nine statements.

1. Phobias are learned responses.
2. Stimuli develop phobic qualities when they are associated temporally and spatially with a fear-producing state of affairs.
3. Neutral stimuli which are of relevance in the fear-producing situation and/or make an impact on the person in the situation, are more likely to develop phobic qualities than weak or irrelevant stimuli.
4. Repetition of the association between the fear situation and the new phobic stimuli will strengthen the phobia.
5. Associations between high intensity fear situations and neutral stimuli are more likely to produce phobic reactions.
6. Generalization from the original phobic stimulus to stimuli of a similar nature will occur.
7. Noxious experiences which occur under conditions of excessive confinement are more likely to produce phobic reactions.
8. Neutral stimuli which are associated with a noxious experience(s) may develop (secondary) motivating properties. This acquired drive is termed the fear-drive.
9. Responses (such as avoidance) which reduce the fear-drive are reinforced. (pp. 81–82)

Disorders of the second kind are the result of failures of conditioning to produce socially desirable habits. An example of the failure of conditioning is psychopathic behavior. The stimulus properties of socially disapproved behavior fail to be conditioned by pairing with punishing unconditioned stimulus events and thus these stimulus properties fail to elicit anxiety as a conditioned response (i.e., "conscience").

Another form of "failure of conditioning" involves the positive reinforcement of socially disapproved behavior. Examples of this phenomenon offered by Eysenck and Rachman are homosexuality and fetishism, the stimulus properties of which may have taken on reinforcing properties as a result of orgasm.

The authors suggest that extinction is not a consequence of the learning conditions producing disorders of the second kind. Thus spontaneous remission should not occur. They suggest that, despite a general lack of evidence, psychiatric opinion concerning the persistence of psychopathic and homosexual behavior patterns is consistent with their conclusions and that therefore extinction does not occur in these disorders.

Sources of Uniformity in Maladaptive Behavior

How does the learning perspective account for the regularities of abnormal behavior? This question is answered by Ullmann and Krasner (1965) in two ways. They assert first of all that the regularities in abnormal behavior may not be so great as has been generally assumed. In order to account for those regularities that do in fact appear, however, three different sources of regularities are identified. They are: (1) role learning, promoted by the general society; (2) the selective reward of behaviors considered "abnormal" by mental health professionals; and (3) the promotion of specific behaviors by the mental hospital itself. We will consider each of these three sources of regularities in abnormal behavior.

It is assumed that role learning is both developed and maintained by systematic reinforcement of the avoidance of certain aversive events. Ullmann and Krasner briefly describe a "sick role" which society tends to reward in certain ways. For example, behavior which is part of the sick role may receive attention and forgiveness which are both considered positive reinforcers. Further, an individual displaying behaviors which are part of the sick role is excused from responsibility and this in turn allows the avoidance of aversive stimuli.

Another potential source of regularity in abnormal behavior is a result of the behavior of the mental health professional himself. Because of the psychiatrist's or psychologist's expectations about the nature of abnormal behavior, he will attend to some behaviors displayed by the patient more than to others. Since attention is a "generalized reinforcer" for Ullmann and Krasner, those behaviors which receive more attention than others will be strengthened and maintained, while others will drop out because they do not receive attention. The result of this sequence of events is that the mental health professional, in the process of doing his diagnostic examination, will attend to some behaviors more than others. In doing so he actually selectively rewards and shapes the abnormal behavior which he expects to occur.

Finally, role learning may occur in a mental hospital itself. In the hospital setting a wide variety of different reinforcing events exist which are presumed to be used to promote a "good patient" role. The good patient role includes behavior such as remaining clean and quiet as well as being cooperative. All these behaviors are assumed to be rewarded both by psychiatrists and by other medical staff members in the mental hospital. Ullmann and Krasner point out that the medical staff has at its disposal a wide range of reinforcers of both the positive and negative variety, ranging from such negative reinforcers as electro-convulsive shock therapy to such positive reinforcers as the granting of privileges. Thus the good patient role is the product of the systematic application of reinforcement.

In summary, the learning perspective argues that there exists a wide variety of sources of reward and punishment within society in general, from mental health professionals, and finally from the mental hospital itself, and that all of these promote the regularities we observe in abnormal behavior.

The Symptom Is the Disorder

There is a final point on which most advocates of the learning perspective are in fundamental agreement. It is argued that the "symptom" or observable behavior is the disorder, rather than some underlying state of affairs. Eysenck and Rachman (1965) make this point quite explicit when they say:

> The point, however, on which the theory here advocated breaks decisively with psychoanalytic thought of any description is in this. Freudian theory regards neurotic symptoms as adaptive mechanisms which are evidence of repression; they are "the visible upshot of unconscious causes." Learning theory does not postulate any such "unconscious" causes, but regards neurotic symptoms as simply learned habits; there is no neurosis underlying the symptom, but merely the symptom itself. *Get rid of the symptom (skeletal and autonomic) and you have eliminated the neurosis.* (p. 10)

Thus, abnormal behavior, at least in the case of neurosis, is not thought to be due to some underlying dynamic or organic set of factors. Similarly, the term "symptom" is regarded only as a convenient label.

> While the term "symptom" may be retained to describe neurotic behavior, there is no implication that such behavior is "symptomatic" of anything. (p. 277)

Most adherents of a learning perspective believe that the assertion that "the symptom is the disorder" provides a clear-cut distinction between their view and that of the illness or psychoanalytic perspective. Furthermore, the assumption that the symptom is the disorder places the behavior therapist in a position to treat the symptom directly without concerning himself with the problem of "symptom substitution."

The notion of symptom substitution—that removal of a symptom will lead necessarily to the development of some new maladaptive behavior— has been vigorously attacked by adherents of the learning perspective (Ullmann & Krasner, 1965; Yates, 1958). Ullman and Krasner (1969) have offered two forms of argument against this notion. They indicate that symptom substitution is much less frequent than is commonly assumed. Rachman (1963) estimates that symptom substitution occurs after symptom removal in no more than 5 percent of the cases examined.

Ullmann and Krasner (1969) also suggest several alternative interpretations when symptom substitution does in fact occur. First, symptom substitution may occur because the individual is resensitized to threatening stimuli to which he had previously been desensitized. Second, a new maladaptive behavior may occur because it is next in response strength in the individual's repertoire. Third, behavioral change in the individual may alter the stimulus situation, thus eliciting new maladaptive behaviors. Finally, symptom removal may lead to inconsistent behavior patterns. That is, newly acquired behavior may not be consistent with other ongoing behavior displayed by the individual and this inconsistency may be perceived as symptom substitution.

The Development of Maladaptive Behavior

A fundamental aspect of the learning perspective is an account of the development of maladaptive behavior in learning terms. Eysenck has focused largely upon the development of neurotic behavior and relies heavily upon the classical conditioning paradigm in its discussion. The Skinnerian group has, on the other hand, formulated an account which relies more heavily upon operant conditioning principles. Despite this difference, both groups attempt to account for a very broad range of behavior and both groups do utilize principles derived from both classical and operant conditioning. Thus the difference is one of emphasis rather than of kind. Since the Eysenck group focuses more upon classical conditioning, we will rely upon their discussion as a basis for remarks concerning this approach to maladaptive behavior.

In their book, *The Causes and Cures of Neurosis* (1965), Eysenck and Rachman develop a three-stage formulation of abnormal behavior. The original experimental work that forms the basis of this paradigm is that of Solomon (1956). The first stage describes the occurrence of traumatic conditioning. A traumatic or series of subtraumatic events may produce intense autonomic reactions in the individual. The autonomic reactions are unconditioned responses and may in themselves produce disorganized behavior. Although this disorganization of behavior is said to be a frequently observed aspect of maladaptive behavior it is not necessarily "neurotic" in character.

The second stage described by Eysenck and Rachman is essentially a restatement of the classical conditioning paradigm in the context of maladaptive behavior.

> . . . We find that in a large number of cases conditioning takes place, in the sense that a previously neutral stimulus, through association, becomes connected with the unconditioned stimuli which give rise to the traumatic, emotional reactions. From now on it will be found that the conditioned stimulus, as well as the unconditioned stimulus, produces the original, maladaptive emotional behavior. (p. 4)

Eysenck and Rachman note that the classical or Pavlovian conditioning mechanism is responsible for many of the behaviors that we consider neurotic, particularly those in which the anxiety appears to have generalized to a variety of previously neutral stimuli.

A corollary observation, that conditioned neurotic responses undergo "spontaneous remission" in many cases, is seen by Eysenck and Rachman as consistent with their formulation. They suggest that conditioned autonomic responses may be extinguished if they are not reinforced by traumatic unconditioned stimuli. As evidence for the phenomenon of spontaneous remission—and, by extension, for extinction—the authors cite data reported by Denker (1946) on the follow-up of 500 severe cases of neurosis. After two years 70 percent of the cases showed recovery without any treatment and after five years over 90 percent had recovered.

The third stage of the Eysenck and Rachman paradigm is designed to explain the observation that not all cases of neurosis show remission. They note that humans are usually in a position to escape or avoid anxiety-evoking conditioned stimuli. Thus Eysenck and Rachman use the mechanism of avoidance to explain the fact that humans will avoid threatening stimuli and thus will fail to extinguish responses to those stimuli. Furthermore, since the avoidance or escape response is reinforced by anxiety reduction, the probability of its occurring is increased, while the original conditioned stimulus retains its power to elicit conditioned emotional reactions. The Eysenck and Rachman formulation can be diagrammed as shown in Figure 5.3.

As we might expect from writers who rely heavily upon Skinnerian

Stage 1: Traumatic Conditioning

Stage 2: Classical Conditioning

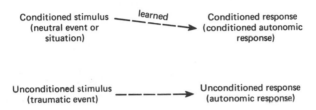

Stage 3: Instrumental Avoidance

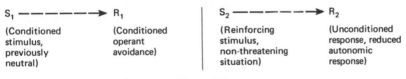

Figure 5.3

principles, Ullmann and Krasner (1965) provide a more detailed account of phenomena which lend themselves to analysis in terms of operant principles. They suggest that two basic paradigms may be offered to account for the development of maladaptive behavior. These are (1) the failure to learn an adaptive response and (2) maladaptive behaviors which have evolved through the systematic application of reinforcement.

Let us first consider phenomena associated with a failure to learn an adaptive response. In particular, Ullmann and Krasner suggest that a failure to learn social skills may result in an individual not receiving the rewards which are actually available to him in a particular situation. The failure to learn adaptive responses associated with social skills not only results in the loss of reinforcement which would occur if these responses were performed; a "vicious cycle" will presumably result as well in many cases. This vicious cycle occurs because the individual's reaction to a situation in which he does not receive appropriate reinforcement may be *in itself* maladaptive and lead to even further withdrawal of reinforcement in subsequent situations of the same kind.

The second paradigm used to explain the development of maladaptive behavior involves direct and systematic positive reinforcement of the maladaptive behavior itself. Perhaps the best way to appreciate the notion that symptoms may develop as a result of the systematic application of positive reinforcement is to examine a demonstration of this principle in some detail.

Haughton and Ayllon (1965) reported a case in which they attempted to develop a "symptom" in an individual and then removed it, thus demonstrating, presumably, the effects of reinforcement on the behavior. The investigators selected a patient from an experimental research ward in a psychiatric hospital, a 54-year-old female patient who had been hospitalized for 23 years. They began by observing the patient every thirty minutes and recording her behavior in terms of both activity and location. After a number of days of observation they found, not surprisingly, that the patient typically stayed in bed, smoked heavily, and refused to work on the ward. Having recorded the necessary base-line data, the patient was deprived of cigarettes with the exception of one cigarette after each meal. Following this, a period of response shaping took place. The investigators selected a response arbitrarily. The response they selected was to stand upright holding a broom. The procedure for instituting this response in the behavior of the patient was described by Haughton and Ayllon (1965) as follows: "a period of response shaping was initiated during which a staff member gave the patient a broom and while she held it, another staff member approached the patient and gave her a cigarette." (p. 96)

Once the response was established, various "reinforcement schedules" were initiated and response shaping occurred. As different reinforcement schedules were applied to the patient's behavior, fewer and fewer reinforcements, that is, cigarettes, were given for longer and longer periods of holding the broom in the prescribed manner. Finally, toward the end of the response shaping period, the patient was receiving the reinforcement of a cigarette as infrequently as every two hundred and forty minutes, and yet the broom-holding "symptom" remained strong. This means that at the end of the response shaping procedure, Haughton and Ayllon's patient would in some cases maintain the prescribed behavior for as long as four hours before being reinforced. During the response shaping period, direct reinforcement by cigarettes was replaced by reinforcement by tokens which were later exchangeable for cigarettes. Thus at the end of the response shaping period, the patient stood and held the broom for long periods simply to receive a token. A final phase of the demonstration involved extinguishing the response. Reinforcement was withdrawn entirely and slowly the behavior disappeared.

A number of interesting behaviors developed as well as the "symptom" that Haughton and Ayllon intended to develop and maintain. The patient's broom holding became quite stereotyped. Furthermore, when other patients asked for the patient's broom, she resisted quite strongly and at times quite aggressively.

Thus we see that the learning perspective argues that symptoms are developed through the systematic application of reinforcement principles. Ullmann and Krasner (1965) place great weight upon Haughton and Ayllon's demonstration and feel that it gives us considerable insight into the nature and evolution of psychiatric symptoms. They say at one point in the introduction to Haughton and Ayllon's paper, "This important paper, which ranks with Watson and Rayner's 1920 'Development of a Phobia,' illustrates that principles of learning are applicable to the development as well as the elimination of maladaptive behavior." (p. 66)

Once maladaptive behaviors are developed, we may ask how they are maintained. The answer is, in essentially the same way they were developed, that is, by reinforcement. Ullmann and Krasner do point out, however, that although reinforcement is assumed to maintain the maladaptive behavior, it is not necessarily true that the reinforcer which led to the development of the behavior will also maintain it. Thus, for example, a behavior may be developed because it allows avoidance of certain aversive consequences in an individual's life. However, once the behavior is developed, it may be maintained by some other positively reinforcing event.

Summary

We have seen that the learning perspective defines abnormal behavior as learned maladaptive behavior. Drawing on the fields of learning, the concepts stimulus, response, and reinforcement provide the basic framework of the perspective. The mechanisms of classical and operant conditioning are invoked both to explain the development of abnormal behavior and to provide a rudimentary taxonomy for the wide variety of abnormal behaviors discussed. Symptoms are said to be learned rather than produced by some underlying process or disposition. Finally, the uniformities and patterns in abnormal behavior are explained by identifying sources of reinforcement in the individual's social environment.

As the basic concepts of the learning approach are applied to new and more molar events outside the learning laboratory, we can see the displacement of concepts in operation. Learning concepts are changed to encompass the phenomenon to be explained. Our conception of the phenomenon itself changes as well when we begin to look at abnormal behavior in terms of stimuli, responses, and reinforcements. Thus mutual adaptation of the original learning concepts and the situation to which they are applied is part of the ongoing process in which the metaphor underlying the learning perspective is elaborated.

For example, the concept of stimulus is extended to refer to persons and complex social situations. Maladaptive behavior consists of responses that are also more complex and wider in variety than originally denoted by the term "response." Reinforcements are often social in nature—even "attention" may be described as a generalized reinforcer (Krasner, 1962).

Another result of mutual adaptation between the original learning concepts and the new situation to which they are applied is that new concepts emerge or are added to the perspective. For example, the concept of adaptation (as in "maladaptive behavior") is found to be necessary as a defining characteristic of abnormal behavior. Similarly, complex response patterns are described as roles (as in the "sick role"). Neither of these concepts is an integral part of learning theories as originally formulated. They become necessary, however, in dealing with complex social behavior and are therefore incorporated as part of the learning perspective.

Commentary

Throughout our discussion of the learning perspective thus far we have focused on questions of how abnormal behavior is defined, how it evolves and how it is maintained. This may create the misleading impression that the learning perspective began as a formulation of abnormal behavior and was then later extended to the problem of treatment. In fact, just the opposite is true. Learning procedures typically have been first applied to clinical problems and, in the formulation of treatment strategies, a conceptual scheme for understanding the "learned" nature of the problem has been worked out.

This sequence of events has led to several interesting consequences. First, persons interested in behavior modification have selected problems which seem particularly amenable to learning-oriented procedures. Thus, clinical problems such as phobias and anxiety were among the earliest problems to be treated and conceptualized in learning terms. Second, as we shall discover later in our commentary, this approach has led some advocates of behavior modification to the untenable position that because a behavior can be modified by the use of learning principles it also follows that those behaviors were produced according to the principles of learning. Finally, as we shall see, the application of learning procedures to complex clinical phenomena has produced a number of conceptual difficulties in the use of concepts such as stimulus, response, and reinforcement.

Another Look at Fundamental Concepts: Stimulus, Response, and Reinforcement

Several of the leading advocates of a learning theory formulation of maladaptive behavior (Dollard & Miller, 1950; Eysenck, 1960) would probably agree with Ullmann and Krasner (1965), who say, "At present only the broadest, most thoroughly established concepts, those common to all learning theory, are used in the clinical setting." (p. 15) If most advocates of the learning perspective on abnormal behavior agree on basic concepts, then it is appropriate to examine the three concepts fundamental to all learning approaches. These concepts are those of *stimulus, response,* and *reinforcement.*

Perhaps one of the best known and most effective attacks on basic learning theory concepts has been launched by Noam Chomsky in his review (1959) of B. F. Skinner's book, *Verbal Behavior* (1957). As a linguist Chomsky was deeply concerned with many of the problems Skinner considered in his attempt to extend a stimulus–response conception to verbal behavior. In many ways the extension of Skinner's thinking from the laboratory to verbal behavior occurring in a natural setting is similar to the extension of learning concepts to clinical phenomena. Thus Chomsky's comments should be especially significant for us.

The concept of stimulus

Chomsky begins by restating what Skinner stated long ago: that stimuli and responses may be called such only if they can be shown to be lawfully related to one another. That is, we can assume that a particular environmental event may be called a "stimulus" only if we can show that this event has "stimulus control" over a particular bit of behavior.

How then, asks Chomsky, can we explain or give an account of any particular response? The answer is that we must do a "functional analysis." Put more simply, this means we must look for the stimulus which was presumably responsible for the response which we have observed. But, Chomsky argues, the "stimulus" cannot possibly be found until the response is known. Thus we can never predict the response from a knowledge of the stimulus alone since the stimulus is inferred *post hoc,* once the response is known. As Chomsky puts it, "We cannot predict verbal behavior in terms of the stimuli in the speaker's environment, since we do not know what the current stimuli are until he responds." (p. 32)

Furthermore, in most cases involving either verbal behavior or clinical phenomena, it is not some physical stimulus of the environment which constitutes the response but instead some psychological property of the physical event. Therefore it follows that many responses are under the "stimulus control" of the psychological properties of a particular object or event. This, says Chomsky, necessarily drives the concept of stimulus back into the organism and is, therefore, nothing but a retreat into mentalism.

Thus Chomsky argues that despite the objective and scientific flavor of the concept of stimulus it may hide more than it reveals about the nature of human behavior and in particular about potentially lawful relationships which may exist between environmental events and the behavior of an organism.

The concept of response

As with the concept of stimulus, the concept of response may be identified as that set of behaviors which can be shown to be functionally related to one or more controlling environmental events or stimuli. Chomsky points out that the concept of response presents us with little difficulty when we are dealing with carefully controlled experimental situations. When the concept of response is extended to the less controlled aspects of behavior such as speech, however, the problem of identifying the response becomes very complex indeed. Chomsky argues that no means of identifying the controlling variables of a particular response, that is, the stimuli, is suggested by Skinner. Furthermore, the boundaries of a particular response are virtually impossible to identify in the stream of behavior. Thus identifying the response and its boundaries in more complex situations such as those involving abnormal behavior becomes an extremely serious problem. Perhaps even the utility of a concept such as "response" may be questioned when one goes beyond the narrowly confined and experimentally controlled limits of laboratory phenomena.

A concept related to that of the response is the concept of *response strength*. Of course, response strength plays an important role in any learning analysis, since it constitutes the basic dependent variable in any such approach. Skinner suggests that response strength may be inferred in verbal behavior from such variables as pitch, speed, rapidity of emission, and immediate repetition. The use of any one of these indicators of response strength is sufficient to infer an increase in response strength according to Skinner. Skinner would suggest, for example, that if we are being shown a prize work of art and exclaim, "Beautiful!" the speed and energy of the response is not lost on the listener. However, this may not be as straightforward as it seems. Chomsky says,

It does not appear totally obvious that in this case the way to impress the owner is to shriek "Beautiful" in a loud, high-pitched voice, repeatedly, and with no delay (high response strength). It may be equally effective to look at the picture silently (long delay) and then to murmur "Beautiful" in a soft, low-pitched voice (by definition, very low response strength). (p. 35)

It would appear that the concept of response strength as it is used within the stimulus–response framework is defined for Skinner by variables for which exceptions can very easily be found. We might suggest that similar problems will be encountered in the complexities of abnormal behavior as well.

In a similar vein, Breger and McGaugh (1965) have been led to express some skepticism concerning the use of the concepts of stimulus and response in describing clinical phenomena. After examining a published account (Bandura, 1961) of Wolpe's counterconditioning technique of behavior therapy, Breger and McGaugh remark that

Without going into great detail, it should be clear from this example that the use of the terms stimulus and response are only remotely allegorical to the traditional use of these terms in psychology. The "imagination of a scene" is hardly an objectively defined stimulus, nor is something as general as "relaxation" a specifiable or clearly observable response. (p. 340)

The concept of reinforcement

Both Chomsky and, more recently, Breger and McGaugh (1965) have undertaken an analysis of the concept of reinforcement. In the *Behavior of Organisms* (1938) Skinner defines the concept of reinforcement:

The operation of reinforcement is defined as a presentation of a certain kind of stimulus or a response. A reinforcement stimulus is defined as such by a power to produce the resulting change (in strength). There is no circularity about this. Some stimuli are found to produce a change, others not, and they are classified as reinforcing and nonreinforcing accordingly. (p. 52)

Breger and McGaugh point out that this is a reasonable definition and is not necessarily circular, particularly if reinforcement is defined according to class membership, but independently of findings which show the occurrence of learning. This is usually done in a case of laboratory examples; however, when attempts are made to use the concept of reinforcement in a broader context, difficulties arise.

Care is usually not taken to define reinforcement independently from learning as indicated by response strength. This leads to a state of affairs where any observed change in behavior is said to occur *because* of reinforcement, when, in fact, the change in behavior is itself the only indicator of what the reinforcement has been. (p. 346)

Of course, this sort of formulation does not avoid the circularity involved in the concept of reinforcement. The stimuli which are assumed to be "reinforcing" cannot be characterized in any other way except in terms of the rather circular assertion that they raise response strength when they follow a particular response.

Chomsky points out that in Skinner's book, *Verbal Behavior* (1957), the term "reinforcement" is used so loosely in many cases that it appears as if a person may be reinforced even if he emits no response at all. In some cases, a "reinforcing stimulus" need not impinge on the individual or even exist as an identifiable event. Chomsky goes on to suggest that the term reinforcement is being used in what can only be characterized as a ritualistic way. It is being used to replace words such as "want," "like," and "wishes." To replace terms of this kind with the term reinforcement adds nothing by way of conceptual clarity or explanatory power. We might note here that the use of reinforcement as an explanatory concept to replace these terms—want, like, wishes—may obscure important differences between these states as well.

All too often, it appears, the concept of reinforcement is not used as it was originally intended by Skinner. As Chomsky points out, when the term reinforcement is extrapolated to behaviors outside of the laboratory setting, even Skinner himself fails to use the concept appropriately. When used in less controlled settings, the concept typically takes on a circularity which blunts any of its explanatory sharpness and tends to be used in a rather mechanical, ritualistic way to account for increases in the probability of an observed behavior. Breger and McGaugh suggest that the concept of reinforcement as an empirical law of performance is accepted by everyone but as such has little explanatory value. However, ". . . reinforcement, conceived as a 'law of learning,' occupies a very dubious status. Like most of the principles of conditioning, it appears to be an unlikely candidate as an explanatory principle of learning." (p. 347)

Thus we see that the logical consistency and coherence of the terms stimulus, response, and reinforcement are seldom maintained when these concepts are extended to events outside the laboratory. In terms of their power to produce a coherent account of the development and maintenance of abnormal behavior, they lend the appearance of rigor rather than the quality itself to the formulation produced.

Some Problems in Defining Maladaptive Behavior

We will recall that Ullmann and Krasner ascribe two principal characteristics to maladaptive behavior. First, it is considered inappropriate by those in a person's life who control reinforcing events for that person. Second, maladaptive behavior is assumed to lead to a reduction in the amount of positive reinforcement received by the individual. Let us examine each of these two characteristics of maladaptive behavior as Ullmann and Krasner discuss them.

The problem with the first characteristic is that maladaptiveness is judged arbitrarily by those individuals who control reinforcements in an individual's life. As a defining characteristic it is not as simple as it might seem at first. As Buchwald and Young (1969) point out, two individuals may display the same behavior toward some person in their life who controls reinforcers, but in one case that person may insist that the behavior is maladaptive while in the other case the person may tolerate the same behavior. Buchwald and Young's remark suggests that the Ullmann–Krasner definition may tell us more about those who judge behavior and choose to reinforce it or not than about those whose behavior is called "maladaptive." Perhaps it was Ullmann and Krasner's intention to adopt this extremely relativistic position. Nevertheless, such a defining criterion does little to reduce our uncertainty concerning the nature of maladaptive behavior.

Let us consider the second criterion of maladaptive behavior as defined by Ullmann and Krasner. Behavior is maladaptive if it leads to a reduction in the amount of positive reinforcement received by the individual. Again, at first glance this appears to be relatively clear and objective. But Buchwald and Young point out that this forces us to define reinforcing events relative to the particular individual. In fact, what is reinforcing to one individual may be aversive to another. Thus, it is virtually impossible to know on our a priori grounds what sort of events are reinforcing to each individual. Thus the "reduction of positive reinforcement" as an indicator of maladaptive behavior becomes considerably less clear than it would seem if examined only superficially.

Is Maladaptive Behavior Learned Behavior?

Much of the evidence offered by Ullmann and Krasner for the idea that maladaptive behavior is learned behavior comes from reported cases of symptom change as a result of learning theory procedures. However, as Buchwald and Young argue, the fact that a particular behavior or set of behaviors can be *changed* by certain procedures does not tell us necessarily anything about how the behaviors were *produced* in the first place. All behavior therapy studies of this sort can do is to demonstrate further the empirical law of effect and the fact that it holds for hospitalized individuals as well as for laboratory animals and normal individuals. To conclude that evidence of the kind tells us anything about how the behavior was originally produced is not warranted. An excellent example offered by Buchwald and Young underscores this point:

> It is important to remember that behavior is a final common pathway, that it is susceptible to a large number of influences. The way in which responses are changed need not parallel the way in which they were originally acquired. The asymmetry between the source of a behavioral disorder and the method of treatment may be illustrated by the case of aphasic patients. They have lost the ability to speak as a result of a vascular accident or other brain lesion, but they can sometimes be taught to speak again. The behavioral loss is due to a physiological insult, but there is no known physiological or medical technique for overcoming this handicap. That the only known successful treatment is a behavioral one implies nothing about the origin of the deficit. Similarly, if a mute schizophrenic can be taught to speak again by shaping and reinforcement (and such efforts have had some limited success), there is no implication that his speech was lost due to the operation of reinforcing factors in his social environment. (p. 618)

This example makes it quite clear that one cannot infer the origin of "maladaptive behavior" from the techniques used to change that behavior. There is no necessary relation between the two, and to suggest that there is can be quite misleading.

Summary

We have suggested that the formulation of the learning perspective on abnormal behavior is to a large degree a byproduct of the application of behavior modification techniques to clinical problems. Thus, our understanding of abnormal behavior from the point of view of the learning perspective is derived primarily from treatment applications.

We also noted that the concepts of stimulus, response, and reinforcement are fundamental to all learning accounts of abnormal behavior. A critical analysis of these concepts suggests that, despite the apparent rigor they seem to provide, they present as many logical problems as they appear to solve. Furthermore, when these concepts are applied to complex human behavior it is seldom possible to do so with the sort of precision that learning oriented clinicians would wish to claim.

The learning perspective definition of abnormal behavior as proposed by Ullmann and Krasner also presents conceptual difficulties. It suffers from an arbitrariness which is difficult to justify and forces the learning theorist to define crucial concepts such as "positive reinforcement" relative to the particular individual under consideration.

Finally, we noted that some advocates of the learning perspective have erroneously concluded that because a particular behavior or symptom can be altered by the application of learning principles, it follows that the symptom originated according to those principles. This is, of course, not necessarily the case.

We should not be too surprised by such unwarranted conceptual leaps. The adherents of most of the perspectives we will discuss are convinced of the power of their own formulation. Consequently, they may extend their explanations to phenomena beyond the scope of their concepts. Often, when such errors are pointed out, the perspective will be altered, but at least as often the proponents of the perspective will steadfastly maintain their position since the admission of exceptions to the perspective tends to subvert it in fundamental ways.

None of these remarks is intended to suggest that the application of learning principles to the treatment of abnormal behavior is invalid or ineffective. On the contrary, behavior modification has provided convincing evidence that the systematic application of reinforcement principles can be quite effective in altering behaviors judged to be abnormal. It is and promises to be a potent tool in the clinician's treatment armamentarium.

References

BANDURA, A.   Psychotherapy as a learning process. *Psychological Bulletin,* 1961, *58,* 143–159.

BREGER, L., & MCGAUGH, J. L.   Critique and reformulation of "learning-theory" approaches to psychotherapy and neuroses. *Psychological Bulletin,* 1965, *5,* 338–358.

BUCHWALD, A. M., & YOUNG, R. D.   Some comments on the foundations of behavior therapy. In C. M. Franks (Ed.), *Behavior therapy: appraisal and status.* New York: McGraw-Hill, 1969.

CHOMSKY, N.   Review of B. F. Skinner, *Verbal behavior. Language,* 1959, *35,* 26–58.

DENKER, R.   Results of the treatment of psychoneuroses by the general practitioner. *New York State Journal of Medicine,* 1946, *46,* 2164–2166.

DOLLARD, J., & MILLER, N. E.   *Personality and psychotherapy.* New York: McGraw-Hill, 1950.

EYSENCK, H. J.   Learning theory and behaviour therapy. In H. J. Eysenck (Ed.), *Behaviour therapy and the neuroses.* London: Pergamon, 1960.

EYSENCK, H. J., & RACHMAN, S.   *The causes and cures of neurosis.* London: Routledge & Kegan Paul, 1965.

HAUGHTON, E., & AYLLON, T.   Production and elimination of symptomatic behavior. In L. Ullmann & L. Krasner (Eds.), *Case studies in behavior modification.* New York: Holt, Rinehart and Winston, 1965. Pp. 94–98.

HILGARD, E. R.   *Introduction to psychology.* (3rd ed.) New York: Harcourt, Brace & World, 1962.

KRASNER, L.   The therapist as a social reinforcement machine. In H. H. Strupp & L. Luborsky (Eds.), *Research in psychotherapy.* Vol. 2. Washington, D.C.: American Psychological Association, 1962.

RACHMAN, S.   Spontaneous remission and latent learning. *Behaviour Research and Therapy,* 1963, *1*, 133–137.

SKINNER, B. F.   *The behavior of organisms.* New York: Appleton, 1938.

SKINNER, B. F.   *Science and human behavior.* New York: Macmillan, 1953.

SKINNER, B. F.   *Verbal behavior.* New York: Appleton, 1957.

SOLOMON, R. L., & BRUSH, E. S.   Experimentally derived conceptions of anxiety and aversion. In M. R. Jones (Ed.), *Nebraska Symposium on Motivation.* Lincoln: University of Nebraska Press, 1956.

ULLMANN, L. P., & KRASNER, L.   *Case studies in behavior modification.* New York: Holt, Rinehart and Winston, 1965.

ULLMANN, L. P., & KRASNER, L.   *A psychological approach to abnormal behavior.* Englewood Cliffs, N. J.: Prentice-Hall, 1969.

WOLPE, J.   *Psychotherapy by reciprocal inhibition.* Stanford: Stanford University Press, 1958.

YATES, A. J.   Symptoms and symptom substitution. *Psychological Review,* 1958, *65*, 371–374.

CHAPTER 6
THE MORAL PERSPECTIVE

The Perspective

Most of the perspectives that we have discussed arc a product of the contributions of a number of different authors whose ideas converge on a single conception. This is not the case with the moral perspective. One man, O. Hobart Mowrer, stands alone as both the source of and the motivating force behind the overwhelming majority of contemporary thinking about abnormal behavior from a moral perspective.

Certainly it is the case that Mowrer has historical antecedants whose work he fully acknowledges. For example, the work of Wilhelm Stekel as summarized in his *Technique of Analytical Psychotherapy* (1950) contains a chapter on "diseases of the conscience" which Mowrer considers an important point of departure from Freud's views on the role of the superego in the development of abnormal behavior. A second important precursor of the modern moral perspective is Anton Boisen, who had anticipated, and may have inspired, some of Mowrer's current views. In his best-known work, *The Exploration of the Inner World* (1936), Boisen suggested that ". . . the real evil in mental disorder is not to be found in the conflict but in the sense of isolation and estrangement. It is the fear and guilt which result from the presence in one's life of that which one is afraid to tell." (p. 281) Thus, Boisen suggests that abnormal behavior may have its roots in moral transgressions rather than in id–ego conflicts (as the psychoanalytic view would suggest) or in a disease process (as the illness perspective would indicate).

Certainly, too, other writers (e.g., Szasz, 1961) have pointed to the undeniable fact that current thinking about abnormal behavior has largely excluded ethical and moral considerations. But only Mowrer has developed a detailed perspective based on ethical, moral, and even religious ideas. In a series of monographs, essays, and books (Mowrer, 1961, 1964a, 1964b, 1965, 1966a, 1966b) he has presented his views on the nature of abnormal behavior and psychotherapy with a remarkable singleness of purpose.

Most professionals who study abnormal behavior consider themselves to be scientists and so they find the view of abnormal behavior as an ethical or moral problem to be alien. Consequently, their reaction to Mowrer's work has been negative for the most part; and often it ranges from mild amusement to outright disdain. As London (1964) puts it,

> It is sometimes the fate of radical theories that they must pass political as well as scientific tests before they become respectable objects of intellectual inquiry. When such theories, by design or otherwise, assault positions that are cherished by established institutions, they are likely to arouse controversy proportionate to the force with which they are presented. This suggests an extension of Newton's Third Law to human behavior, in which one useful index of the seminal quality of a new theory would be the extent to which it is publicly reviled. If so, then the theory of the origin and treatment of neurosis put forth by O. H. Mowrer may deserve more serious attention than any such theory since Sigmund Freud's psychoanalysis, for in the two generations that lie between them, no other mental health theorist has been subjected to such voluble and vituperative criticism. (p. 134)

Mowrer is an intellectual renegade of the first rank. It is no wonder that one prominent critic has stated that adopting Mowrer's position "would, in my opinion, turn back the psychiatric clock twenty-five hundred years" (Ausubel, 1961, p. 70).

Mowrer's current views have deeply personal origins. In a recent monograph (Mowrer, 1966b) he details both his personal and intellectual development, including his own experiences in psychoanalysis and several "breakdowns," at least one of which led to psychiatric hospitalization. There seems to be little doubt that these personal experiences have significantly affected his views on the nature of abnormal behavior. Within this context we will examine Mowrer's views and the moral perspective on abnormal behavior.

Opposition to the Freudian Viewpoint

Mowrer's perspective on the nature of abnormal behavior gains much of its impetus from its opposition to the traditional Freudian view of neurosis.

The origin of his ideas may be traced to an early paper in which he proposes a guilt theory of anxiety (Mowrer, 1950). Anxiety, Mowrer argues, is not a result of the individual's fear of his own primitive impulses, as the Freudian view would suggest. Instead, anxiety is more accurately described as guilt. Mowrer assumes that the individual feels guilty because of some act he has actually committed in the past, rather than because he is fearful of his own impulses as the psychoanalytic view would suggest.

> The view here proposed is that anxiety comes, not from acts which the individual would commit but dares not, but from acts which he has committed and wishes that he had not. It is, in other words, a "guilt theory" of anxiety rather than an "impulse theory." (p. 537)

A second major theme in Mowrer's thinking is reflected in his paper "Learning Theory and the Neurotic Paradox" (1948). Mowrer himself describes his emerging orientation in the following way:

> In one crucial respect . . . I had broken with the whole psychoanalytic tradition: on a scale of socialization or social-competence, I was putting the so-called neurotic *midway* between the criminal (or sociopath) on the extreme left (low end of the scale) and the normal person on the extreme right. Freud had repeatedly asserted—it was, in fact, the very heart of his argument—that the neurotic is very strongly, indeed excessively, socialized and therefore to be placed at the far right on a socialization continuum with the normal individuals occupying an intermediate position. (Mowrer, 1966b, p. 28)

Thus we can see two major points of departure from the Freudian view in Mowrer's early thinking. First, anxiety is the result of guilt concerning acts the individual has already committed but knows he should not have; second, neurotic individuals are actually undersocialized rather than oversocialized. We shall see these early working assumptions asserted repeatedly throughout Mowrer's view of abnormal behavior.

The Dynamics of Neurosis

In outlining his conception of the dynamics of neurosis, Mowrer again opposes himself to the traditional Freudian viewpoint. The Freudian version of the dynamics of neurosis as Mowrer views it is described in Figure 6.1.

We can see that in this scheme the superego is enlarged and appears stronger than other structures in the system. Mowrer indicates that this is

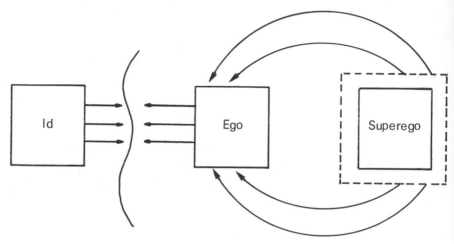

Figure 6.1   Freudian view of the dynamics of neurosis. (Redrawn from O. H. Mowrer, Abnormal reactions or actions? (An autobiographical answer.) In J. A. Vernon (Ed.), *Introduction to psychology: A self-selection textbook*. Dubuque, Iowa: Wm. Brown, 1966. Reproduced by permission.)

consonant with the Freudian assumption that the superego is disproportionately strong because of socializing influences on the individual. The curved arrows in the diagram suggest that the superego takes over the ego functions of the individual. In this situation, the ego is forced to reject the instinctual demands of the id. As a result, a barrier is constructed between the ego and the id. Repression now occurs (as represented by the barrier) as the motives and instincts of the id are held back. In this scheme, the neurosis is due to anxiety. The anxiety, in turn, is a response to the danger which the ego senses from the possibility of being overwhelmed by id impulses.

Mowrer offers a revised version of this system. His revision employs the same elements as the original Freudian version, but the arrangement of these elements has been cleverly changed. The revised system is shown in Figure 6.2.

Now the ego is taken over by the id rather than by the superego. In this scheme, it is the *superego* which is repressed. The voice of conscience is being stifled. Anxiety now is assumed to be a result of guilty knowledge; or to use Mowrer's picturesque phrase, anxiety is a result of "the unheeded railings and anger of conscience." (Mowrer, 1966b, p. 31)

What are the implications of each of these two schemes? Mowrer argues that his modified scheme accounts adequately and more completely for the appearance of certain clinically observed symptoms. Of particular interest are the frequently observed clinical symptoms of "withdrawal."

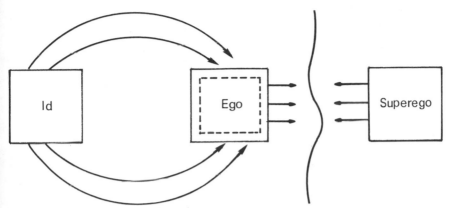

Figure 6.2 Mowrer's view of the dynamics of neurosis. (Redrawn from O. H. Mowrer, Abnormal reactions or actions? (An autobiographical answer.) In J. A. Vernon (Ed.), *Introduction to psychology: A self-selection textbook.* Dubuque, Iowa: Wm. Brown, 1966. Reproduced by permission.)

Withdrawal is assumed to have relatively mild manifestations in neurotics such as stage-fright or shyness. In psychotics, however, withdrawal is both more severe and more pervasive. The symptoms of withdrawal in cases of psychosis include a generalized fear of other people, seclusiveness, and mutism. If Freud's idea of a strongly overdeveloped superego were in fact correct, then both neurotics and psychotics should be "well integrated socially" (Mowrer, 1966b, p. 30). This conclusion follows, Mowrer suggests, because it is assumed within the Freudian scheme that it is the superego which is directing the individual's actions.

But, Mowrer argues, the "clinical facts" favor his version of the dynamics of neurosis. If the individual is cut off or isolated from his superego, then it follows that he will also be cut off from his society which represents the values of the superego. Thus, the clinical symptom of withdrawal and accompanying feelings of alienation are a result of concealed misdeeds, or "sins." The concealed misdeeds result in guilt, and the feelings of guilt then lead the individual to "withdraw" from social contacts.

Mowrer's scheme differs from the Freudian scheme in both the direction and the content of repression. The Freudian scheme argues that the id is repressed by the ego which has in turn been taken over by the superego. Mowrer's scheme, on the other hand, argues that the superego has been repressed by the ego, which has itself been taken over by the id.

We can see from this that Mowrer has opposed his own view of the dynamics of neurosis to that of the Freudian version using the same dynamic mechanisms and the same structures of personality.

Two Typological Corollaries

Mowrer extends his argument concerning the nature of abnormal behavior to include what he would describe as two typological corollaries. Again, he has opposed the Freudian typology of abnormal behavior to his own, and again he has managed to rearrange cleverly certain elements in the Freudian scheme to serve the ends of his own argument. The essence of his argument can be grasped from a look at Figure 6.3 in which he describes the Freudian view.

The continuum along which various types of individuals are distributed may be assumed to be a continuum of socialization. The neurotic is on the right of the distribution, suggesting that he was "oversocialized." Here, the direction of therapy is opposite to that of socialization and the goal of therapy to soften or weaken the motives of the superego. The normal individual is put in the middle of this continuum, placing him in correspondence with both statistical and psychological normality. The psychopath or sociopath is placed on the left side of the distribution, since he shows the least effect of socialization.

Mowrer suggests that at least two arguments may be directed against this sort of arrangement. The first argument has to do with the inconsistency of this typology with certain clinical phenomena. How can this scheme deal with the "psychopath, mixed type"? This type of individual is assumed to show symptoms which are characteristic of both the psychopath on the one hand and the neurotic on the other. A mixture of neurotic traits and psychopathic traits, according to this scheme, would produce a normal individual. But a brief examination of the clinical phenomenon argues against this conclusion. The "psychopath, mixed type" in fact bears

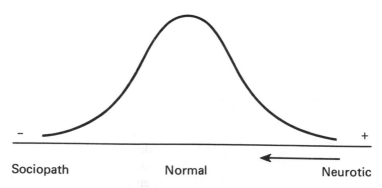

Figure 6.3 Psychoanalytic version of distribution of character types with respect to socialization. (Redrawn from O. H. Mowrer, Abnormal reactions or actions? (An autobiographical answer.) In J. A. Vernon (Ed.), *Introduction to psychology: A self-selection textbook*. Dubuque, Iowa: Wm. Brown, 1966. Reproduced by permission.)

little or no resemblance to the normal individual, but the Freudian typology seems to have difficulty in handling this possibility.

The second argument leveled against the Freudian scheme concerns the outcome of therapy. We may recall that the goal of conventional Freudian therapy is to soften the superego. However, Mowrer states that typically there are two possible results of psychoanalytic therapy (Mowrer, 1961, p. 235). The first result is that therapy is "technically unsuccessful." That is, the individual fails to develop a softened or a less strict superego and, as a result, does not move along the socialization continuum in the direction of becoming less socialized. The second outcome of psychoanalysis is that it is "technically successful." In the case of a technically successful analysis, the individual develops a "character disorder" and becomes sociopathic in his behavior. Now Mowrer argues that these outcomes are not consistent with the typology we have outlined above. He reasons that if the Freudian typology is correct, then the individual who has had a technically successful analysis should move into the normal range and stop instead of developing sociopathic or psychopathic tendencies.

Mowrer's alternative to the Freudian typology can be seen in Figure 6.4. Again there is a continuum of socialization moving from left to right. However, in this case it is not the normal distribution which is used to

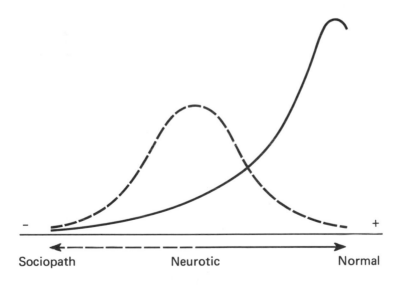

Figure 6.4 Mowrer's J-curve distribution of character types on a socialization continuum. (Redrawn from O. H. Mowrer, Abnormal reactions or actions? (An autobiographical answer.) In J. A. Vernon (Ed.), *Introduction to psychology: A self-selection textbook.* Dubuque, Iowa: Wm. Brown, 1966. Reproduced by permission.)

depict the relative frequency of various types of individuals. Instead, it is the "J-curve." Another significant change in Mowrer's version of the typological scheme involves the fact that now the normal individual is placed on the far right; the neurotic is placed in the middle of the continuum; and, as before, the psychopath or sociopath is placed on the far left. The arrow going toward the left depicts the direction of psychoanalytic therapy. However, Mowrer suggests that the arrow moving to the right indicates the direction of effective therapy.

How can the logical difficulties pointed out by Mowrer be handled within this modified structure? First, where does the "psychopath, mixed type" fall in this scheme? He may be located now between the neurotic and the psychopath on the socialization continuum. Thus one inconsistency is resolved by the new scheme. Second, what is the result of psychoanalysis according to this new scheme? The "technically successful" analysis will move the neurotic individual in the direction of psychopathy. On the other hand, the direction of "effective therapy" will move the neurotic to the right along the socialization continuum and will "help the neurotic person get better (psychologically) by being better (morally) not worse." (Mowrer, 1966b, p. 32)

Mowrer suggests that if his modified scheme is correct, then previous therapeutic efforts have been damaging and detrimental both to individuals who undergo psychoanalysis and to society in general. He argues that the Freudian ethic has promoted the notion that both the individual and society will benefit by becoming less socialized. On the contrary, the goal of therapy, as Mowrer sees it, is actually to *increase* the socialization of the psychopathic and the neurotic individual in order to move them along the socialization continuum toward normality.

In discussing the implications of his typology, Mowrer also formulates the dynamics of paranoia and sociopathy. Paranoia, in Mowrer's view, is a condition in which the individual has learned to blame others for his difficulties rather than blaming himself. The Freudian ethic, on the other hand, is assumed by Mowrer actually to encourage paranoia. In *The Crisis in Psychiatry and Religion* (1961), Mowrer summarizes his view of the dynamics of paranoia: "The distinguishing feature of the paranoid is that unlike the depressive, he typically projects his own outraged conscience out upon others and then perceives *them* as "after" him and *against* him." (pp. 238–239)

Thus, according to Mowrer, the paranoid has internalized the norms and values of his culture but rejects those norms. The paranoid may experience these values and norms only in projected form as delusions concerning others' attitudes and feelings towards him. The demands of conscience are no longer seen by the paranoid as internal to himself, but instead are embodied in the attitudes of others toward him.

The sociopath is another unfortunate product of the Freudian ethic.

The views of Freud and his followers, Mowrer argues, have encouraged parents in the first half of the twentieth century to raise their children permissively. This practice has produced children who have been raised "without character." As a result of these permissive rearing practices, the sociopath or psychopath has not internalized the norms and values of society enough to feel any guilt concerning his own misconduct. The psychopath or sociopath does not take responsibility for his antisocial acts because he has been raised virtually without a conscience.

Schizophrenia as the Concealment of Misdeeds

Mowrer (1961) offers yet another fascinating example of his view that abnormal behavior is the result of concealed sin. He describes a paper published in the *Journal of Abnormal and Social Psychology* anonymously in 1958 entitled, "A New Theory of Schizophrenia." The paper was written by a 34-year-old man residing in the closed ward of a mental hospital who had received a diagnosis of paranoid schizophrenia.

I propose that the motive force of schizophrenic reactions is *fear,* just as fear motivates, according to Freud, neurotic mechanisms—but with this difference; in the case of schizophrenia, the chronic fear is more properly called terror, or concealed panic, being of the greatest intensity; and second, as is not the case in neurosis, the fear is conscious; third, the fear itself is concealed from other people, the motive of the concealment being fear. In neurosis a sexual or hostile drive, pointing to the future, is defended against. In schizophrenia, by my view, detection by others of a guilty deed, the detection pointing to the past, is defended against.

My hypothesis may be called the Dick Tracy theory loosely in honor of the familiar fictional, human bloodhound of crime.

Motivated in the very first place by fear, the schizophrenic psychoses originate in a *break with sincerity,* and not in the classically assumed "break with reality." The patient's social appetite (an instinctive drive in primates, I believe), including love and respect for persons and society, is consciously anticathected or forsaken and ultimately repressed with the passage of time, since full satisfaction of sociality entails, more or less, communicative honesty, faith, and intimacy. Also, the tension set up in interpersonal intimacy by the withholding of emotionally important (although perhaps logically irrelevant) information causes unbearable pain. This repression of sociality accounts for the well-known "indifference" of schizophrenics. But if safety can be achieved by means of "perjury" alone without great discomfort, then no further defenses are adopted. Perjury is here defined as avoiding telling the whole truth and nothing but the truth. If, for many possible reasons, perjury is not an adequate and comfortable guarantee of safety, as it usually is not, then "cutting" of social contacts is progressively pursued—all in the interest of safety in respect to avoiding possible punishment. Suppression and repression of the social appetite or instinct is thus central to schizophrenia. I believe that repression of sexual and hostile drive is *not* primary in schizophrenia, although it is secondary, as will be explained further on.

Schizophrenia is the cultivation of a lie. A lie is "proved" to be the "Truth." The real truth is that the schizophrenic is responsibly guilty for some crucial misdeeds. . . .

A semi-instinctive deceptive stratagem leads schizophrenics, like pursued rabbits, to "zigzag," thus baffling the pursuer's expectations. Unpredictability is the stock-in-trade fetish of schizophrenics. The proximate goal is to avoid being understood. The ultimate goal is to avoid punishment. They "non-want" punishment. . . .

As Freud found Shakespeare's Hamlet to be representative of neurosis, I take Shakespeare's Lady Macbeth to typify schizophrenic psychoses. The motto of the schizophrenic might well be, "Out, damned spot!" and that of the therapist working with schizophrenics, "Find the crime!" (pp. 86, 87, 88)

Mowrer notes that he obtained the reactions of several clinical psychologists to the paper. "The evaluation fell into two categories. Some hold that the paper is just what it purports to be, an original and highly reasonable *theory* of schizophrenia—while others insist that it is a classical exhibit of the *disease itself*" (Mowrer, 1961, p. 85). It should by now be clear to the reader which view Mowrer holds.

Language of the Moral Perspective

Our discussion to this point should provide us with a general introduction to Mowrer's thinking. We are now in a position to examine some of the key concepts of the moral perspective in more detail. The language of the moral perspective is a curious mixture of traditional psychiatric terms, such as "symptom" and "cure," with terms having a clearly religious tone, such as "God" and "sin." The definitions given below are based on some of Mowrer's own writings (Mowrer, 1961, 1966a, 1966b) and on London's (1964) discussion of Mowrer's perspective.

Sin   Behavior that violates social norms. In general, behavior thought to be deviant or abnormal is considered sinful.

Guilt   A normal emotion that results from an actual or objective transgression or sin. Guilt is often referred to as "real guilt" to distinguish it from the Freudian concept of guilt which refers to guilty feelings concerning feelings or thoughts rather than actions.

Symptom   Attempt on the part of the individual to cope with his feelings of guilt. Concealment is a typical symptomatic attempt used to effect self-cure. Symptoms are not to be confused with abnormal behavior, i.e., sin.

God   The "idealized objective of the socialization process" (London, 1964, p. 139). Also, an internal manifestation of socialization.

Confession   Disclosure of past sins to significant others in one's life. Confession is a necessary but not a sufficient condition for cure.

Expiation   The only effective method of self-cure. Once confession has occurred, the individual must recommit himself to society and engage in behaviors that support social norms rather than violate them.

The Role of Behavior, Symptoms, and Emotions in Abnormal Behavior

Mowrer's most recent and most general accounts of the moral perspective (Mowrer, 1965, 1966b) consider the relationship between behavior, symptoms, and emotions. As in many of his arguments he contrasts the conventional view with his own.

According to Mowrer the conventional view suggests that irrational or inappropriate behavior by other persons results in an individual's abnormal emotions; he then exhibits symptoms as in Figure 6.5. In this view, an

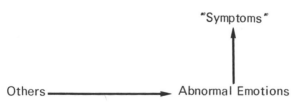

Figure 6.5   Conventional view of the relation between emotions, symptoms, and the behavior of others. (Redrawn from O. H. Mowrer, Abnormal reactions or actions? (An autobiographical answer.) In J. A. Vernon (Ed.), *Introduction to psychology: A self-selection textbook.* Dubuque, Iowa: Wm. Brown, 1966. Reproduced by permission.)

individual's own behavior is not seen as "causal," or as a determining factor in the disorder. Only the behavior of others is seen as "causal." Furthermore, according to this conventional view, whatever the person does is seen as a "symptom" of some deep underlying problem or difficulty. Within this scheme little responsibility is ascribed to the individual. Instead, all responsibility for the abnormal behavior of the individual is attributed to the irrational and inappropriate behavior of others.

The moral perspective suggests a very different view, shown in Figure 6.6. Here the deviant life style of the individual *is* the abnormal behavior. As the brackets in the diagram suggest, this deviant or sinful behavior is often concealed from others. Because the individual is engaging in behavior which is contrary to society's norms, he experiences quite *normal* emotions, such as real guilt, feelings of inferiority, and anxiety.

Symptoms occur as a further result of these normal emotions. According to this view, the individual's own bad or "sinful" behavior is seen as the principal determinant of his difficulties. Furthermore, symptoms result from emotional discomfort (normal emotion) which the individual deserves because of some sinful or deviant act that he has performed. Finally, the individual's own conduct and responsibility are considered to be primary rather than secondary.

Figure 6.7 brings together the assumptions we have just discussed and provides an even more complete picture of Mowrer's view of the relation between abnormal behavior, emotions, and symptoms. The symptoms that an individual displays are assumed to be an attempt at "self-cure." That is, they represent attempts to deal with the emotion the person is experiencing. Naturally, Mowrer argues, symptomatic behavior is an attempt to relieve the individual's discomfort, although he will not be successful. Sympto-

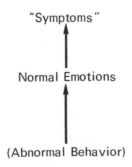

Figure 6.6 Mowrer's view of the relation between abnormal behavior, symptoms, and emotions. (Redrawn from O. H. Mowrer, Abnormal reactions or actions? (An autobiographical answer.) In J. A. Vernon (Ed.), *Introduction to psychology: A self-selection textbook.* Dubuque, Iowa: Wm. Brown, 1966. Reproduced by permission.)

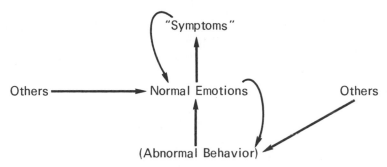

Figure 6.7 Relation between abnormal behavior, symptoms, emotions, and the behavior of others. (Redrawn from O. H. Mowrer, Abnormal reactions or actions? (An autobiographical answer.) In J. A. Vernon (Ed.), *Introduction to psychology: A self-selection textbook.* Dubuque, Iowa: Wm. Brown, 1966. Reproduced by permission.)

matic attempts at self-cure of emotional discomfort will fail because it is incorrectly assumed that the emotions themselves are the center of the problem.

The only effective therapeutic intervention that is possible involves the effort of other individuals to actually change the abnormal behavior which is the true cause of the problem. That is, efforts by others must be directed to change the individual's wrongdoing and sinful behavior. This involves both openly confessing one's guilt and also expiation.

Thus, for Mowrer, the basic problem is misconduct or "sin" on the part of the individual. The misconduct results in guilt and other quite normal emotions which in turn lead to ineffective symptomatic attempts to relieve the emotional discomfort. It is noteworthy that in this scheme abnormal behavior and symptoms are not synonymous. Instead, abnormal behavior is sinful misconduct, while symptoms are attempts at self-cure which eventually result from the misconduct.

Summary

Because the basic metaphor of the moral perspective is religious, it stands as a radical departure from other perspectives. Deviant or abnormal acts are sins. Confession and expiation are the sinner's only sources of permanent relief from his feelings of real guilt. It is certainly true that Mowrer retains a number of concepts that are not explicitly religious in nature. For example, he repeatedly refers to "neurosis" and to "symptoms." But the basic spirit of his perspective is, nevertheless, religious.

We should realize that Mowrer's use of a religious metaphor does not assume a theism as well. In outlining the history of the early Christian church (Mowrer, 1966b), he notes that the central concern of religious groups was the rehabilitation of neurotic or alienated persons.

> What I refer to is the fact that early Christianity was basically a small-groups movement in which alienated, sinful, "neurotic" persons confessed before and did penance under the guidance of the particular "congregation" (or "house church") to which they belonged or wished to belong. From all indications . . . this type of experience was highly "therapeutic," and it seems likely that this early version of Christianity survived and spread not because of the supposedly miraculous "powers" it had borrowed from the earlier Greek and Egyptian mystery cults . . . but because it was redemptive and rehabilitative in an intensely practical, psychologically and socially important way. (p. 35)

Thus the emphasis on interpersonal responsibility and community is what Mowrer finds attractive in the religious metaphor, rather than its theistic aspects.

Commentary

Sin or Disease?

Ausubel (1961) has severely criticized Mowrer's statements concerning the nature of abnormal behavior. One paper of Mowrer's in particular, "Sin, The Lesser of Two Evils" (1960), has served as a target for Ausubel's attack. In that paper Mowrer proposes that we give up the concept of mental illness and replace it with the concept of sin.

Ausubel (1961) admits that it is possible that most formulations of abnormal behavior have been in error by omitting ethical and moral considerations. But he suggests that we can acknowledge this error without necessarily asserting that personality disorder is a reflection of sin, and he offers four arguments to support this assertion.

First, Ausubel says that, as a rule, we can distinguish between immorality and mental illness. We have considered this criticism previously in discussing the illness perspective. We noted then that Ausubel defines disease as "any marked deviation, physical, mental, or behavioral, from normally desirable standards of structural and functional integrity." (p. 71) It is doubtful that a definition of this level of generality can exclude immorality as Ausubel would wish.

Second, Ausubel admits that guilt may contribute to personality disorder but indicates that guilt is not a principal cause. He substantiates this assertion by noting that guilt, when uncomplicated by other factors, is transitory in nature. Furthermore, he argues that guilt is not a prominent part of a number of different abnormal reactions including schizophrenia, inadequate personality, and psychopathy.

Certainly Ausubel has raised an important point when he notes that not all forms of abnormal behavior have guilt as a prominent component. Mowrer's rejoinder to this objection would probably be that some people, notably psychopaths, have been reared virtually without character or conscience and therefore do not experience guilt for their transgressions. Still, this reply does not weaken Ausubel's criticisms substantially, since it admits that guilt is not a necessary condition for the occurrence of abnormal behavior. Thus Mowrer would have to admit that the occurrence of psychopathic behavior is clearly an exception to his assumption that guilt is instrumental in the production of abnormal behavior.

Third, Ausubel argues that it is as unreasonable to hold individuals suffering from mental illness responsible for their symptoms as it is to hold persons responsible for their physical symptoms. Whether it is possible to dispense with the problem of responsibility in this way depends, of course, on the validity of the analogy between mental and physical illness. We have suggested that some writers have leveled compelling arguments against this analogy (Marzolf, 1947; Sarbin, 1967). Furthermore, recent research (Braginsky, Braginsky, & Ring, 1968) indicates that mental patients do have at least some control over and therefore presumably some responsibility for their symptoms.

On the other hand, we may ask whether persons suffering from physical symptoms may be said in some cases to have responsibility for those symptoms. Certainly, to the degree that individuals knowingly allow circumstances to occur which may result in physical symptoms we may attribute some responsibility to them for the occurrence of those symptoms. For example, are we to assume that the diabetic who deviates from his prescribed diet or the epileptic who fails to take his medication is in no way "responsible" for his symptoms?

We would argue that Ausubel's analogy between physical and mental symptoms does not convincingly deal with the problem of responsibility. This is a complex and important question and cannot be dismissed by the application of a facile analogy.

Finally, Ausubel argues that even if all personality disorders were due to sin it would not be necessary to deny the concept of disease. But, by the same token, if Mowrer's argument is correct concerning the etiology of abnormal behavior, then the importance of the disease concept would be greatly diminished.

Mowrer Versus Freud:
How Different Are Their Views?

Throughout Mowrer's account of the nature of abnormal behavior he emphasizes his opposition to the traditional Freudian point of view concerning the dynamics of neurosis. How different are Mowrer's views from Freud's? Perhaps the principal difference is in emphasis rather than a fundamental difference in theoretical orientation.

Mowrer's view of the dynamics of neurosis argues that the superego is repressed by the ego which has in turn been taken over by the id. How different is this from Freud's concept of *moral anxiety?* According to Freud's concept of moral anxiety the individual feels anxiety and discomfort because of the warning of the superego. In the case of moral anxiety the individual has either thought of or has actually performed an act which is not consistent with the values of the superego or conscience. Thus it appears that little substantial difference exists between Mowrer's guilt theory of neurosis and Freud's idea of moral anxiety. As London (1964) puts it, "For what is 'guilt' but 'moral anxiety' as Freud observed?" (p. 143)

Perhaps Freud provided a strong emphasis upon neurotic anxiety (which was presumed to be fear of the ego being overwhelmed by the superego) because he was writing at the turn of the century, within the context of the Victorian era. At this time society's attitudes toward immoral behavior were considerably more strict than they are today. Hence it is likely that most of Freud's experience was with clinical phenomena which were a result of "neurotic anxiety." Today, on the other hand, Mowrer emphasizes moral anxiety, perhaps correctly so. Mowrer's society is more permissive than Freud's was, and the nature of clinical difficulties may have shifted from those involving neurotic anxiety to those involving moral anxiety.

The irony is that Freud may have actually changed the phenomena which he was writing about by the very act of discussing it. There is much to be said for Mowrer's argument that we have been strongly affected by the "Freudian ethic." Considerable permissiveness has been the rule rather than the exception in the first half of the twentieth century. Much of that permissiveness has been justified on the grounds that strict controls may lead to dangerous repressions. Thus Mowrer's reaction may be justified in that it responds to a change in emphasis in our socialization practices which, in turn, may have been due to Freud's original influence.

State of the Evidence

Empirical evidence bearing directly on the moral perspective is scarce. Although Mowrer's propositions in many cases appear to be stated explicitly enough for empirical test, little work has actually been done. Perhaps this is because Mowrer's ideas are not popular among psychologists with a research orientation. The language he uses to convey his ideas sounds "unscientific." Whatever the reason, even Mowrer himself has appeared to be content with case history observations or with hearsay evidence supplied by his colleagues.

The J-curve hypothesis

An example of this surprisingly casual attitude is displayed in the support Mowrer offers for the argument that his typology of neurotic, normal, and psychopathic behavior is more "consistent with the facts" than is the Freudian typology. His argument rests heavily upon the assumed outcome of psychoanalysis. The Freudians, Mowrer says, argue that psychoanalysis can have one of two outcomes. The "technically unsuccessful" outcome is one in which the neurotic's superego remains overly strict. The "technically successful" outcome is one in which the neurotic's superego becomes less strict, and the individual then becomes sociopathic in his behavior. One may ask, what is Mowrer's evidence for these outcomes? An answer to this question may be found in Mowrer's essay "Footnotes to a Theory of Psychopathology" (1961).

> I was quite unprepared to have an analyst tell me, a few years ago, the following concerning the findings of the psychoanalytic institute of which he was a member. Typically, he said he and his colleagues have found that psychoanalysis has one of two outcomes: either the analysis is technically unsuccessful, which means that it fails to lessen the presumed over-severity of the superego, with the result that the patient continues to be neurotic; *or* the analysis is technically successful, i.e., the superego is softened-up and inner conflicts are resolved, but the patient then develops a "character disorder" and begins "acting out." (Mowrer, 1961, p. 235)

For an individual who has spent a large part of his professional career dealing with empirical evidence, Mowrer is surprisingly willing to take the word of an "analyst friend" on this crucial piece of evidence. Since his argument for the typology which he offers rests so strongly on these facts, one would expect Mowrer to take greater care to document his evidence.

Additional evidence on the validity of Mowrer's typology is available, however. In an impressively careful and thorough study Peterson (1967) has attempted a test of Mowrer's "J-curve hypothesis." We will recall that Mowrer has suggested that neurotics should fall midway between psychopaths and normals on a scale of socialization with psychopaths falling at the low end and normals showing the greatest degree of socialization. The

Freudian assumption, on the other hand, predicts that neurotics should be oversocialized and therefore should display the greatest degree of socialization followed in order by normals and psychopaths.

Peterson selected groups of junior high school students on the basis of factorially derived indicators (Peterson, 1961) of conduct problems and personality problems. A third group was selected that manifested no problems at all. Peterson carefully qualified his conclusions concerning the question of whether these groups could be legitimately described as psychopaths, neurotics, and normals. At the very least, there is a strong analogy between conduct problems and psychopathy, and between personality problems and neurosis. Thus, as a preliminary test of the hypothesis, these groups appear to be at least adequate. Subjects in each group were administered the socialization scale of the California Psychological Inventory and the distribution of their socialization scores was examined.

The major results of this study were consistent with Mowrer's rather than Freud's formulation. Children with no problems showed a negatively skewed distribution of socialization scores. That is, the majority of the problem-free children fell at the high end of the socialization scale, as the J-curve hypothesis predicted. Conduct-problem children had the lowest socialization scores, which is consistent with both Mowrer's and the Freudians' formulations. Finally, children in the personality problem group fell below the no-problem group but above the conduct-problem group.

Peterson makes it clear that these results say nothing about the actual misconduct of neurotics, the process of socialization among the groups, or the appropriate mode of treatment for conduct or personality problems. He also is careful to qualify his interpretation of the socialization measure. Despite these caveats, the weight of evidence is clearly in favor of Mowrer's propositions concerning socialization among conduct and personality problem groups rather than the Freudian formulation.

Sexual behavior and psychopathology

Swensen (1962) has attempted to test Mowrer's proposition that neurosis is the result of behavior which is not consistent with the dictates of conscience. He compared the reported sexual behavior of 25 female college students who had sought psychotherapy with a matched sample of 25 girls from the same college population. Swensen reasoned that, if Mowrer is correct, then people who seek psychotherapy for neurotic complaints should have violated the conventionally accepted moral code more frequently than normal people coming from the same background.

A comparison of case history variables for both groups indicated that girls in the patient group had engaged in significantly more sexual behavior than girls in the control group. In addition, girls in the control group had engaged in significantly more social activity than those in the group needing psychotherapy. An examination of both groups indicated that all but two of the girls who engaged in extensive sexual activities also reported psychological symptoms or recurring psychosomatic complaints. Of course, it is not possible to decide on the basis of these findings whether the misconduct was the antecedent or the consequence of the psychological symptoms, but the findings are suggestive, at least.

Thus two studies that attempt to bring evidence to bear on Mowrer's hypotheses have yielded findings consistent with his view. This at least represents a beginning.

Mowrer and the Religious Metaphor

Despite the fact that Mowrer's concept of abnormal behavior is deeply rooted in Christian traditions, it can be argued that many, if not all, of his arguments could be presented without explicit reference to such terms as "sin" or "confession." It is certainly true that Mowrer's ideas have a deeply personal flavor that results from his own life experience with abnormal behavior. However, there may be something more to his use of the Christian–religious metaphor.

Some hint of Mowrer's intention appears at the beginning of Chapter 3 of his book, *The Crisis in Psychiatry and Religion* (1961).

> As long as one adheres to the theory that psychoneurosis implies no moral responsibility, no error, no misdeed on the part of the afflicted person, one's vocabulary can, of course, remain beautifully objective and "scientific." But as soon as there is so much as a hint of personal accountability in the situation, such language is, at the very least, wide of the mark and, conceivably, quite misleading. Therefore, if "moral judgment" does enter the picture, one might as well beard the lion and use the strongest term of all, *sin*. (Mowrer, 1961, p. 40)

Thus we see that Mowrer uses the religious metaphor intentionally to emphasize the *moral* aspects of man's behavior with his fellow man. As we have suggested in the introduction to this chapter, from the point of view of modern psychological theory, this is a unique departure. Mowrer has a long personal history of scientific achievement, yet has departed from the scientific tradition in order to explore what he believes to be a crucial aspect of abnormal behavior.

But there is also a strong flavor of pragmatism in his use of metaphor. Mowrer has always been deeply invested in the social implications of his work in psychology. Further on in his paper, we begin to sense his feeling of urgency about the problem of personality disorder.

The unassailable, brute fact is that personality disorder is the most pervasive and baffling problem of our time; and if it *should* turn out that persons so afflicted regularly display (or rather *hide*) a life of too *little*, rather than too much, moral restraint and self-discipline, the problem would take on an empirical urgency that would require no fine-spun argument. (p. 42)

It seems that Mowrer uses the concept of sin in part because he hopes that it will have great impact on those who heed his arguments. Thus we may infer that Mowrer's use of the religious metaphor has two purposes. First, it is intended to point to the moral aspects of abnormal behavior, and second, it is intended to lend impetus to his crusade for the acceptance of the moral perspective.

Summary

At this point it is worthwhile to review the strengths and weaknesses of the moral perspective. First, we have noted that Mowrer's approach seems to *require* that some misdeed or sin has occurred before a person may be regarded as disturbed and in need of therapeutic help. This is certainly a strong assumption, and, at the same time, one which is particularly difficult to document. Yet it would appear that much of Mowrer's argument turns on this crucial question.

Second, an important element of psychopathology is the existence of guilt in the disturbed individual. Yet, as Ausubel (1961) has pointed out, it is not difficult to point to personality disorders where guilt plays little or no role.

Third, Mowrer consistently opposes himself to the Freudian view of neurosis and argues that anxiety is not the result of the repression of id impulses but instead is guilt about acts which have actually been committed. We may ask how different Mowrer's notion of guilt is from Freud's idea of "moral anxiety."

To his credit, Mowrer has offered a number of propositions which are accessible to empirical test. One important example we have discussed involves the question of whether neurotics are actually undersocialized or oversocialized when compared with normal individuals. We will recall that the evidence (Peterson, 1967) favored Mowrer's prediction that neurotics are undersocialized rather than the Freudian view that they are oversocialized. But as London (1964) has noted, support for one part of a particular perspective does not necessarily mean that other aspects of the perspective are equally valid, and we should certainly reserve judgment concerning the validity of other propositions Mowrer offers us.

Perhaps the single most important contribution of the moral perspective is its emphasis on personal responsibility. This is not a popular stand to take in a time when rigorous approaches to the problem of abnormal behavior find no room for concepts like morality and strive to avoid value judgments concerning the question of whether an act is good or bad, right or wrong.

London (1964) captures the essence of Mowrer's moral perspective when he says that

> Without certainty of what goodness is, it proposes that men must try to be good, striving for an ideal which may not require definition to achieve fulfillment. Without a doubt, this is a thoroughly pretentious theory. But perhaps any theory that pretends to less than this risks denying man both cherished and valid parts of his humanity. (p. 145)

References

AUSUBEL, D. P.   Personality disorder *is* disease. *American Psychologist,* 1961, *16,* 69–74.

BOISEN, A. T.   *The exploration of the inner world.* New York: Harper & Row, 1936.

BRAGINSKY, B. M., BRAGINSKY, D. D., & RING, K.   *Methods of madness: The mental hospital as a last resort.* New York: Holt, Rinehart and Winston, 1969.

LONDON, P.   *The modes and morals of psychotherapy.* New York: Holt, Rinehart and Winston, 1964.

MARZOLF, S. S.   The disease concept in psychology. *Psychological Review,* 1947, *54,* 211–221.

MOWRER, O. H.   Learning theory and the neurotic paradox. *American Journal of Orthopsychiatry,* 1948, *18,* 571–610.

MOWRER, O. H.   *Learning theory and personality dynamics.* New York: Ronald Press, 1950.

MOWRER, O. H.   "Sin," the lesser of two evils. *American Psychologist,* 1960, *15,* 301–304.

MOWRER, O. H.   *The crisis in psychiatry and religion.* Princeton, N. J.: Van Nostrand, 1961.

MOWRER, O. H.   Freudianism, behavior therapy, and "self-disclosure." *Behavioral Research and Therapy,* 1964, *1,* 321–337 (a).

MOWRER, O. H.   *The new group therapy.* Princeton, N. J.: Van Nostrand, 1964(b).

MOWRER, O. H.   Learning theory and behavior therapy. In B. Wolman (Ed.), *Handbook of clinical psychology*. New York: McGraw-Hill, 1965.

MOWRER, O. H.   The basis of psychopathology: Malconditioning or misbehavior? *Journal of National Association of Women Deans & Counselors*, 1966, *29*, 51–58(a).

MOWRER, O. H.   Abnormal reactions or actions? (An autobiographical answer). In J. A. Vernon (Ed.), *Introduction to psychology: A self-selection textbook*. Dubuque, Iowa: Wm. Brown, 1966(b).

PETERSON, D. R.   Behavior problems of middle childhood. *Journal of Consulting Psychology*, 1961, *25*, 205–209.

PETERSON, D. R.   The insecure child: Over-socialized or under-socialized? In O. H. Mowrer (Ed.), *Morality and mental health*. Skokie, Ill.: Rand McNally, 1967.

SARBIN, T. R.   On the futility of the proposition that some people be labeled "mentally ill." *Journal of Consulting Psychology*, 1967, *31*, 447–453.

STEKEL, W.   *Technique of analytical psychotherapy*. New York: Liveright, 1950.

SWENSEN, C. H.   Sexual behavior and psychopathology: A test of Mowrer's hypotheses. *Journal of Clinical Psychology*, 1962, *18*, 406–409.

SZASZ, T. S.   *The myth of mental illness*. New York: Hoeber, 1961.

CHAPTER 7
THE HUMANISTIC PERSPECTIVE

The Perspective

Introduction

In the study of abnormal behavior, particularly in the United States, two perspectives have until recently been dominant forces. These viewpoints are behaviorism and psychoanalysis. Recently, however, a third approach has captured the imagination of mental health professionals and laymen alike. The name usually given to this "third force" is humanistic psychology (Sutich & Vich, 1969).

Although "third force" suggests a monolithic or univocal point of view, this is not accurate. Instead the humanistic perspective has at least three distinct viewpoints: self-theories, some elements of existentialism, and some of phenomenology. Among the authors usually identified with the humanistic perspective are Rogers (1959, 1961), Maslow (1954, 1955), May (1967, 1969), Laing (1959, 1967), and Bugental (1965).

What unifies these various authors under the rubric of humanistic psychology is a general *view of man*. Sutich and Vich (1969) suggest what this view is when they contrast it to behaviorism and psychoanalysis.

> Two main branches of psychology—behaviorism and psychoanalysis—appear to have made great contributions to human knowledge, but neither singly nor together have they covered the almost limitless scope of human behavior, relationships and possibilities. Perhaps their greatest limitation has been the inadequacy of their approach to the positive human potentialities and the maximal realization of those potentialities. (p. 1)

The concern of humanistic psychologists is with concepts like growth, values, creativity, being, autonomy, existence, meaning, and psychological health.

Although this perspective has only recently appeared, a great deal of writing and activity has marked its past. As Sutich & Vich (1969) point out, the founding of the *Journal of Humanistic Psychology* in 1961 represents an important landmark in the development of the humanistic perspective, as does the founding of the American Association for Humanistic Psychology in the period 1961–1963. In addition, the humanistic movement has stimulated increasing interest in sensitivity training and centers for growth-engendering techniques such as Esalen Institute at Big Sur (Schutz, 1967).

As we have suggested, self-theory, phenomenology, and some forms of existentialism have all been part of the humanistic movement. In choosing a single proponent of humanistic psychology for presentation we have selected Carl Rogers as being representative. Although Rogers is basically a self-theorist, his approach exhibits the optimistic view of man so characteristic of the humanistic perspective. Furthermore, Rogers is, at least in part, a phenomenologist, deeply concerned with the phenomena of individual human experience.

> There is one attitude which I hold, which I believe has relevance for the proper evaluation of any theory I might present. It is my belief in the fundamental predominance of the subjective. Man lives essentially in his own personal and subjective world, and even his most objective functioning, in science, mathematics, and the like, is the result of subjective purpose and subjective choice. (Rogers, 1959, p. 191)

Furthermore, many of the concepts Rogers uses—"actualization," for instance—are a part of the intellectual tradition of the humanistic perspective and have been discussed by other major representatives of the perspective (e.g., Maslow, 1954).

Rogers' view of personality originally began as an approach to therapy he sketched in *Client Centered Therapy* (1951) and *On Becoming a Person* (1961). It is more formally presented in a chapter in Koch's *Psychology: A Study of a Science* (Rogers, 1959). We will select from it those portions of Rogers' theory that are directly relevant to the development of abnormal behavior.

One other point influenced our choice of Rogers. His work is more articulate and systematic than that of many writers in the humanistic tradition. Thus it provides a solid base for the discussion of other humanistic viewpoints.

The Language of Rogers' Perspective

We will include in this section only terms that are directly related to the development of abnormal behavior. (For a more complete list of Rogers' concepts see Rogers, 1959.) A number of the terms we will examine here are used by other authors in the humanistic tradition with slightly different meanings.

Actualizing tendency   The actualizing tendency is the tendency of the organism as a whole to develop all its potentialities in a manner that serves to maintain or enhance itself. The actualizing tendency involves both meeting biological needs and striving for autonomy from external forces. It is the only motive postulated in Rogers' system.

Experience (as a noun)   Experience includes both physiological and psychological events—all that is going on in the organism at a given moment in time. These events are potentially available to awareness.

Experience (as a verb)   To experience is to receive the impact of exterior and interior events at a given moment in time. Events that are perceived at the level of consciousness are said to be experienced.

The self   The self is an organized set (Gestalt) of perceptions and characteristics of the "I" or the "me." The term refers to both the characteristics of the "I" or "me" and the perceptions that we have about others. The perceptions of the self may also include values that are associated with these perceptions. The self is not necessarily in awareness, but it is potentially available to awareness. The self is also variously called the "concept of self" or "self-structure."

Self-experience   The self-experience is the "raw material" from which the self-concept is formed. This includes any experiences the individual has that he identifies as involving the "me," "I," or "self."

Ideal self   The ideal self is the concept of that self which the individual would most like to have, the self-concept upon which he places the highest value.

Incongruence   Incongruence refers to a discrepancy or conflict the organism experiences. The discrepancy is between the self as the individual perceives it and the actual experience of the organism. For example, the individual may perceive himself as having one set of characteristics, but an accurate symbolization of his experience would indicate a different set of characteristics. A state of incongruence in the organism may be characterized as internal confusion or tension.

Anxiety   Anxiety, as it is experienced by the person phenomenologically, is a state of tension or uneasiness for which no known cause exists. Anxiety is likely to occur when the awareness of incongruence between the self and experience is impending.

Vulnerability   Vulnerability refers to the potential for psychological disorganization that exists because of the incongruence between the self and experience. Thus an individual is vulnerable to anxiety when incongruence exists but is not yet perceived in awareness.

Threat   Threat is the state that exists when the individual actually perceives incongruence between the self and experience.

Defense   Defense is the organism's response to threat. The goal of defense is to maintain the self-structure as it currently exists. Defense achieves the maintenance of the existing self-structure in the face of incongruity by distorting experience in awareness. A distortion serves to reduce the incongruity between the current state of self and the discrepant evidence of experience. Denial and distortion are forms of defense that serve the same general purpose.

Psychological maladjustment   This exists when the organism denies or distorts experiences in awareness in such a way that these experiences cannot be incorporated into the self. Thus incongruence is produced. The term psychological maladjustment is used when a person experiencing incongruence is viewed from a social point of view. He may display signs of unhappiness, anxiety, or disorganization.

Positive regard   Positive regard is the perception of a self-experience in another person, which leads to favorable or pleasant experience for that perceiver. When this occurs, the perceiver is said to be experiencing positive regard for that individual. The need for positive regard is learned early in childhood.

Unconditional positive regard   Unconditional positive regard is positive regard experienced toward an individual irrespective of that individual's values or behavior. As Rogers (1959) puts it: "If self-experiences of another are perceived by me in such a way that no self-experience can be discriminated as more or less worthy of positive regard than any other, then I am experiencing unconditional positive regard for this individual." (p. 208)

Early Development of the Person

In order to understand Rogers' ideas about the development of abnormal behavior, we must first examine his theory of the development of the normal individual from infancy.

Characteristics of the infant

For Rogers (1959) the infant's experience constitutes the whole of his reality. Only that particular infant has access to his unique internal frame of reference. Furthermore, the infant has an inherent tendency toward actualizing himself. The goal-directed behavior of the infant—his reaching, sucking, touching—is an attempt to actualize himself in terms of his reality as he perceives it.

Thus the infant comes to value experiences which he perceives as serving that actualizing process. Similarly, the infant learns to avoid unpleasant experiences which he finds are hindering the actualization of his biological and psychological being.

Development of the self

As the child engages in the actualizing process, his experiences become more and more differentiated from each other. He begins to symbolize, that is, he begins to view his own behavior as a separate entity. His emerging awareness of his own behavior and his own functions is the beginning of his experience of himself as an independent entity.

As the child continues to grow and interact with other people, his self-experience develops into the *self-concept*. The self-concept then becomes a perceptual object which the child may experience when he thinks of the "me" or "I." He may come to think of himself as good or bad, clever or ineffective as a result of his experience with others and their reactions to him.

The need for positive regard and positive self-regard

As the child's self-concept develops, he also develops a need for others' positive regard. Rogers avoids any explicit statement of whether the need for positive regard is learned or inherent, but he does hold that it is a pervasive and persistent characteristic of the individual. For Rogers the need for positive regard is a "universal" need.

The need for positive regard is usually satisfied by the child in a reciprocal way. That is, in satisfying another person's need for positive regard he will also satisfy his own need. However, we must realize that this need may become more compelling than the need for actualization. The child may seek positive regard from others rather than seeking experiences that would serve to actualize himself.

Positive regard applied to oneself or to those experiences that refer to the self is termed positive self-regard. The need for positive self-regard is a learned need, and the child comes to value or devalue himself independently of how others may see him.

The development of conditions of worth

Conditions of worth develop in the person when he selectively responds to his self-experiences as more or less worthy of positive regard. If a child always experienced unconditional positive regard, then no conditions of worth would develop and the child would experience himself in terms of positive self-regard regardless of his external experience. He would in this case remain psychologically adjusted. In reality, however, conditions of worth exist for everyone since no child receives only unconditional positive regard from others.

Thus the child is valued for competent performance in school or play and less valued for poor performance. He is valued for "good" behavior and less valued when he is "bad." As we shall see, the child who has incorporated many or intense conditions of worth is vulnerable to threat or anxiety when he encounters experiences which are contrary to his conditions of worth.

The Development of Incongruence

As the individual grows he continues to need self-regard, but, as we suggested above, he has also acquired conditions of worth. That is, he comes to value certain behaviors and experiences which he finds others value. Similarly, he devalues those behaviors and experiences which others do not value or disapprove of or punish.

Since the person retains his need for self-regard, he begins to perceive his experience in a selective fashion. He either denies awareness to or selectively views those experiences that are contrary to his conditions of worth, even to the point of making them appear to be conditions of worth. He may deny or rationalize a failure, for example.

As a result of this distortion or selective perception an incongruence develops between the person's actual experience and his concept of self. The individual is now vulnerable to anxiety and, to some degree, is psychologically maladjusted.

Rogers (1959) describes the dilemma of incongruence in the following way:

This, as we see it, is the basic estrangement in man. He has not been true to himself, to his own natural organismic valuing of experience, but for the sake of preserving the positive regard of others has now come to falsify some of the values he experiences and to perceive them only in terms based upon their value to others. Yet this has not been a conscious choice, but a natural—and tragic—development in infancy. The path of therapy is the undoing of this estrangement in man's functioning, the dissolving of conditions of worth, the achievement of a self which is congruent with experience, and the restoration of a unified organismic valuing process as the regulator of behavior. (pp. 226–227)

Thus for Rogers the development of incongruity and, therefore, man's estrangement from himself are natural consequences of the socialization process.

That Rogers' concept of incongruence is very closely tied to his notion of conditions of worth is central to his idea of psychopathology. It tells us, as well, a good deal about his view of man and the humanistic tradition in which his theory clearly fits.

The Development of Defensive Behavior

When incongruity exists in the person, he is vulnerable to threat. The basic threat is that experiences which are incongruent with the self-structure endanger the integrity of the self as a consistent structure or Gestalt. He will not meet his conditions of worth and will then experience anxiety.

Defensive behaviors develop as the person attempts to prevent the anxiety from occurring. In general defensive behavior is a distortion or selective perception of experience that makes the experience consistent with the self-structure as it currently exists. Rogers (1959) offers the following examples of defensive behavior:

Let us consider for a moment the general range of defensive behaviors from the simplest variety, common to all of us, to the more extreme and crippling varieties. Take first of all, rationalization ("I didn't really make that mistake, it was this way . . ."). Such excuses involve a perception of behavior distorted in such a way as to make it congruent with our concept of self (person who doesn't make mistakes). Fantasy is another example ("I am a beautiful princess, and all men adore me."). Because the actual experience is threatening to the concept of self (as an adequate person, in this example), this experience is denied, and a new symbolic world is created which enhances the self, but completely avoids any recognition of the actual experience. (p. 228)

In Figure 7.1, the development of defensive behavior is shown in schematic form. Our diagram recapitulates the development of the person as Rogers describes it. The lack of unconditional positive regard and un-

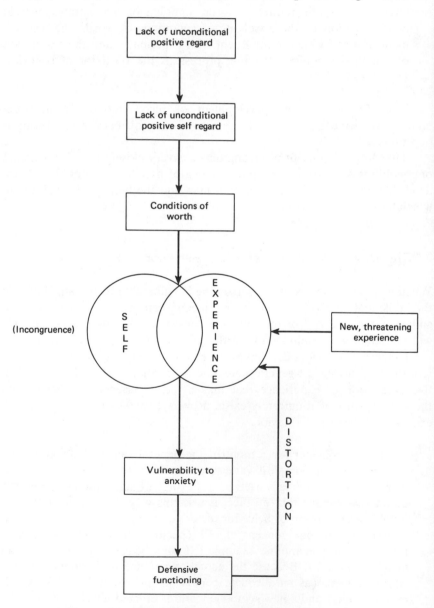

Figure 7.1   The development of defensive behavior.

conditional positive self-regard in the life of the person leads to conditions of worth. Once conditions of worth are firmly established as part of the self-concept, the person may encounter threatening experiences which are incompatible with his self-concept. Thus, incongruence may develop between his self-concept and his experience.

Incongruence makes the individual vulnerable to anxiety, an unpleasant state. At this point the person's defenses come into play. Defenses serve the purpose of distorting his experience to make it more compatible with the self-concept. But it is an artificial compatibility, one that occurs only at the expense of distorted experience.

Rogers makes a general distinction between defensive behaviors as we have just described them and disorganized behaviors. This distinction provides a crude typology of abnormal behavior. Among the defensive behaviors are included behaviors conventionally thought of as "neurotic"— for example, rationalization, projection, phobias—as well as some behaviors often regarded as psychotic—for example, paranoid behaviors such as suspicion or projection. Disorganized behaviors, on the other hand, include much of what is usually associated with "acute psychotic" reactions. We will now turn to the development of this second type of abnormal behavior.

The Development of Disorganized Behavior

The degree of incongruence between the self and experience may be great for a particular individual. Furthermore, one may undergo an experience that confronts him with the incongruence suddenly and without warning. If this occurs, the process of defense may not operate successfully. When defenses are unable to operate with any degree of effectiveness the experience will not be distorted but instead will be symbolized accurately in experience. In this case disorganization, rather than defensiveness, will result.

Rogers suggests that in cases of disorganization, the behavior pattern that will result is one in which at times the person will act in terms of his self-concept and at other times in terms of his discrepant experiences, thus his behavior will alternate between these two modes. Examples of disorganized behavior are the "psychotic break" or the "acute psychotic episode."

Once an individual has shown the psychotic behavior, he may resort to two possible processes of defense. First, he may defend against his awareness of himself. He may in effect deny his identity and perhaps even take on a different identity. The person may, for example, be perplexed about who he is or he may even claim he is some famous figure in the past. The latter claim is usually regarded as a "paranoid delusion." A second possibility is for the concept of self to change, and, as Rogers puts it, now exist as ". . . a self-concept which includes the important theme, 'I am a crazy, inadequate, unreliable person who contains impulses and forces beyond my control.' Thus it is a self in which little or no confidence is felt." (Rogers, 1959, p. 230)

In Figure 7.2, the development of disorganized behavior is sketched. We can see that the early stages of the development of disorganized behavior are the same as those of defensive behavior. In this case, however,

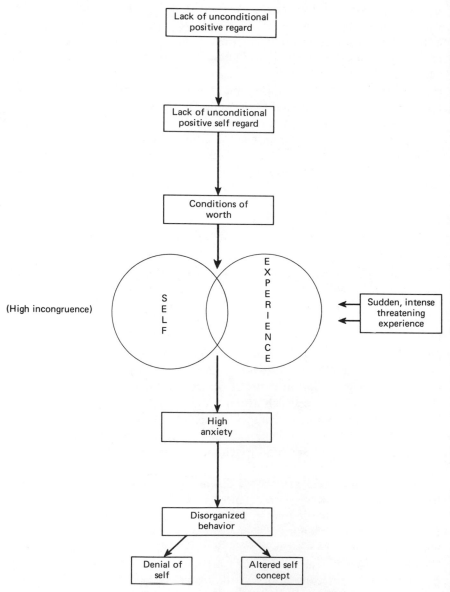

Figure 7.2   The development of disorganized behavior.

the incongruence-evoking experience is sudden and intense, producing extreme incongruence and high anxiety. The defenses are unable to operate under such circumstances, and the result is disorganized behavior which is resolved either by the denial of the current self-concept or an altered self-concept.

Summary

The humanistic perspective or "third force" is the study of abnormal behavior encompassing portions of self-theory, existentialism, and phenomenology. Moreover, this perspective conveys a general attitude about man that is optimistic and focuses on the realization of human potential. This fulfillment of human potential is usually termed "actualization." The humanistic view sees abnormal behavior as a failure to achieve that actualization.

Carl Rogers stands as perhaps the best known adherent of the humanistic perspective. He views the organism as having an inherent drive to actualize its potentials. As a child grows he begins to develop a conception of himself. At the same time he develops a need for positive regard from others and, by extension, from himself. Further socialization leads the person to experience conditions of worth. He comes to value aspects of himself, not because they enhance his own actualization, but because other people in his world value these aspects of him.

While the person begins to view himself and his world in terms of conditions of worth, he may have experiences which are not consistent with these conditions. The result is a state of incongruence between himself and his experience that leaves the person vulnerable to anxiety.

The person now may adopt certain defensive behavior as a way to cope with his vulnerability. Defensive behavior serves to distort his view of his experience and is thus an attempt to restore congruence between the self and experience. Often defensive behaviors are "neurotic" in character but they may also include behaviors that are viewed as "psychotic." Examples are suspicion and paranoid thinking.

If the incongruity between the self and experience is very great, the person's anxiety will be correspondingly great and defensive measures may be ineffective in coping with it. In this case disorganization results. Disorganized behavior is characterized by actions that are consistent with the person's self-concept at some times and with his experience at other times. The person's behavior will appear confused and ambivalent and may also appear "psychotic." At least two possible resolutions of this state of disorganization are possible according to Rogers. First, the person may try to take on a new "identity" (which others may see as delusional), or he may accept his identity as an inadequate, confused, "crazy" person.

This account relies heavily on conditions of worth as the predisposing factor in the development of abnormal behavior. The precipitating factor is the introduction of threatening experiences that are not congruent with the self-concept. It is implied that the factors which lead a person to react in defensive or disorganized ways are basically quantitative. That is, extreme conditions of worth or extremely threatening experiences, or both, should make it more likely that the person would develop disorganized rather than defensive behavior.

People who do not develop strong conditions of worth but who instead have grown up in an atmosphere of unconditional positive regard from others are much less likely to be vulnerable to anxiety because of incongruent experiences. Implicit in Rogers' theory is the idea that unconditional positive regard is the crucial ingredient both for healthy development and for effective psychotherapy. In both cases, valuing the person for what he is rather than for what he should be is the first step in his self-actualization.

Commentary

Maslow's Concepts of Self-Actualization, Need Hierarchy, and Psychological Health

Unlike most perspectives on psychopathology, the humanistic movement places at least an equal emphasis on the positive aspects of man's behavior. The single most important theme that runs through the work of many theorists within this movement is the concept of *self-actualization*. Goldstein (1939) was one of the first to use the term "self-actualization"; Erich Fromm (1941) described the concept as "the productive orientation." Karen Horney (1950) used the term "the real self and its realization," while for Allport (1955) the concept was best expressed as "creative becoming."

What sort of person is a self-actualized individual? Maslow (1954) has attempted to provide a general description by a list of characteristics. He indicates that these are not merely speculative ideas but the result of his study of a number of self-actualizing people.

Maslow believes that the self-actualizing person is more efficient in perceiving reality, more accepting of himself and others, more spontaneous, more problem centered, and capable of being detached and objective. In addition he is autonomous, capable of a fresh appreciation of things, and open to mystical experiences. The self-actualizer shows a good deal of interest in his fellow man, possesses a democratic character structure, experiences deep and profound interpersonal relationships, and is able to discriminate between means and ends. Finally, the self-actualizer has a sense of humor, is creative, and yet at the same time is able to resist many of the forces of the culture in which he lives.

These characteristics are by no means mutually exclusive but overlap with each other to a great extent. In addition, it is fairly clear that Maslow owes much to Erich Fromm (1955), since his list is quite similar to Fromm's description of the characteristics of persons with a "productive orientation." Yet it serves to provide an explicit example both of what is meant by the concept of self-actualization, and at the same time, of the positive, optimistic orientation so typical of the humanistic perspective.

Maslow (1954, 1955) postulates a hierarchy of needs, with the most basic needs at the bottom; as one progresses up the hierarchy, these needs become less basic to human existence. He argues that the higher needs only function when lower needs have been satisfied. Further, Maslow believes that these needs are universal and independent of specific cultural influences. Thus he describes them as "instinctoid," by which he means that although they exist in all men, many of these needs are not strong enough to be observed unless conditions are favorable.

Maslow places the *physiological needs* at the bottom of the hierarchy. These are needs such as hunger and thirst. Since in our society few people are in danger of starvation, this need is almost always satisfied.

Second in the hierarchy are the *safety needs.* Like the physiological needs, the safety needs may dominate behavior if they are not satisfied. Among the safety needs are, for a child, the need to protect oneself from sudden noises or being dropped, or, in slightly older children, the need to protect oneself from strangers. In times of war, disease, or natural catastrophe, the safety needs dominate behavior.

Next in the hierarchy are the *belongingness* or *love needs.* In general, these needs are manifested by the hunger for affectionate relationships with other people. Again, this need will not manifest itself until prior needs in the hierarchy are fulfilled. Maslow believes that belongingness and love needs are often frustrated and this frustration is an important basis for the development of maladjustment or abnormal behavior.

Next are the *esteem needs.* These needs represent a desire for a firmly based high evaluation of oneself. The need for self-esteem or self-respect and a need for respect from others are examples of esteem needs. In adults these esteem needs often show themselves as a desire for dominance, recognition, prestige, or status. When these needs are gratified, the person will feel self-confident, strong, capable, and adequate.

Finally, the highest need in the hierarchy is that of *self-actualization.* The characteristics of self-actualizing people that have already been outlined implicitly describe the needs of the self-actualized person. They include the need for spontaneity, the need to be creative, and the need to show an interest in one's fellow man.

Maslow believes that the gratification of all of the needs in the hierarchy is crucial to the psychological well-being of the individual. When these needs are not met, there exist, Maslow says, "deficiency conditions." Maslow argues that the hierarchical needs are basic to mental health for a number of reasons. First, if these needs are not satisfied, psychological health is not possible. Second, when these needs are satisfied, illness is prevented. Third, if a person is already maladjusted, the satisfaction of the needs will overcome the maladjustment. Finally, Maslow believes that in healthy, fully functioning persons, these needs are fulfilled (Maslow, 1955).

It is interesting to note that Maslow strongly believes that this hierarchy of needs is not specific to any particular culture but is universal. Unlike Freud, who holds a relatively pessimistic view of man, the growth theorists such as Maslow and Rogers hold as a basic premise the idea that destructiveness is not instinctual in man's nature. Instead, the growth theorists view aggression and destructiveness as learned reactions.

Thus, it is not man who is indicted as the "cause" of abnormal behavior but society. Both Maslow's concept of "deficiency conditions" and Rogers' idea of "conditions of worth" are central to their view of how abnormal behavior develops. Both concepts attribute the source of man's unhappiness not to man himself but to his society and to the socialization process. We will see this theme again later in our commentary.

Some Problems with the Concept of Actualization and the Humanistic Definition of Mental Health

We can identify a number of difficulties with Maslow's description of the concept of actualization and definition of mental health. Although these difficulties arise from Maslow's conceptions, they apply with almost equal force to Rogers' view and those of other advocates of the humanistic perspective.

First, we should note that Maslow's major source of evidence for the concept of actualization comes from his study of self-actualizing people. Although Maslow has referred to these people repeatedly in his writings, we know surprisingly little about them which would allow us to make the inference that self-actualization is a potential characteristic of everyone. For example, are these people typical of the general population? Or is it the case that they are more intelligent, exist in more fortunate circumstances, or enjoy more affluence than most of us? It is quite possible that these people are really untypical of the general population in a number of ways, and consequently form an unrepresentative basis for generalization about the nature of human potential for happiness or mental health.

Second, we noted earlier that the humanistic view of man suggests that man is essentially good. The destructive elements of man are accounted for by arguing that these are learned elements or that they may be attributed to socializing influences. Again, little evidence for this assumption is offered. The indictment of society by the humanistic perspective has the status of an ideological or political stance rather than of an assumption potentially verifiable by empirical methods.

Third, the humanistic perspective asserts that actualization and mental health are universal rather than culturally determined. The possibility of cultural relativity of definition of mental health is ignored despite considerable evidence in favor of the relativistic position.

Finally, perhaps the greatest weakness of the humanistic view is its conceptual unclarity and imprecise language. As Cofer and Appley (1964) remark,

> The emphasis on self-actualization (and its philosophical relative, existentialism) suffers, in our opinion, from the vagueness of its concepts, the looseness of its language, and the inadequacy of the evidence related to its major contentions. It is difficult to see how it can foster meaningful investigations in view of its vague language. The first prerequisite for further development and evaluation of this viewpoint, it seems to us, is the formulation of the important ideas in language that is relatively precise. It then may be possible to carry out investigations related to the basic premises. (p. 692)

Abnormal Behavior as Growth

Nearly all perspectives on abnormal behavior view the development of symptoms in an individual as a negative, unfortunate turn of events. Typically the terms used to denote the development of psychological disturbance are negative. Behavior is described as "maladaptive," "disorganized," "disintegrated," or "regressed." However, there is a small but growing group of theorists, especially within the humanistic tradition, who regard some forms of abnormal behavior not as negative events but as a hopeful and positive indication of the possibilities of personal growth.

Such a conception may well sound unfamiliar or alien to us. Yet this idea may force a genuine shift in our perspective. Assumptions that are shared by other perspectives—for example, the idea that all abnormal behavior is negative—may not be obvious to us until we are confronted with an exception to the implicit assumption. Thus, the idea that abnormal behavior may actually be an opportunity for personal growth not only represents a genuine shift in our view of abnormal behavior but also exposes an assumption which we may previously have accepted unquestioningly.

Among the major proponents of this view are R. D. Laing (1959, 1967), Kazimierz Dabrowski (1964), and John Perry (1962). As yet, no single account of this basic idea has emerged, but there are similarities. Let us examine, briefly, the general views of Laing and Dabrowski.

In *The Divided Self*, Laing argues that "madness" is actually a breakdown of an earlier split between the person's real or true inner-self and a false outer-self. As the child develops, he may develop a false outer-self which is conforming and compliant and which attempts to fulfill others' expectations. This false outer-self leads other people to believe that the child is adjusted and happy. But meantime a true inner-self is developing which protects itself by withdrawing and disengaging from the relentless demands of others. Thus the person may smile but he does not necessarily feel amusement or friendliness. Phenomenologically, he is isolated and alone.

For Laing, psychosis or madness, in some people at least, is the sudden stripping away of the false outer-self revealing beneath it the preoccupation, distortions, and fears of the true inner-self. The precariously maintained split or dissociation between the true inner-self and the false outer-self is dissolved, revealing all of the terror and anger that had remained hidden.

However, the psychotic break or onset of madness may actually represent a possibility for personal growth. Laing believes once the person has become mad, the split between the inner-self and the false outer-self may now be healed.

But "healing" is not accomplished by the reestablishment of the false outer-self. Instead, for Laing, therapy consists of allowing the person to explore his inner-self freely, since he assumes that only through such exploration and support from others can the person achieve a whole and vital embodied self.

There are several striking parallels in the thinking of Rogers and Laing concerning the development of abnormal behavior. For both Laing and Rogers abnormal behavior arises from a background involving a great deal of pressure to please others. For Laing this results in a "false outer-self"; for Rogers the result is "conditions of worth." Rogers suggests that incongruity is reflected in a discrepancy between the self and experience while Laing describes much the same thing when he suggests that a split develops between a true inner-self and a false outer-self. Finally, the source of these difficulties is attributed by both Laing and Rogers to an oppressive socialization process which values people for what they do rather than what they are.

In *Positive Disintegration* (1964) the Polish psychiatrist Kazimierz Dabrowski gives a somewhat different account from Laing's, but emphasizes a similar theme. In his theory of positive disintegration, Dabrowski views all personality development as the result of disintegration. Disintegration is seen as a conflict or disharmony in the individual and his adaptation to his environment.

One's personality develops only when he is dissatisfied with the self as it currently exists. The developing self evolves through a period of disintegration, then a period of secondary integration. The period of disintegration usually involves anxiety, regression, and neurosis. Secondary integration then follows at a higher level and is characterized by the individual's ability to adapt to his environment. For Dabrowski growth can occur only after a period of disintegration.

People who are likely to undergo positive disintegration, according to Dabrowski, tend to be intelligent and creative. They are people involved in developmental crisis with their whole being. But Dabrowski makes clear that not all disintegration is positive. Negative disintegration may also occur, either because the developmental crisis is poorly handled or because the individual does not have the capacity to deal with the crisis of disintegration.

To better appreciate what these theorists are describing let us examine briefly a clinical example. James Gordon (1971) describes the case of Mary, a woman who had been seeing R. D. Laing in psychotherapy for some years before her crisis occurred. Mary had been hospitalized previously and had been diagnosed as a schizophrenic. She had since left the hospital but continued to lead a dreary, anxiety-laden life in which she continually put up a rigid, constricted front.

Mary went to Kingsley Hall shortly after R. D. Laing opened this special institution. Soon after her admission she began to regress. At night she would tear off her clothes and lie on the floor smearing her feces. For a time, she stopped eating solid food and was fed milk from a bottle by Laing and his colleagues. At one point, Mary regressed even further and even stopped drinking milk from a bottle or performing any other bodily function. Then, slowly, Mary began to recover from her madness. She began to wear clothes again and to play like a child, dancing and playing ball. Throughout this time, Laing and his fellow therapists continued to support her but made no attempt to intervene or to in any way alter the evolution of her psychosis. Soon she began to draw profusely. She drew all over the wall and then began to draw on strips of paper. Since then, Mary has been painting steadily. Dozens of paintings and drawings have appeared on boards, sheets of paper, and the walls. She describes her fascination with painting as her salvation and has become a full-time artist, still living in Kingsley Hall but, nevertheless, by her own account, a new person.

Such a dramatic account of madness and the resulting dramatic personality change may lead us to ask whether Mary's case is an extraordinary exception or whether it is typical of a much larger group of people who have once been "mad." There is some evidence to indicate that some patients diagnosed as schizophrenic may actually benefit from their psychotic experience as Mary did.

Silverman (1970) suggests that patients who improve after the onset of their symptoms are typically people for whom symptom onset is sudden. They have experienced a definite life crisis or precipitating event immediately before their psychotic break.

He also points out that, in other cultures, behavior which we call schizophrenic may be treated very differently and thought of as a kind of initiation rite. He suggests that many religious figures, among them Saint Theresa, Saint Paul, and George Fox (the founder of the Quakers), went through experiences which we might today regard as psychotic episodes. But these were individuals who, in their own cultural setting, were valued for the special insights that their psychosis seemed to provide.

Silverman also suggests that, for these people, the immediate introduction of psychoactive drugs in an attempt to control the symptoms of psychosis may actually harm rather than benefit the patient. He cites a recent study of Goldstein, Judd, Rodnick, and LaPolla (1969) in which it was found that acute nonparanoid schizophrenic patients who were treated with tranquilizers, particularly chlorpromazine, actually showed increases in thought disorder over a period of several weeks. A similar group of patients on placebos showed decreases in thought disorder during the same period. As Silverman points out, "tranquilizers seem to reduce regressed and agitated schizophrenic behavior, and most psychiatrists take this as evidence of improvement. Unfortunately, regressed and disorganized behavior may be essential parts of schizophrenia's problem-solving process" (p. 64).

The work of Goldstein and his colleagues is not the only research following the theoretical lead of Laing, Dabrowski, and others. Silverman (1970) reports that at Agnew's State Hospital in San Jose, California, he is attempting to identify people who are engaged in what appear to be growth-engendering psychotic experiences. In this project researchers are withholding antipsychotic tranquilizers from some of the patients who would ordinarily be heavily drugged. As in the Goldstein study, Silverman is interested in the question of whether or not these individuals will actually benefit from the schizophrenic experience if antipsychotic medication is withheld from them.

It is also interesting to note the implications of the views of Laing, Dabrowski, and Silverman for Rogers' account of the development of disorganized behavior. We will recall that Rogers (1959) suggests two possible results of severe behavioral disorganization. First, the person may finally deny his own identity and even take on a new "delusional" identity. Second, he may finally accept an identity as an incompetent, confused, "crazy" person. If the view that abnormal behavior may in some cases be the precursor of a growth experience has any validity, then we may add yet a third possible outcome to the two that Rogers has outlined. In some cases the development of behavioral disorganization may actually signal the beginning of positive personality growth.

Research on Self-Concept and Maladjustment

The humanistic view has not generated a large body of empirical research directed at systematically testing hypotheses derived from the basic perspective. There is, however, a reasonably large body of research stimulated by Rogers' thinking concerning the relationship between maladjustment and self-concept. Since we have discussed his approach to abnormal behavior in some detail, it is appropriate to look at some examples of research on this problem.

Rogers suggests that maladjustment may be defined in terms of the degree of discrepancy between the concept of self and experience. If this discrepancy increases anxiety will presumably result, leading to disorganization of the self-structure, defensiveness, and in extreme cases psychological breakdown.

One of the most widely used measures of incongruence in the psychological literature has been a measure of the magnitude of the discrepancy between the self-concept and the ideal self. The usual technique for obtaining this measure is to ask the person being studied to rate self-descriptive items, first as he actually sees himself and second as he would ideally want to be. The correlation between these two sets of scores is taken to reflect the discrepancy between the self-concept and the ideal self. High correlations reflect low discrepancy and low correlations reflect high discrepancy.

A study by Davids and Lawton (1961) suggests that negative self-concepts are associated with maladjustment. These investigators studied two groups of boys ages 9 to 12. The maladjusted group was composed of emotionally disturbed youngsters undergoing psychiatric treatment, while the control group consisted of 30 boys at a YMCA camp. Davids and Lawton found that self-concept as measured by means of an adjective checklist was considerably lower among the maladjusted group. It should be noted that this study reflects not self-ideal discrepancy, but only the fact that maladjusted groups tend to view themselves less positively than apparently normal groups.

A second study which bears more directly on the question of self-ideal discrepancy was done by Chase (1957). Chase studied psychiatric patients in a Veterans Administration Hospital and a control group consisting of medical and surgical patients. All subjects were given a 50-item Q-sort which measured self-concept and ideal self. Correlations between self and ideal self were obtained for each group. The average correlation for the control group was .64, significantly higher than that for the maladjusted group, which was .36. Interestingly, Chase also found that subjects in both the psychiatric and the control groups had similar conceptions of the ideal self. The differences in correlations were due to the fact that the psychiatric patients had significantly lower self-concept scores than did the control group.

Results such as these might lead one to conclude that there is a linear relationship between degree of incongruity between the self and ideal self and maladjustment. However, this is not necessarily true. There is evidence suggesting that the maladjustment could be reflected either in a large discrepancy between the self and ideal or in an unrealistically low discrepancy. This would suggest a curvilinear rather than a linear relationship between adjustment and self–ideal discrepancy.

Some research which bears on this point is the work of Hillson and Worchel (1957). They compared measures of self-concept for normal subjects, neurotic patients in treatment, and hospitalized schizophrenic patients. Surprisingly, they found that neurotics had a higher self–ideal discrepancy score than normals or psychotics. Psychotics did not differ from normals in self-satisfaction. Similar results have been reported by Friedman (1955), who compared normals, neurotics, and paranoid schizophrenics on a self-description measure and found that the positive self-concepts of normals and the negative self-concepts of neurotics tended to be based on realistic self-appraisal, whereas schizophrenics' positive self-concepts were usually based on unrealistic self-appraisal and self-enhancing defenses.

Most of the research dealing with maladjustment and self-concept has focused on the self–ideal discrepancy, despite the fact that Rogers explicitly defines incongruence in terms of the discrepancy between self-concept and experience. Mehrabian (1968) has suggested a measure that perhaps more closely approximates the self–experience discrepancy. He proposes a measure of self-concept obtained by asking subjects to rate various statements, such as "I am a responsible person" or "I feel adequate," on a 7-point scale ranging from "most like me" to "least like me." This would provide a measure of self-concept. As a measure of "experience" he suggests that the same items be rated by an acquaintance or friend of the subject as the acquaintance actually perceives him. The self–experience discrepancy would then be measured in terms of the correlation between the subject's self-concept and the acquaintance's perceptions. Thus a low correlation would presumably reflect a high discrepancy between self and experience and high maladjustment, while a high correlation would reflect a low discrepancy between self and experience and presumably better adjustment. Mehrabian points out that correlations between 0 and +1.0 are relatively easy to interpret, but negative correlations are somewhat more difficult.

Negative correlations in this case indicate that the self-concept of the person is systematically opposite to the perceptions of the observer. This suggests the interesting possibility that zero correlations are more likely to be associated with *disorganized states,* while negative correlations are more likely to be associated with *defensive states.*

Mehrabian goes on to suggest possible measures of two other basic concepts within the Rogerian framework. The concept of conditional-positive self-regard could be measured using a questionnaire that would assess the individual's attitudes toward himself. Items would be of the following kind: "I lose confidence in myself when I make minor mistakes," or "Depending on what I do, I sometimes think of myself as a good person, and at other times I think of myself as a bad person" (p. 48).

Research of the kind we have briefly described is certainly within the humanistic tradition. Unfortunately, the rigor and intensity of empirical research inspired by the humanistic perspective is not nearly as great as that generated, for example, by the learning or illness perspective. However, empirical research will be necessary if the humanistic perspective is to move from its current status as a perspective to that of a theory which can stake its own claim to having aided in our understanding of abnormal behavior.

Values and the Goals of Science

As we might expect, the humanistic perspective holds strong views concerning the nature of science, particularly the science of man. Perhaps the best known expression of these views exists in the now famous Rogers–Skinner debate (Rogers & Skinner, 1956). This debate paired proponents of two of the major perspectives discussed in this book—the learning perspective, espoused by Skinner, and the humanistic perspective, of which Carl Rogers is a major advocate.

In this symposium, Rogers and Skinner are concerned with the place of science in human endeavor. More specifically, both are concerned with the issue of the control of human behavior. It is not surprising that the question of control would be a pivotal question in the conflict existing between the learning perspective and the humanistic view.

Science and human control

Skinner opens the debate by pointing to the fact that our power to influence, to change, to control human behavior has been steadily increasing. He suggests that three broad areas of human behavior supply good examples of our increasing ability to control. There is first the area of personal control, in which men influence each other in face-to-face relationships.

Second, there is the area of education, where again, Skinner points out, our concept of education implies the control and shaping of human beings. Finally, at the most general level, Skinner points to government as an explicit example of control.

Skinner does not believe that the capacity for human control is necessarily evil, only that it is necessary. Perhaps the best example of a Skinnerian conception of what government control can be like at its best is portrayed in his utopian novel, *Walden II* (1948). Skinner suggests that his intention in writing *Walden II* was to propose a behavioral technology which would lead to the construction of an effective, productive, workable pattern of government. He notes that his idea met violent reaction and that attitudes concerning the inherent freedom of man directly conflicted with his notion of what a utopian society would be if it systematically applied learning principles to human behavior. Skinner expresses some surprise at the reaction and says:

> One would scarcely guess that the authors are talking about a world in which there is food, clothing, and shelter for all, where everyone chooses his own work and works an average of only 4 hours a day, where music and the arts flourish, where personal relationships develop under the most favorable circumstances, where education prepares every child for the social and intellectual life which lies before him, where—in short—people are truly happy, secure, productive, creative, and forward looking." (p. 1059)

Skinner summarizes his argument by calling for a new conception of human behavior which is compatible with what he feels are the implications of scientific analysis. In short, Skinner asks us to accept the fact that all men control and are controlled. This is a basic fact of our lives. He sees the wise use of this control as a basic challenge to our scientific ingenuity.

Science and value choice

Rogers' reply to Skinner illustrates well the humanistic attitude toward the question of human control. Rogers, although he believes that Skinner presents an optimistic view, feels he underestimates the problem of power in societies which value control.

But Rogers' major objection to Skinner's analysis is that he believes that Skinner and his fellow scientists grossly underestimate the place of means and ends, goals and values in their relationship to science. Rogers' principal point is that "in any scientific endeavor—whether 'pure' or applied science—there is a prior subjective choice of the purpose or value which brings the scientific endeavor into being which must always lie outside of that endeavor and can never become a part of the science involved in that endeavor" (p. 1061). Rogers points out that, although the techniques for engaging in the experimentation may be the province of science, to choose to experiment is in itself a value choice. Thus, any endeavor in science is carried on in pursuit of a purpose or value which is at bottom subjectively chosen. He argues further that this basic value choice can never be studied by scientific means, and that therefore any discussion of the control of human beings must first concern itself with the subjectively chosen purposes which science is intended to implement.

Since for Rogers science must begin with the value choice, and that value choice is subjectively chosen, Rogers offers a very different set of initial values and purposes from those he attributes to Skinner. He suggests that, instead of valuing control, we might value man as a process of becoming and value the goal of developing the potentiality of each individual. In short, Rogers suggests that we turn the methods of science toward discovering how each person can ultimately engage in the self-actualizing process. Rogers argues that the choice between the goal of control and the goal of man as a self-actualizing being cannot be reconciled. But, we can "choose to use the behavioral sciences in ways which will free, not control; which will bring about constructive variability, not conformity; which will develop creativity, not contentment; which will facilitate each person in his self-directed process of becoming; which will aid individuals, groups, and even the concept of science to become self-transcending in freshly adaptive ways of meeting life and its problems" (p. 1064).

It appears, however, that Rogers has not had the last word in this debate. Recently Skinner (1971) has reopened the controversy with his book, *Beyond Freedom and Dignity*. In it he argues that the solution to society's problems lies in the systematic application of the principles of his behavioral technology. The book is a frontal attack on many of the most fundamental concepts of the humanistic perspective. Predictably, the reaction has been violent and the debate continues without a resolution or an end in sight.

Thus we see yet another point of conflict between two of the perspectives we have discussed. For the learning perspective, the goal of the science of man is clear. We must face the fact of human control, develop our ability to control human behavior and use it wisely. For the humanistic perspective, the goals of the science of man are value choices which are outside the province of that science and are subjectively chosen.

The Humanistic Movement as a Reaction to the Dilemmas of Modern Man

The humanistic movement is a relatively recent phenomenon, though, as we have seen, many of its themes have been anticipated by earlier theorists.

We might wonder why the humanistic perspective, with its optimistic flavor, its emphasis on the individual, and its concern with values, should enjoy such a rapidly growing popularity today.

A number of writers see the humanistic movement as a reaction to a number of features of our contemporary life. Conditions like those described below are thought to have set the stage.

> Problems of identity and alienation in a technocratic and overly crowded society provided fertile ground for the growth of new systems of thought that attempted to address explicitly discrepancies in the social system, in man's relationship to himself, and in the relationship between the two. The threat of nuclear annihilation, the rapid technological changes that interfered with long accepted roles and modes of existence, the tendency to value man for what he did rather than what he was—all of these confronted man with a gap between himself as an individualistic, unique person and the demands of a scientifically based industrial society. (Anonymous, 1970, p. 13)

In an essay entitled "Modern Man's Loss of Significance," Rollo May (1967) expresses a similar idea. He suggests that there is ample evidence that modern man has lost his sense of self and his sense of individual significance or importance. Among the examples he cites are the student protests against the "facelessness of students in the modern factory university" (p. 26). He suggests that modern man is a victim of feelings of helplessness and insignificance when he confronts the ever-present spectre of thermonuclear war. Finally May discusses the problem of the organization man, who paradoxically can only gain personal significance by giving up his individual significance and becoming a "team man." For May (1967) the results of these dilemmas are:

> . . . the loss of the experience of one's own significance which leads to that kind of anxiety that Paul Tillich called the anxiety of meaninglessness, or what Kierkegaard terms anxiety as the fear of nothingness. We used to talk about these things as psychological theories, and a couple of decades ago when I was undergoing my psychoanalytic training, we discussed them as psychological phenomena shown by "neurotic" people. Now such anxiety is endemic throughout our whole society. These are some of the considerations which impel me to suggest that there is "no hiding place" with respect to the psychological dilemmas of our time (p. 37).

Although our conclusion can only be speculative, it certainly seems plausible that the dilemmas which May cites have provided fertile ground for the growth of a perspective on human behavior and pathology which attempts to reassert man's sense of self and individuality.

Summary

In our commentary we have tried to point up some of the issues and implications which flow from a humanistic view of abnormal behavior. This view is first and above all one which sees abnormal behavior, not so much as a pathological process or as a learned response, but as a failure in the growth process. The concept of actualization implies a fulfillment for which man must strive, and Maslow has attempted to exemplify this ideal of actualization by describing persons who have in some way attained this ideal. But he points out that before actualization can take place other needs of the person must be met. The failure to meet these needs is for Maslow an important determinant in psychological maladjustment.

One extraordinary product of this view is the idea that abnormal behavior can serve as an avenue to actualization and personal growth. Laing and others have suggested that some people whom we have called psychotic may in fact benefit from their "pathological" experiences and their disorganization may be the precursor of a new, higher level of personality organization.

Research on the self-concept suggests that there does appear to be a relationship between self-concept and maladjustment, but not perhaps the simple relationship some researchers have anticipated. Instead it is likely that both very low and very high discrepancies between the person's self-concept and his ideal self may be indicative of maladjustment.

Humanistic psychology is a psychology concerned with science and its goals. The conflict between the humanistic perspective and the learning perspective is brought into sharp focus in the Rogers–Skinner debate. While Skinner argues that the control of human behavior is a fundamental goal of science and a fact of our lives, Rogers argues that the goals of science require prior value choices that are subjectively chosen. For Rogers the goals of science should be to free man, not to control him.

Finally, we have suggested that the humanistic movement has been at least in part a reaction to the dilemmas of modern man. Rollo May points out that, faced with increasing dehumanization and the threat of annihilation, it is not surprising that people would turn to a view of man that emphasizes individual identity, one which sees the "etiology" of modern man's anxiety in his dehumanized and increasingly technological society.

The cry for a new view of man as one who reacts intensely and subjectively to the growing loss of his own identity is perhaps best expressed by Rogers (1969) when he says:

It is my judgment, as I try to understand the vigorous thrust of this phenomenological-existential movement in a variety of other fields, as well as in psychology, that it represents a new philosophical emphasis. Here is the voice of subjective man speaking up loudly for himself. Man has long felt himself to be a puppet in life—molded by economic forces, by unconscious forces, by environmental forces. He has been enslaved by persons, by institutions, by the theories of psychological science. But he is firmly setting forth a new declaration of independence. He is discarding the alibis of *un*-freedom. He is choosing himself, endeavoring, in a most difficult and often tragic world, to *become* himself—not a puppet, not a slave, not a machine, but his own unique individual self (p. 46).

References

ALLPORT, G. W.   *Becoming: Basic considerations for a psychology of personality*. New Haven: Yale University Press, 1955.

ANONYMOUS.   Phenomenology in perspective: Is there schizophrenia? *Schizophrenia Bulletin*, 1970, *2*, 11–14.

BUGENTAL, J. R. T.   *The search for authenticity: An existential-analytic approach to psychotherapy*. New York: Holt, Rinehart and Winston, 1965.

CHASE, P. H.   Self concepts in adjusted and maladjusted hospital patients. *Journal of Consulting Psychology*, 1957, *21*, 495–497.

COFER, C. N., & APPLEY, M. H.   *Motivation: Theory and research*. New York: Wiley, 1964.

DABROWSKI, K.   In J. Aronson (Ed.), *Positive disintegration*. Boston: Little Brown, 1964.

DAVIDS, A., & LAWTON, M. J.   Self-concept, mother concept and food aversion in emotionally disturbed and normal children. *Journal of Abnormal and Social Psychology*, 1961, *62*, 309–314.

FRIEDMAN, I.   Phenomenal, ideal, and projected conceptions of self. *Journal of Abnormal and Social Psychology*, 1955, *51*, 611–615.

FROMM, E.   *Escape from freedom*. New York: Holt, Rinehart and Winston, 1941.

FROMM, E.   *The sane society*. New York: Holt, Rinehart and Winston, 1955.

GOLDSTEIN, K.   *The organism*. New York: American, 1939.

GOLDSTEIN, M. J., JUDD, L. L., RODNICK, E. H., & LaPOLLA, A.   Psychophysiological and behavioral effects of phenothiazine administration as a function of premorbid status. *Journal of Psychiatric Research*, 1969, *6*, 271–287.

GORDON, J. S.   Who is mad? Who is sane? R. D. Laing: In search of a new psychiatry. *The Atlantic*, January, 1971, 50–66.

HILLSON, J. S., & WORCHEL, P.   Self concept and defensive behavior in the maladjusted. *Journal of Consulting Psychology*, 1957, *21*, 83–88.

HORNEY, K.   *Neurosis and human growth.* New York: Norton, 1950.

LAING, R. D.   *The divided self.* London: Tavistock, 1959.

LAING, R. D.   *The politics of experience.* New York: Ballantine, 1967.

MASLOW, A. H.   *Motivation and personality.* New York: Harper and Row, 1954.

MASLOW, A. H.   Deficiency motivation and growth motivation. In M. R. Jones (Ed.), *Nebraska symposium on motivation.* Lincoln: University of Nebraska Press, 1955, pp. 1–30.

MAY, R.   *Psychology and the human dilemma.* Princeton, N. J.: Van Nostrand, 1967.

MAY, R.   *Existential psychology.* (2nd ed.) New York: Random, 1969.

MEHRABIAN, A.   *An analysis of personality theories.* Englewood Cliffs, N. J.: Prentice-Hall, 1968.

PERRY, J. W.   Reconstitutive process in the psychopathology of the self. *Annals of the New York Academy of Sciences*, 1962, *96*, 853–876.

ROGERS, C. R.   *Client centered therapy.* Boston: Houghton-Mifflin, 1951.

ROGERS, C. R.   A theory of therapy, personality, and interpersonal relationships, as developed in the client-centered framework. In S. Koch (Ed.), *Psychology: A study of a science.* Vol. 3. New York: McGraw-Hill, 1959, pp. 194–235.

ROGERS, C. R.   *On becoming a person.* Boston: Houghton-Mifflin, 1961.

ROGERS, C. R.   Toward a science of the person. In A. Sutich & M. Vich (Eds.), *Readings in humanistic psychology.* New York: Free Press, 1969.

ROGERS, C. R., & SKINNER, B. F.   Some issues concerning the control of human behavior: A symposium. *Science*, 1956, *124,* 1057–1066.

SCHUTZ, W. C.   *Joy: Expanding human awareness.* New York: Grove, 1967.

SILVERMAN, J.   When schizophrenia helps. *Psychology Today*, 1970, *4,* 62–65.

SKINNER, B. F.   *Walden Two.* New York: Macmillan, 1948.

SKINNER, B. F.   *Beyond Freedom and Dignity,* New York: Knopf, 1971.

SUTICH, A. J., & VICH, M. A. (Eds.)   *Readings in humanistic psychology.* New York: Free Press, 1969.

CHAPTER 8

THE SOCIAL PERSPECTIVE

The Perspective

Introduction

A rapidly growing movement—exemplified by writers such as Goffman (1959, 1961, 1963a, 1963b, 1967), Becker (1963, 1964), Lemert (1951), and Scheff (1966, 1967)—is developing a unique perspective on abnormal behavior. The central thesis of the approach can be put quite simply, although its implications are far from simple. Rosenhan (1968) captures the spirit of the perspective when he says: "Beauty, we know, exists in the eye of the beholder. But what of madness? Is it possible that a profitable conceptualization of madness can emerge from the examination, not of the mad, as both psychoanalysts and learning theorists have done, but of those who call them mad?" (p. 360).

This approach offers a direct challenge to the essentially individual orientations to abnormal behavior that have their roots in psychiatry and clinical psychology and have dominated the field for so long. Sociologists and social psychologists, perhaps because of the unique viewpoint of their discipline, have offered us a fresh look at abnormal behavior.

The social perspective differs from others in at least two important ways. First, for the most part, psychiatrists and clinical psychologists think of mental illness or abnormal behavior as something arising within the individual. The social view, on the other hand, argues that "mental illness is something ascribed to persons as a function of the definition given certain types of acts by certain audiences" (Spitzer & Denzin, 1968, pp. v–vi). Second, the social perspective focuses upon the ascription process. That is, the perspective asks "who is labeled as mentally ill and under what circumstances?"

These viewpoints have a number of consequences. One consequence of adopting the social perspective is that considerably more attention will be given to the social context in which the abnormal behavior occurs. One of the strongest criticisms made by proponents of the social view is that other approaches have isolated the symptoms displayed by individuals from the context in which they occur. The social view attempts to remedy this deficiency, sometimes emphasizing context at the expense of descriptive precision of the symptoms themselves.

Another consequence of adopting the social perspective is that new elements are introduced into the problem. Whereas individual approaches to abnormal behavior operate in what is essentially a contextual vacuum, the social approach focuses on social reactions to symptoms, the social institution of mental illness, and the diagnostician as well as those who are diagnosed. Thus, the social rule which is broken and the consequences of breaking it become at least as important as the rule-breaker himself.

Looking at abnormal behavior through the eyes of the sociologist or social psychologist gives us a sense of immediacy about the problem. One reason for this is the wide range of data on which he draws. Material from newspapers, television, and our own social experience appears in a new light and the commonplace takes on new meaning. The sociologist looks where we have been looking all along but sees things there we never saw.

In our discussion of the social perspective we will rely heavily on the work of Thomas Scheff (1966). His writing is particularly suited to our purpose because it represents a clear example of the social perspective, is moderately well formalized, and reflects the thinking of some of the most influential theorists in this area, most notably Becker and Goffman. Scheff summarizes his own approach in the following way:

> The theory of mental illness outlined . . . is that the symptoms of mental illness can be considered to be violations of residual social norms, and that the careers of residual deviants can most effectively be considered as dependent upon the societal reaction and the processes of role-playing, when role-playing is viewed as part of a social rather than an exclusively individual system (1966, p. 169).

Scheff's account traces the career of the person as he becomes a mental patient. The story begins innocently enough with the breaking of rules for face-to-face interaction. By the time our story is finished, however, we should be able to fully appreciate Goffman's (1959) comment that "one could say that mental patients *distinctively* suffer not from mental illness, but from contingencies" (p. 127).

Language of the Social Perspective

Each of the perspectives we have discussed thus far has a group of terms and concepts of its own. In the case of the social perspective it is particularly important that we present these concepts at the outset since a grasp of the perspective is heavily dependent on understanding their meaning.

Norms   The agreed-upon rules of conduct or demeanor of the group.

Social role   "A pattern of behavior associated with a distinctive social position, e.g., that of father, teacher, employer, or patient" (Broom & Selznick, 1963, p. 16).

Status   A socially acknowledged position in a group.

Rule-breaking   Behavior that clearly violates agreed-upon rules of the group, e.g., crime, perversion, drunkenness, or bad manners.

Residual rule-breaking   Rule violations that do not have an explicit label associated with them but which may result in others labeling the rule violator as "mentally ill."

Deviance   The response of other people to the rule breaker. Deviance is a quality of people's response to an act and not a characteristic of the act itself.

Career   The sequence of movements from one position to another in a social or occupational system.

Deviant career   "The sequence of movements from one stigmatized position to another in the sector of the larger social system that functions to maintain social control" (Scheff, 1966, p. 39).

Career contingency   Those factors on which the individual's mobility from one social position to another depends.

Stigma   A stigmatized person is one with a discrediting identity. Persons who have been labeled as "mentally ill" or as "ex-mental patients" are usually said to be stigmatized.

Residual Rule-Breaking

The concept of residual rule-breaking is crucial to the formulation of a social perspective on abnormal behavior. We have already given a brief definition of this concept but a deeper understanding of its meaning requires some elaboration.

Scheff (1966) offers us a more detailed discussion in the following quote:

> . . . we can categorize . . . psychiatric symptoms as instances of residual rule-breaking or residual deviance. The culture of the group provides a vocabulary of terms for categorizing many norm violations: crime, perversion, drunkenness, and bad manners are familiar examples. Each of these terms is derived from the type of norm broken, and ultimately, from the type of behavior involved. After exhausting these categories, however, there is always a residue of the most diverse kind of violations, for which the culture provides no explicit label. For example, although there is great cultural variation in what is defined as decent or real, each culture tends to reify its definition of decency and reality, and so provides no way of handling violations of its expectations in these areas. The typical norm governing decency or reality, therefore, literally "goes without saying" and its violation is unthinkable for most of its members. For the convenience of society in construing those instances of unnameable rule-breaking which are called to its attention, these violations may be lumped together into a residual category: witchcraft, spirit possession, or, in our own society, mental illness. In this discussion, the diverse kinds of rule-breaking for which our society provides no explicit label, and which, therefore, sometimes lead to the labeling of the violator as mentally ill, will be considered to be technically *residual rule-breaking*" (pp. 33–34).

Thus we can see that residual rule-breaking is a kind of norm violation in which the "norm" is never explicitly stated. Of course for our discussion psychiatric symptoms are the most important examples of residual rule-breaking.

Goffman (1963a) has described a number of acts which fall into the category of residual deviance and are also taken to be psychiatric symptoms. Perhaps the best example of this sort of norm violation is what Goffman calls the "away." The away violates norms of involvement. When an individual allows his attention to wander or when he sinks into reverie in the presence of others who are engaged with him in social interaction he is violating involvement norms. However, the act of "away" is not in itself a norm violation and will not in itself bring censure. Only when these acts are performed in inappropriate social contexts or by unqualified persons will they be seen as a breach of the implicit rules of face-to-face interaction. Under these circumstances violations of involvement norms may be seen as "withdrawal" or "hallucination" and be taken as evidence of "mental illness."

Having gained a somewhat clearer idea of the nature of residual rule-breaking, we may ask some additional questions. What are the origins of residual rule-breaking? How frequently does it occur? What is the public response to residual rule-breaking? Scheff (1966) offers answers to each of these questions.

For Scheff, residual rule-breaking arises from diverse causes. Four general sources are mentioned. These include organic defects typically involving genetic or physiological disturbances. A second source is the psychological background of the individual. Scheff refers to this source only generally, assuming that any variables having to do with child-rearing are included. A third general cause cited is external stress. Included in this category are a variety of phenomena such as food deprivation, sleep deprivation, and combat stress. A final source of residual rule-breaking is volitional acts. Scheff cites two movements in history as examples of deliberate breaking of residual rules: French Impressionism and Dadaism. Both of these movements engaged in deliberate rule breaking that evoked strong societal reaction but in time actually changed social and esthetic evaluations. Perhaps a more contemporary example of volitional breaking of residual rules can be found in the Youth International Party or "Yippie" movement (Hoffman, 1968).

The actual sources of residual rule-breaking are of only marginal interest to Scheff and this is typical of the social perspective. As we suggested in the introduction, the social viewpoint focuses upon the social reaction to rule-breaking and has little interest in the origins or "etiology" of the behavior in question. We shall discuss this point in more detail in the commentary.

How frequent is residual rule-breaking? Scheff argues that "relative to the rate of treated mental illness, the rate of unrecorded residual rule-breaking is extremely high" (p. 47). As evidence for this Scheff cites a number of epidemiological studies which have attempted to estimate the actual or "true" rate of mental illness in various populations and which compare that rate to the rate of actual treatment. After reviewing a number of different studies, Scheff concludes that approximately 14 untreated cases exist in a community for every case that is actually treated. Hence his statement that the unrecorded (untreated) rate is high.

Thus relatively few cases of residual rule-breaking actually receive social recognition and censure or treatment. The residual rule-breaker is not necessarily given the status of one who is "mentally ill."

We may ask then what processes are operating to allow the rate of actual residual rule-breaking to be so much higher than that of recognized or treated cases? This leads us to Scheff's next proposition. He argues that the vast majority of instances of residual rule-breaking tend to be "denied" and are of little or only transitory significance. By denial, Scheff means that people respond to much residual rule-breaking by inattention, ignoring the behavior, or rationalizing its existence.

Although evidence on this point is scanty, at least two pieces of research offer support for Scheff's proposition that much residual rule-breaking is denied, or at least minimized, by significant others in the rule-breaker's environment. A study by Yarrow, Schwartz, Murphy, and Deasy (1955) examined the reactions of wives to their husbands' behavior prior to the husbands' first psychiatric hospitalization. The most striking finding in their study was that wives tolerated prolonged and extreme amounts of deviant behavior from their husbands before reluctantly acknowledging the possibility of a "mental" problem. Hallucinations, delusions, physical abuse, and even threats on the wife's life were rationalized, excused, or "normalized" by elements in the husband's past behavior that were consistent with his current bizarre actions. In many cases, only when it was abundantly clear that the husband or wife's life was in danger would the wife recognize the problem as one requiring psychiatric attention.

Another example of minimization of residual rule breaking is offered by Bittner (1967) in his study of police discretion in dealing with mentally ill persons.

> In one observed instance a young man approached an officer in a deteriorating business district of the city. He voiced an almost textbook-type paranoid complaint. From the statements and the officer's responses it could be gathered that this was a part of a sequence of conversations. The two proceeded to walk away from an area of high traffic density to quieter parts of the neighborhood. In the ensuing stroll the officer inspected various premises, greeted passers-by, and generally showed a low level of attentiveness. After about twenty-five minutes the man bade the officer goodbye and indicated that he would be going home now. The officer stated that he runs into this man quite often and usually on the same spot. He always tried to lead the man away from the place that apparently excites his paranoid suspicions. The expressions of inattentiveness are calculated to impress the person that there is nothing to worry about, while, at the same time, the efforts the man must make to hold the officer's interest absorb his energies. This method presumably makes the thing talked about a casual matter and mere small-talk. Thus, the practices employed in sustained contacts involve, like the practices of "psychiatric first aid," the tendencies to confine, to disregard pathological material, and to reduce matters to their mundane aspects. (p. 290)

Although the reasons for denial and minimization of residual rule-breaking may be diverse, evidence that even extreme cases may be denied exists, as Scheff suggests.

So far we have seen that there are diverse causes of rule-breaking and that not all rule-breaking will be of the "residual" sort which may or may not be classified as symptomatology. Furthermore, even if the rule-breaking is of the residual sort it will not necessarily be recognized or labeled as a manifestation of mental illness. The vast majority of residual rule-breaking will be episodic and transitory, and will be denied or go unrecognized.

What of the behavior that *is* recognized as mental illness? What mechanisms transform the residual deviant into an individual who embarks on a career of chronic deviance? Scheff suggests an answer to this question.

> The hypothesis suggested here is that the most important single factor (but not the only factor) in the stabilization of residual rule-breaking is the societal reaction. Residual rule-breaking may be stabilized if it is defined to be evidence of mental illness, and/or the rule-breaker is placed in a deviant status, and begins to play the role of the mentally ill. (pp. 53–54)

In the following section we will examine the processes that transform the social identity of the residual rule-breaker into that of chronic mental patient.

Sources of the Deviant Role

If, as Scheff suggests, the chronic residual deviant is a person who has accepted certain role prescriptions and is playing the role of mental patient, then at least two conditions must be fulfilled: first, the chronic residual deviant must have available to him the basic elements of the role; and second, he must be willing to accept the deviant role. Put another way, he must have knowledge of how mental patients behave, and he must be motivated to act that way himself.

The first question raised by this analysis is, how does the chronic residual deviant know how to behave like one who is mentally ill? Among the sources of the final stabilization of the deviant role adopted by the residual rule breaker is the stereotyping of mental symptoms. Scheff offers two propositions concerning the stereotyped imagery of mental illness that are intended to establish the fact that these stereotypes are (a) learned early in childhood and (b) continually reinforced and reaffirmed in our everyday life.

Let us consider Scheff's (1966) first proposition concerning the stereotypy of mental disorder. Scheff states that "stereotyped imagery of mental disorder is learned early in childhood" (p. 64) He suggests that it is commonly observed that children learn the literal meaning of the word "crazy" early in life. Furthermore, adults are often evasive and unclear in their responses to questions concerning the meaning of the term "crazy." Hence the stereotypes that arise around the term "crazy" continue to have associated with them many of the childhood uncertainties and fears typified by concepts such as "the bogeyman."

His second general proposition concerning the stereotype of mental disorder takes the following form: "The stereotypes of insanity are continually reaffirmed, inadvertently, in ordinary social interaction" (p. 67). Scheff draws on a wide variety of evidence to support this assumption. In particular he implicates the mass media. Both traditional stereotypes of mental disorder learned early in childhood and more sophisticated views may exist side by side in individuals whom one would presume to have a more informed notion of abnormal behavior. Scheff argues that the mass media tend to reinforce our stereotype of mental disorder, and he draws upon data from the work of Nunnally (1961) to support his claim. For example, Nunnally shows that of all the televised films depicting mental illness in some form the vast majority of such programs are fictional rather than documentary programs. Typically, these features and films use the stereotype of mental disorder while there are few documentaries that attempt to produce a more realistic picture of the disorder.

The following quote from Scheff (1966) concerning the manner in which newspapers strengthen our traditional stereotypes of mental disorder speaks for itself.

> In newspapers it is a common practice to mention that a rapist or a murderer was once a mental patient. Here are several examples: Under the headline, "Question Girl in Child Slaying," the story begins, "A 15-year-old girl *with a history of mental illness* is being questioned in connection with a kidnap-slaying of a 3-year-old boy." A similar story under the headline, "Man Killed, Two Policemen Hurt in Hospital Fray" begins *"A former mental patient* grabbed a policeman's revolver and began shooting at 15 persons in the receiving room of City Hospital No. 2 Thursday."
>
> Often acts of violence will be connected with mental illness on the basis of little or no evidence. For instance, under the headline, "Milwaukee Man Goes Berserk, Shoots Officer," the story describes the events and then quotes a police captain who said, "He may be a mental case." In another story under the headline, "Texas Dad Kills Self, Four Children, Daughter Says," the last sentence of the story is "One report said Kinsey (the killer) was once a mental patient." In most large newspapers there is apparently at least one such story in every issue.
>
> Even if the coverage of these acts of violence was highly accurate, it would still give the reader a misleading impression because negative information is seldom offset by positive reports. An item like the following is almost inconceivable: "Mrs. Ralph Jones, an ex-mental patient,

was elected president of the Fairview Home and Garden Society at their meeting last Thursday" (pp. 71–72).

It seems clear from examples like those given above that Scheff is justified in asserting that the stereotypes of mental disorder are reaffirmed and strengthened by our mass media. Thus the individual who may embark on a career of chronic deviance has available the elements necessary to learn the mental illness role. Now it remains for us to examine the mechanisms by which he is actually compelled to adopt the role.

Processes Which Lead to the Acceptance of the Deviant Role

If we accept Scheff's description of the nature of residual rule-breaking as well as the proposition that the cultural stereotypes of mental disorder are learned early and continually reinforced, we still must ask a basic question: What sorts of processes lead the deviant individual to accept his stigmatized role as one who is mentally ill? Scheff offers several propositions which constitute an attempt to answer this question.

His first assumption argues that "labeled deviants may be rewarded for playing the stereotyped deviant role" (p. 84). Scheff cites a number of different sources of reward for the acceptance of deviant roles. The therapeutic psychiatrist systematically rewards patients' "displays of insight." In many cases other patients in a psychiatric setting exert social pressure on a new arrival for him to accept being "sick."

> *New Patient:* "I don't belong here. I don't like all these crazy people. When can I talk to the doctor? I've been here four days and I haven't seen the doctor. I'm not crazy."
> *Another Patient:* "She says she's not crazy." (Laughter from patients.)
> *Another Patient:* "Honey, what I'd like to know is, if you're not crazy, how did you get your ass in this hospital?"
> *New Patient:* "It's complicated, but I can explain. My husband and I . . ."
> *First Patient:* "That's what they all say." (General laughter.) (Scheff, 1966, p. 86)

A second process Scheff describes to account for the stabilization of the deviant role is that of punishment. Scheff summarizes his assumption in this way: "Labeled deviants are punished when they attempt to return to conventional roles." (p. 87) The general idea of this proposition is that entry into nondeviant roles is blocked for any individual who has already been labeled as mentally ill. Ex-mental patients have more difficulty finding jobs, entering into conventional social groups, or otherwise attempting to regain their status as normal members of the community. We shall have more to say about this in the following section.

Another mechanism by which the individual becomes stabilized in his deviant role has to do with the crisis that occurs when an individual who breaks residual rules is publicly exposed for his rule-breaking and is labeled as a result. Scheff summarizes this assumption in the following way: "In the crisis occurring when a residual rule-breaker is publicly labeled, the deviant is highly suggestible, and may accept the proffered role of the insane as the only alternative." (p. 88)

A summary of this proposition may be given as follows. First, an individual may break residual rules and be recognized for doing so. An issue is then made of the residual rule-breaking. At this point the rule-breaker is expected to become confused and ashamed, but most important of all, he should also become *suggestible*. Naturally, to those around the rule-breaker in the crisis situation, his behavior is incomprehensible. This leads to a strong need among the rule-breaker's associates for collective action. Furthermore, the need for collective action and the action itself is typically based on the stereotype of mental disorder. Because the rule-breaker is sensitive to the cues of others and because he accepts their evaluation of his behavior, he begins to behave according to the stereotype. As Scheff puts it, "when a residual rule breaker organizes his behavior within the framework of mental disorder, and when his organization is validated by others, particularly prestigeful others such as physicians, he is 'hooked' and will proceed on a career of chronic deviance." (p. 88)

Scheff argues that one factor is more important than all others in starting residual rule-breakers on chronic careers of residual deviance. That factor is labeling. Once the individual has been labeled or publicly described as suffering from mental illness, a large number of social contingencies come into play. Each of the factors that are assumed to stabilize an individual in the role of residual deviance begins to operate once the individual has been labeled. The individual may be rewarded for retaining his role of deviant behavior. He may be punished for attempts to escape the role of deviant. And finally, labeling may precipitate the crisis which makes the deviant more suggestible and therefore more willing to accept his deviant role.

Stigma

Sociological thinking about abnormal behavior has emphasized the idea that persons who have been labeled as mentally ill are stigmatized. Their social identity as mental patients or even as ex-mental patients is deeply discrediting.

One of Scheff's propositions—that the labeled deviant is punished for attempts to return to conventional roles—takes account of the phenomenon of stigma but does not treat the problem in detail. The stigma phenomenon is worthy of more extended discussion, both because it illustrates the potential power of the labeling phenomenon so well and because it emphasizes the importance of audience reaction to the labeled deviant. These are both central themes in the sociological perspective. In addition, the phenomenon of stigma extends our view well beyond the narrower limits to which other perspectives of abnormal behavior adhere.

Goffman (1963b) describes the origin of the idea of stigma in the following way:

> The Greeks, who were apparently strong on visual aids, originated the term *stigma* to refer to bodily signs designed to expose something unusual and bad about the moral status of the signifier. The signs were cut or burnt into the body and advertised the bearer as a slave, a criminal, or a traitor—a blemished person ritually polluted, to be avoided, especially in public places. Later, in Christian times, two layers of metaphor were added to the term: the first referred to bodily signs of holy grace that took the form of eruptive blossoms on the skin; the second, a medical allusion to this religious allusion referred to bodily signs of physical disorder. Today the term is widely used in something like the original sense, but is applied more to the disgrace itself than to the bodily evidence of it. (Goffman, 1963b, pp. 1–2)

One of the most notable things about the stigma of mental illness is that it occupies what Hughes (1945) has described as a "master status" in the minds of others. That is, a person who has been socially defined as mentally ill is considered mentally ill or deviant above all else. All other attributes or social roles that the individual may carry are relegated to the background. Consequently, when the patient is released from the hospital —even if he has been described as "cured" by the hospital staff—he cannot be cured of the stigma of mental illness from which he will suffer. Although society provides a wide variety of rituals to allow the normal individual to gain entrance to deviant status there are no formal rituals for removing the stigma of mental illness from an individual so designated.

The stigma associated with having been a mental patient may affect both the way in which others view a person and behave toward him and the way he views himself. Miller and Dawson (1965) have interviewed over a thousand ex-mental patients one year after discharge from mental institutions. They have found that one third of their patients reported difficulty in obtaining or maintaining a job once prospective employers discovered that they had previously been mental patients. In addition, many ex-mental patients reported that once they had been identified as ex-mental patients, this strongly affected the way in which their families and friends related to them.

Of course, the stigma of mental illness has the quality of a self-fulfilling prophecy. An employer may reject an applicant because he has been a mental patient. It may also be that ex-mental patients are viewed as unemployable because employers reject them. Thus the discrimination associated with the stigma of mental illness may in a sense "create" the social fact of the mental patient's inferiority.

The stigma of institutionalization can affect the relatives of the mental patient as well. The behavior of the wife of a mental patient provides a good example.

> Concealment often becomes cumbersome. Thus, to keep the neighbors from knowing the husband's hospital (having reported that he was in a hospital because of suspicion of cancer), Mrs. G. must rush to her apartment to get the mail before her neighbors pick it up for her as they used to do. She has had to abandon second breakfasts at the drugstore with the women in the neighboring apartments to avoid their questions. Before she can allow visitors in her apartment, she must pick up any material identifying the hospital, and so on. (Goffman, 1963b, p. 89)

The wife of another mental patient reports,

> But I've cut off all our other friends [after citing five who "knew"]. I didn't tell them that I was giving up the apartment and I had the phone disconnected without telling anyone so they don't know how to get in touch with me.
>
> I haven't gotten too friendly with anyone at the office because I don't want people to know where my husband is. I figure that if I got too friendly with them, then they would start asking questions, and I might start talking, and I just think it's better if as few people as possible know about Joe. (Goffman, 1963b, p. 99)

The effect of such stigma is not restricted to persons who have been hospitalized at some time in psychiatric institutions. A study by Phillips (1963) indicates that the act of seeking help for psychological problems is *in itself* ground for rejection by other members of an individual's community. Phillips found that members of the community display increasing amounts of rejection toward an individual depending upon where he has gone for help. For identical descriptions of disturbed behavior, the amount of rejection increased according to what help the person sought: no help, a clergyman, a physician, a psychiatrist, hospitalization in a mental hospital. Thus the act of seeking help may identify the person as someone with mental problems and may in turn discredit his identity.

A person who has been identified as a mental patient or someone with mental problems may attempt to hide this fact and to "pass" for normal (Goffman, 1963b). Passing provides the possibility of re-entry into normal role status, but it may provide pitfalls of its own. A person who attempts to conceal the fact that he has been in a mental hospital or has had psychiatric difficulties may go to great lengths in order to accomplish his act of passing. Difficulty may arise when his attempts to conceal his stigmatized status become in themselves instances of residual rule-breaking. If this occurs, or if the individual is discovered concealing his status, this may lead to a new cycle of disturbed behavior and a new public crisis. The unsuccessful passer will then be relabeled as a mental patient and again embark on his career of deviance.

We can see, then, that the stigma of mental illness and the failure to pass as normal successfully may lead the deviant even deeper into his career of chronic deviance.

Summary

The sociological perspective begins with an analysis of rules for social interaction. Most rules for social interaction are unnamed social conventions or "residual rules." The breaking of residual rules is thought of as residual deviance and may be the result of a variety of biological, psychological, and social factors. Most residual rule-breaking is denied, minimized, or ignored by others despite the fact that the prevalence of residual rule-breaking is quite high.

However, some residual rule-breaking becomes labeled as mental illness. It is at this point in the crisis—when the rule-breaker is publicly labeled as deviant or mentally ill—that he may become highly suggestible and accept the label as the only alternative. Now the rule-breaker is embarked on a career of chronic deviance and may begin to play the role of one who is mentally ill.

The labeled deviant is a product of our culture and as such knows a good deal about the social institution of insanity and how "crazy" people are supposed to behave. From early childhood he has been exposed to stereotypes of madness. As he proceeds in his career of chronic deviance, he is rewarded for playing the stereotyped role and is punished for any attempts to leave the role. "Insight" into the fact that he is "sick" will be rewarded by his therapist and the stigma of his identity as a mental patient will block his entrance into normal roles when he seeks a job after release from the hospital. Thus the stability of his career as a mental patient is assured. He has become a chronic mental patient.

In Figure 8.1 Scheff has summarized his theory of stable mental disorder in a flow chart. Various propositions of the theory are depicted as

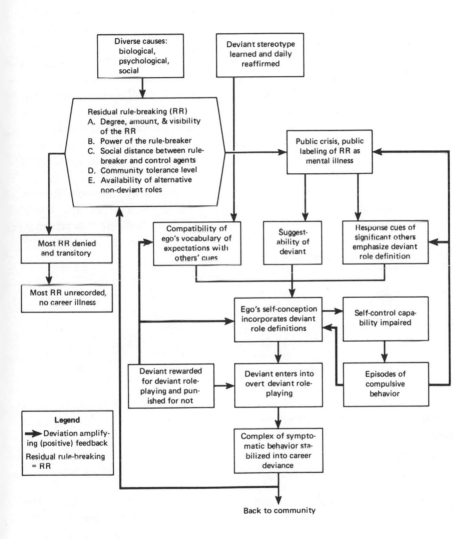

Figure 8.1 Flow chart—Stabilization of deviance in a social system. (Redrawn from T. J. Scheff, *Being mentally ill: A sociological theory.* Chicago: Aldine, 1966. Reproduced by permission.)

"system modules"; the arrows leading from one system module to the next specify the relations which are hypothesized to exist between propositions in the theory.

One of the notable features of this summary chart is that it includes a large number of "feedback loops." These feedback loops are intended to characterize situations in which the deviant may be caught in a "vicious circle" in the social system. To take an example from the flow diagram, a public crisis may lead to increased suggestibility of the deviant, incorporation of the deviant role definition, and impairment of self-control capability, followed by episodes of "compulsive" behavior, which in turn lead back to the crisis module; the same process may be repeated almost indefinitely. A number of different feedback loops of this kind exist within the system. As Scheff points out, these feedback loops may serve to create a *stabilized* or even amplified system.

The social perspective has given us yet another way in which we may view the problem of abnormal behavior. More important, perhaps, it has broadened our conception of what is relevant to the problem. Social rules, roles, and societal reaction have now become part of our conceptual framework in understanding abnormal behavior.

Commentary

Deviance as a Role

At this point it should be clear that the concept of *role* is central to a social formulation of abnormal behavior. The chronic deviant is playing a role which he has thoroughly learned through years of presentation of stereotyped concepts of mental illness. The stability and uniformity of that role is accounted for largely in terms of the multiple sources of support it receives in our society.

In a recent paper, "Schizophrenic Thinking: A Role-theoretical Analysis," Theodore Sarbin (1969) has offered a detailed account of the role transformations that an individual may undergo in the successive stages involved in becoming a mental patient.

Sarbin's account begins with the description of a typical sequence of events in the career of a mental patient. The sequence is divided into four periods, three of which denote specific stages in the patient role. The first stage describes remote ecological events as well as postulated genetic and constitutional events. The second stage describes the prepatient role, and the third describes the unsettled patient role. Stage four describes the stabilized patient role. Sarbin has set himself an ambitious task, since he wishes not just to describe career contingencies in the life of the mental patient but also to suggest how "the language and thought defects noted in hospitalized schizophrenics are *products, resultants,* or *outcomes* of certain describable social events associated with labeling a person as mentally ill and with the attendant instrumental acts and rituals carried out by medical, legal, or other professional personnel" (p. 192).

The first stage provides us with a description of the events which predispose the person to later difficulty. When a person finds himself unable to ascribe meaning to events in his life, that is, when the inputs he receives do not match the structure of his cognitive organization, he is said to be in a condition of "cognitive strain." Cognitive strain almost always has physiological activation as a concomitant and the result is often described clinically as an "anxiety state."

Typically the person tries to engage in adaptive behaviors which will reduce the strain. Although these behaviors can take a variety of different forms, Sarbin suggests that they usually involve such acts as changing beliefs and values, redeploying attention, or engaging in behavior which has a tranquilizing function.

Any of these behaviors may or may not be useful to the person in reducing his cognitive strain but it is important to realize that these behaviors are also *social events* for others in the person's life. Since these behaviors may have social impact, they may be judged by others and either rewarded or punished.

We should also note that these adaptive behaviors are not unique to people who ultimately become mental patients. Everyone engages in some or perhaps all of these adaptive behaviors at some time in his life.

In any case, once these adaptive behaviors become social events an important turning point in the career of the potential mental patient is reached. If these adaptive behaviors reduce cognitive strain or if they are tolerated or rewarded by others, little else will occur. But on the other hand, if the significant persons in the individual's life find themselves threatened or have no norms for dealing with these behaviors they may come to regard him as "sick." At this point the person enters the second stage in Sarbin's sequence: the *prepatient role.*

Several important changes occur once the person has entered prepatient stage. First, as a person who is regarded as "sick" the prepatient will be absolved of many of the social roles and responsibilities he would normally undertake. For example, he may leave his job. While reducing the prepatient's responsibilities may appear to be humane, it also has the effect of reducing the choices of role enactments he has available. He is now treated as a person who can only enact roles with minimal obligations. A second important change in the life of the prepatient is that other people in his life may feel obliged to see that his "sickness" is attended to; thus he may be sent to the family doctor for examination. If the prepatient shows none of the usual physical signs of illness but continues to enact the role of a sick person—perhaps even with the encouragement of his family and friends who continue to regard him as sick—it may be concluded that his illness is "emotional" or "mental."

It is interesting to note, as Sarbin does, that if the prepatient passively accepts his role it may confirm the expectations of others while if he resists particularly vehemently this too can be regarded as evidence of his emotional illness. At this point he may be locked in a psychiatric ward for observation and he enters the third stage in the sequence, the *unsettled patient role*. He may be legally committed for hospitalization or he may not, but whatever the case he will lose still more of his opportunities for normal role enactment. Once hospitalized he loses even the opportunity for functioning that he might have had as a prepatient in his home setting.

As Sarbin points out, once hospitalized, "the events associated with mental disease may include everything the patient does or does not do." (p. 200) The patient is forced by the hospital setting and routine into a submissive, docile role that Sarbin calls a "nonperson role." It is important to note that this situation pushes the person even further in looking for adaptive techniques to reduce his cognitive strain. Often he will utilize one of the few adaptive behaviors available to him, that of attention redeployment in the form of fantasy or withdrawal.

Even at this point it is possible that the patient may be able to return to the community, particularly if the community is satisfied that he is "cured." If not, the person may move to the fourth stage in the sequence, the *stabilized patient role*. The stabilized patient role is characterized by a minimum of obligations and is a role in which there is only very limited reciprocity of interaction. Placed in a stabilized nonperson role, the patient will resort even more frequently to fantasy and attention redeployment.

Thus far we have described the sequence of events leading to the stabilized patient role. But, we may ask, how does Sarbin propose to account for the repeated observation that hospitalized persons diagnosed as "schizophrenic" display disorders of language and thought?

Sarbin begins by pointing out that it is the group of persons who are already in the stabilized patient role which provides the pool of cooperative subjects for experiments intended to clarify the nature of schizophrenic thought disorder. He also suggests that much of the cognitive work carried out by persons who have been desocialized is done in private and is characterized by various shortcutting devices. Thus the thought processes become more and more stimulus-bound and "concrete." Sarbin concludes:

So when the investigator compares the cognitive behavior of schizophrenics and nonschizophrenics and discovers differences, the problem becomes one of identifying the correct antecedent conditions. The widely employed—often tacit—disease model asserts that the differences noted are symptoms of an underlying disease, either organic, psychic, or both. The social role model asserts that the differences are cognitive effects of social withdrawal and desocialization (pp. 203–204)

We should note that Sarbin has posed a direct point of conflict between the social role perspective and the illness perspective. He has suggested that abnormal behavior in the form of language and thought disorder may be accounted for not by an illness process, but by the effects of interpersonal and social events.

Sarbin's use of the concept of role has another important impact on our thinking. By introducing the concept of role and using it as he has, he provides an important conceptual linkage between individual psychological events and social events. In other contexts Sarbin (1968) has used the concept of role in describing the "transformation of social identity" and has shown how it can be applied to the social events that lead to the identification of "dangerous" persons (Sarbin, 1967).

In addition, Sarbin's role-theoretical account of schizophrenic thinking makes it clear that it is not merely that deviant behavior may be thought of as a social role but also that there is a concomitant loss of other more legitimate roles involved in the process. Adopting this perspective allows us to see that a number of behaviors which we may have previously believed to be products of disease or organic defect may also be seen as the products of social forces operating in the transaction between the mental patient and his audience.

Individual Differences in Deviant Behavior

The fact that deviant behavior can take a variety of different forms is for the most part neglected by the social perspective. Certainly it is true, as Scheff has suggested, that there are no specifications of residual rule-breaking since it literally goes "without saying."

There are at least two reasons for this failure to take account of individual differences. The first is that the audience's reaction to the behavior, not the behavior itself, is what interests the adherents of the social perspective. Furthermore, what is considered deviant in one social group will not necessarily be considered deviant in another. Behavior that is residual rule-breaking for a business executive may not be residual rule-breaking for a laborer. Thus we can appreciate the desire to focus on the process that unifies all varieties of deviant behavior. That process is the *attribution of deviance* rather than the specific behavior that is called deviant.

The second reason is that advocates of the social perspective in general have a strong belief in the power of situational variables to mold and shape the behavior of different people. Goffman (1961) illustrates this point quite well.

Persons who become mental hospital patients vary widely in the kind and degree of illness that a psychiatrist would impute to them, and in the attributes by which laymen would describe them. But once started on the way, they are confronted by some importantly similar circumstances and respond to these in some importantly similar ways. Since these similarities do not come from mental illness, they would seem to occur in spite of it. It is thus a tribute to the power of social forces that the uniform status of mental patient cannot only assure an aggregate of persons a common fate and eventually, because of this, a common character, but that this social reworking can be done upon what is perhaps the most obstinate diversity of human materials that can be brought together by society (p. 129).

Goffman recognizes individual differences in the behavior of mental patients. But he suggests that social forces operating in mental institutions tend to reduce this variability, since all patients must react to essentially the same environmental pressures.

Goffman does offer us a description of how social forces can produce individual differences in deviant behavior. In his discussion of total institutions, he (1961) describes what he calls adaptation styles to the "total institution" environment.

Before we can appreciate these adaptation styles it is necessary to describe briefly what Goffman means by the concept of "total institution." Prisons, mental hospitals, the army, and concentration camps are all examples of total institutions, which have the following features: first, all aspects of the individual's life occur in the same place and under the same authority. Second, each phase of the member's life—for example, sleep, work, or play—is carried out in the immediate company of others who are treated alike and are required to do exactly the same things. Furthermore, all activities are tightly scheduled and the scheduling is imposed from above by a body of officials. Finally, all activities are part of a single, overall plan that is designed to fulfill the aims of the institution.

Typically, because of their very nature, total institutions engage in what Goffman calls a "stripping" process which leads to "mortification" of the inmates. For example, upon entering a total institution personal possessions are removed and stored and other symbols of personal identity are taken away. The patient must wear a uniform. Family occupational roles stop, and usually a stigmatized status is substituted. Finally, autonomous decision-making is eliminated and replaced by a group routine.

Naturally, the member of a total institution who has undergone the stripping and mortification process must learn to adapt to the environment of the total institution. The adaptation styles that Goffman suggests prevail in total institutions are as follows. The first is the patient's engaging in "situational withdrawal." He withdraws his attention from all but the most immediate events in his life. In mental hospitals this adaptation style is often called "regression," in prisons it is described as "prison psychosis," and in concentration camps it is "depersonalization." The second adaptation style is "rebellion." The individual rebels by challenging the institution and its rules in every way possible. Rebellion, of course, requires strict attention to the rules since the rebel must know what the rules are in order to break them. Although rebellion often results in high morale among the inmates, it is a temporary reaction and usually leads to some other form of adaptation. The third adaptation style is that of "colonization." Colonization occurs when the inmate becomes contented with his existence and decides to make the most of the situation. At this point he is no longer oriented to the outside world, and the total institution is now his home. If discharge is imminent the colonized inmate may actually behave in ways to forestall his being discharged. The final adaptation style is that of "conversion." The process of conversion occurs when the inmate takes over the staff view of himself and tries to act like a "perfect inmate." The converted inmate is typically moralistic and zealous and has completely internalized the values of the total institution.

Goffman has provided a unique solution to the problem of individual differences in deviant behavior. For him the institution itself plays an important role in the production of individual differences in adaptation style.

What Are the Causes of Residual Rule-Breaking?

The social perspective gives us a fairly complete account of abnormal behavior and the reaction of others to that behavior once residual rule-breaking has already occurred. But this perspective has very little to say about the origins of residual rule-breaking. At least in part this is because the emphasis of the perspective is on audience reactions and social reactions to deviance. Scheff (1966) discusses the origins of residual rule-breaking only very briefly, and his discussion of this vital problem adds very little to our knowledge.

But there is a sense in which society can be said to "create" deviance. Becker (1963) describes this notion:

[This is] the central fact about deviance: it is created by society. I do not mean this in the way it is ordinarily understood, in which the causes of deviance are located in the social situation of the deviant or in "social factors" which prompt his action. I mean, rather, that *social groups create deviance by making the rules whose infraction constitutes deviance,* and by applying those rules to particular people and labeling them as outsiders. From this point of view, deviance is not a quality of the act the person commits, but rather a consequence of the application by others of rules and sanctions to an "offender." The deviant is one to whom that label has successfully been applied; deviant behavior is behavior that people so label. (pp. 8–9)

The implications of Becker's remarks are obvious. Society creates the rules for conduct. Without rules there can, quite obviously, be no deviation from rules. Thus, society's propensity for rule making can be thought of as a "causal" factor in the production of deviance. In this sense, at least, society creates deviance.

We have not yet mentioned the more traditional view held by sociologists, which suggests that social factors such as socioeconomic status or ethnic group identification can also operate as causal factors in the production of abnormal behavior. The analysis of large numbers of epidemiological studies (e.g., Hollingshead & Redlich, 1958) indicates a much higher frequency of abnormal behavior among lower socioeconomic groups. The meaning of this finding remains unclear, however. Students of society have been prone to interpret this finding as evidence for the causal role of social factors in the production of abnormal behavior. Students of genetics, on the other hand, have interpreted this same finding as evidence of the operation of social selection processes whereby the genetically better endowed individuals tend to rise to, or at least maintain, high status and those disabled by their poorer genetic endowment tend to drift to lower socioeconomic status or fail to rise. Until recently, no empirical means have been available to choose between these two very different interpretations of the relationship between social class and mental disorder.

Recent work by Dohrenwend and Dohrenwend (1969) offers what they believe is a crucial test of this etiological question. Their test involves examining relative rates of disorder according to social class and ethnic status. Their experimental design yields differential predictions for the rate of disorder among advantaged and disadvantaged ethnic groups of higher and lower class status.

Dohrenwend and Dohrenwend have based their research strategy on three basic assumptions. First, they assume that there is a nearly universally shared norm that upward social mobility is desirable. Thus, members of lower class groups will attempt to rise to higher class status. Second, they assume that serious psychological disorder will result in a decrease in the chances of upward social mobility and increase the chances of downward social mobility. Finally, they assume that disadvantaged ethnic groups (e.g., Negroes and Puerto Ricans in New York City) will experience more downward social pressure than will people in the same social class who are not disadvantaged (e.g., white Anglo-Saxon Protestants or Jews in New York City).

With these basic assumptions it is possible to make differential predictions concerning the rate of psychological disorder according to social class and ethnic status. These predictions bear directly on the question of whether psychological disorder is a result of societal factors (social causation hypothesis) or genetic factors (social selection hypothesis).

Let us consider the predictions made by the social hypothesis as described by Dohrenwend and Dohrenwend which are shown in Table 8.1. We can see that in general the rate of disorder among lower class individuals is higher than among higher class individuals. This prediction is consistent with the general findings of epidemiological studies. If the rate of disorder is a result of genetic endowment then *within a given class* we should expect the more able individuals to rise in class and the less able either to drift downward or be unable to rise in class. However, since the downward social pressure is assumed to be greater among disadvantaged ethnic groups, fewer of the able members of that group should be able to rise to the higher class. This will result in a lower rate of psychological disorder among lower class disadvantaged groups because the rate of disorder will be, in effect, "diluted" by the able members of this group who are unable to rise in status. On the other hand, the able members of the advantaged ethnic groups will be able to rise in status more easily and will do so leaving a "residue" of less able persons in the lower class advantaged group. Thus, the rate of psychological disorder should be higher in this group.

The social causation hypothesis makes a different set of predictions and these are shown in Table 8.2. If the rate of psychological disorder is a result of the social pressures exerted on disadvantaged social groups, then the rates should be higher in disadvantaged rather than advantaged groups within a given class level.

This is an intriguing set of differential predictions which would appear to be testable simply by collecting the appropriate data. However, a number of factors complicate this enterprise. Standards vary widely as to what

TABLE 8.1: Predictions Based on the Social Selection (Genetic) Hypothesis. Rates of Disorder Ranked from Lowest (1) to Highest (4)

| | | Ethnic Group Status | |
		Advantaged	Disadvantaged
Class Status	Higher	2	1
	Lower	4	3

From Dohrenwend & Dohrenwend, *Social Status and Psychological Disorder*, 1969, p. 56. Reprinted by permission.

TABLE 8.2: Predictions Based on the Social Causation Hypothesis. Rates of Disorder Ranked from Lowest (1) to Highest (4)

| | | Ethnic Group Status | |
		Advantaged	*Disadvantaged*
Class Status	Higher	1	2
	Lower	3	4

From Dohrenwend & Dohrenwend, *Social Status and Psychological Disorder*, 1969, p. 56. Reprinted by permission.

constitutes a "case" in different epidemiological studies. Furthermore, respondents in different ethnic and class groups differ in the modes they employ to express distress as well as in their willingness to admit the existence of symptoms. These problems are potentially soluble, however, and experimental strategies of the sort Dohrenwend and Dohrenwend propose promise to clarify the causal status of social variables in the production of psychological disorders.

The Neglected Role of the Patient

The social perspective places considerable emphasis on the process of labeling and its consequences for the mental patient. Scheff (1966) has argued that the social fact of labeling is perhaps the single most important factor in establishing an individual in a career of chronic deviance. Certainly labeling represents an important part of the social institution of mental illness. Audience reaction to the labeled deviant is a crucial element of the social perspective. Yet this emphasis may lead us to neglect the role of the labeled deviant or predeviant himself in the social process, as Spitzer and Denzin (1968) point out.

> This view of deviant behavior has quite profitably shifted attention in research to the interactional settings within which the labeling and deviance ascription process occurs; yet, it has deficiencies which may mislead the researcher. Most notable has been a tendency to slight the role played by the deviant or pre-deviant in the actual labeling process. Erikson, Kitsuse, and H. Becker have insightfully noted that the actual province of a sociology of a deviant behavior is "audience reactions," but it must be recognized that the actor himself may and, in fact, quite frequently does play an important determining part in the labeling process. If the burden of theoretical attention is placed upon the audi-

ence's reaction to social acts, the implication is that the pre-deviant is under the complete control of the audience members whenever interpretation of social acts becomes an issue . . . It is our position that investigators in the sociology of mental illness, regardless of theoretical orientation, have overlooked the fact that quite frequently persons labeled as mentally ill react to this label and often attempt to dissuade audience members of their allegations. (p. 462)

Evidence is now available to suggest that hospitalized psychiatric patients are at least capable of engaging in a variety of interpersonal strategies in order to fulfill their own goals. Braginsky, Braginsky, and Ring (1969) have reported a series of studies showing that mental patients are able to manage the impressions they make upon hospital staff in order to remain at or leave the hospital, remain on a custodial ward, or to achieve whatever their goal is. Evidence of this sort will certainly counteract any overemphasis on audience reactions implied in the social perspective. In addition, the integration of this information into the perspective will provide a more complete account of the social processes involved in becoming deviant.

Ideological Commitments

Despite all attempts at "objectivity," students of abnormal behavior have ideological commitments. Often the researcher may not be aware that he has such commitments and may vigorously deny any bias if he is asked about the possibility. The social perspective certainly may contain such a bias. Spitzer and Denzin (1968) suggest what it may be:

By ignoring the process of self-indication in social interaction, theorists have presented what at times appears to be an ideological defense for the underdog—e.g., "the poor mental patient." While this defense is seldom if ever explicitly stated, the implication is that the mental patient has virtually no control over his environment and that once he has been so labeled, he will carry for life a deeply discrediting and stigmatizing label. (p. 462)

There may well be a place for such ideological commitments in the study of abnormal behavior. However, if such commitments are going to be made they should be explicit, and their implications must be fully explored. Unfortunately this is seldom done. Instead, sociological data are often examined and interpreted as if no value orientation or ideological commitment existed.

Becker (1964) distinguishes between two types of ideological commitment that can occur in social research. The first type he calls "conventional sentimentality." The social scientist who refuses to examine the possibility of professional incompetence in the disposition of persons who become labeled as mental patients is guilty of conventional sentimentality. In many cases the error of conventional sentimentality takes the form of unquestioning acceptance of myths that mental health workers hold about themselves or their profession. For example, they may commit the "sentimental" fault of believing that the treatment that mental patients receive is "for their own good" and that therefore these people's rights are not being violated. Perhaps worse, the acceptance of a conventional sentimentality may lead social scientists to design their research in ways which do not allow evidence of possible incompetence to be gathered.

A different sort of error is what Becker (1964) calls "unconventional sentimentality." The unconventional sentimentalist assumes that things are always worse than they appear. Furthermore, he does not acknowledge any evidence that refutes his assumption. He may believe that the underdog is always right or perhaps that the mental patient is always the "poor mental patient" who is being systematically discriminated against and mistreated.

Much of the research and theory on the problem of abnormal behavior written from the social perspective has erred in the direction of unconventional sentimentality. Becker (1964) suggests that "this, after all, is the lesser evil. If one outrages certain conventional assumptions by being unconventionally sentimental, a large body of opinion will be sure to tell him about it. But conventional sentimentality is less often attacked, and specious premises stand unchallenged." (pp. 5–6)

Perhaps the ideal stance for the student of society to take in investigating the problem of abnormal behavior might be described as the study of "folk medicine" (Scheff, 1967). This idea, which borrows a term from anthropology, implies that the researcher seeks to describe the way in which members of a particular society (including the society's "medicine men") behave toward illness and those who are designated as ill without necessarily subscribing to the assumptions made by that society about the illness. It is likely that specious assumptions and inadequately examined beliefs will fall into disrepute when exposed by the social scientist in this way.

Advantages of a Sequential Account
of Deviant Behavior

The social perspective uses a particular method of description. Following Becker (1963) we will use the term "sequential" to describe it. As we shall see, the sequential method of description has a variety of useful features.

Becker (1963) distinguishes between simultaneous and sequential approaches to the description of abnormal behavior. The principal methodological tool of simultaneous methods is multivariate analysis. An assumption often made when multivariate analysis is the methodology employed is that all of the factors which produce the event or phenomenon we are studying operate "simultaneously." The question implicit in the multivariate approach is: what variables or combination of variables will best predict the occurrence of the behavior being studied? For example, in the study of abnormal behavior, we might wish to ask what variables predict whether psychiatric hospitalization will occur, and we might begin by trying to discover whether socioeconomic class, marital conflict, traumatic childhood events, or a combination of these factors are involved.

However, we know that these factors do not operate at the same time and we need instead an approach that accounts for the fact that *behavior patterns develop in sequence.* The idea of events being sequential is of great importance, because a particular factor may have to occur at a certain point in the sequence in order to operate in a causal fashion. If it occurs at other points in the sequence its effects may be negligible.

Becker (1963) offers the example of habitual drug use:

> Let us suppose, for example, that one of the steps in the formation of an habitual pattern of drug use—willingness to experiment with the use of the drug—is really the result of a variable of personality or personal orientation such as alienation from conventional norms. The variable of personal alienation, however, will only produce drug use in people who are in a position to experiment because they participate in groups in which drugs are available; alienated people who do not have drugs available to them cannot begin experimentation and thus cannot become users no matter how alienated they are. Thus, alienation might be a necessary cause of drug use, but distinguish between users and nonusers only at a particular stage in the process. (pp. 23–24)

Perhaps now we can better appreciate the reason for the use of the term "career" in the social perspective. The concept of career implies a sequence of movements from one social position to another. In addition, the idea of career contingencies—those factors which are responsible for mobility from one position to another—may seem more real and useful to us.

Social accounts of the development of deviant behavior often have the idea of career contingencies implicit in them. For example, Goffman (1959) writes of the "moral career of the mental patient" and Becker (1963) describes "becoming a marijuana user."

The flow diagram used to describe Scheff's (1966) account of the career of the chronic residual deviant is a specific application of the sequential approach. Buckley (1966) notes that this method of description is a product of modern systems research; to place a general verbal theory within this more rigorous context, he finds, carries with it a number of advantages.

First, such a system allows the explicit labeling of propositions and variables within the theory and allows relations and potential relations between propositions to be made specific. Second, as a result of this increase in explicitness, research hypotheses are easily formulated from an examination of the propositions and the relationship that exists between them. Third, the systematic nature of theories cast in this form implies not merely the consideration of the relations of single variables to each other but also the relations between whole complexes of variables. The variety of problems as elaborate as those posed by the systematic study of abnormal behavior seems to require an approach that allows enough complexity to consider the problem at hand.

Finally, an approach of this kind incorporates as a natural part of the system certain mechanisms that seem important in capturing the process involved in the development of abnormal behavior. For example, within Scheff's own system, a number of "feedback loops" are incorporated to depict the manner in which sets of events lead from one to another and may produce stabilized or even amplified sequences of events.

Thus a sequential approach to the description of abnormal behavior, particularly if it is cast in a flow chart, would seem to recommend itself strongly to the study of abnormal behavior. Perhaps other perspectives on abnormal behavior considered in this way could profit from the explicitness of this approach.

Summary

In our commentary we have seen that the concept of role as Sarbin describes it can serve as an important mediator between individual psychological events and social events in the career of the mental patient. Furthermore, Sarbin's account provides us with a social explanation for abnormal behavior (thought disorder) which was previously thought to be best understood by the illness perspective.

In Goffman's description of the total institution we noted that a variety of adaptation patterns of inmates may account, in part at least, for the individual differences we observe in the behavior of institutionalized persons.

The social perspective provides at least two types of "causal" explanations for the occurrence of abnormal behavior. First, Becker has argued that society "creates" abnormal or deviant behavior by making the social rules whose infraction constitutes deviance. Second, Dohrenwend and Dohrenwend have suggested that abnormal behavior may be at least in part the result of social pressure on disadvantaged ethnic and social groups.

Although many social accounts describe the mental patient as the passive victim of social forces, we suggested that this is certainly not always the case. At times the patient may play an active part in either entering or forestalling his entrance into the patient role.

Many but certainly not all social accounts may contain an ideological bias. The social perspective often contains an element of "unconventional sentimentality." That is, the argument is cast in a form which constitutes an indictment of society and a depiction of the mental patient as the "underdog." We have suggested that as long as they are made explicit, such ideological commitments are not necessarily detrimental to scientific progress.

Finally, we pointed out that the social perspective uses a sequential form of analysis. The sequential approach, particularly when carefully formalized, has a number of conceptual advantages that help to clarify the nature of the mental patient's career.

References

BECKER, H. S. *The other side: Perspectives on deviance.* New York: Free Press, 1963.

BECKER, H. S. *Outsiders: Studies in the sociology of deviance.* New York: Free Press, 1964.

BITTNER, E. Police discretion in emergency apprehension of mentally ill persons. *Social Problems,* 1967, *14,* 278–292.

BRAGINSKY, B. M., BRAGINSKY, D. D., & RING, K. *Methods of madness: The mental hospital as a last resort.* New York: Holt, Rinehart and Winston, 1969.

BROOM, L., & SELZNICK, P. *Sociology.* (3rd ed.) New York: Harper and Row, 1963.

BUCKLEY, W. A methodological note. In T. J. Scheff, *Being mentally ill: A sociological theory.* Chicago: Aldine, 1966, pp. 201–205.

DOHRENWEND, B. P., & DOHRENWEND, B. S. *Social status and psychological disorder: A causal inquiry.* New York: Wiley-Interscience, 1969.

GOFFMAN, E. The moral career of the mental patient. *Psychiatry: Journal for the Study of Interpersonal Processes,* 1959, *22,* 123–131.

GOFFMAN, E. *Asylums: Essays on the social situation of mental patients and other inmates.* Garden City, N. Y.: Anchor, 1961.

GOFFMAN, E. *Behavior in public places: Notes on the social organization of gatherings.* New York: Free Press, 1963.(a)

GOFFMAN, E.   *Stigma: Notes on the management of spoiled identity.* Englewood Cliffs, N.J.: Prentice-Hall, Inc., 1963. (b)

GOFFMAN, E.   *Interaction ritual: Essays on face-to-face behavior.* Garden City, N. Y.: Anchor, 1967.

HOFFMAN, A.   *Revolution for the hell of it.* New York: Dial, 1968.

HOLLINGSHEAD, A. B., & REDLICH, F. C.   *Social class and mental illness.* New York: Wiley, 1958.

HUGHES, E. C.   Dilemmas and contradictions of status. *American Journal of Sociology,* 1945, *1,* 353–359.

LEMERT, E. M.   *Social pathology: A systematic approach to the theory of sociopathic behavior.* New York: McGraw-Hill, 1951.

MILLER, D., & DAWSON, W. H.   Effects of stigma on re-employment of ex-mental patients. *Mental Hygiene,* 1965, *49,* 281–287.

NUNNALLY, J. C., Jr.   *Popular conceptions of mental health.* New York: Holt, Rinehart and Winston, 1961.

PHILLIPS, D. L.   Rejection: A possible consequence of seeking help for mental disorders. *American Sociological Review,* 1963, *28,* 963–972.

ROSENHAN, D. L.   Madness: In the eye of the beholder. (Review of T. J. Scheff, *Being mentally ill.*) *Contemporary Psychology,* 1968, *13,* 360–361.

SARBIN, T. R.   The dangerous individual: An outcome of social identity transformations. *British Journal of Criminology,* 1967, *7,* 285–295.

SARBIN, T. R.   The transformation of social identity: A new metaphor for the helping professions. In L. Roberts, N. Greenfield, & N. Miller (Eds.), *Comprehensive mental health: The challenge of evaluation.* Madison: University of Wisconsin Press, 1968.

SARBIN, T. R.   Schizophrenic thinking: A role-theoretical analysis. *Journal of Personality,* 1969, *37,* 190–206.

SCHEFF, T. J.   *Being mentally ill: A sociological theory.* Chicago: Aldine, 1966.

SCHEFF, T. J. (Ed.)   *Mental illness and social processes.* New York: Harper and Row, 1967.

SPITZER, S. P. & DENZIN, N. K.   *The mental patient: Studies in the sociology of deviance.* New York: McGraw-Hill, 1968.

YARROW, M. R., SCHWARTZ, C. G., MURPHY, H. S., & DEASY, L. C.   The psychological meaning of mental illness in the family. *Journal of Social Issues,* 1955, *11,* 12–24.

PART THREE
INTEGRATION
AND APPLICATION

CHAPTER 9

OVERVIEW
And a Look to the Future

A Brief Summary of Perspectives
on Abnormal Behavior

It should be clear at this point that the perspectives we have discussed differ in a variety of ways and that therefore direct comparison is difficult. Nevertheless a brief summary of the perspectives may be useful. In Table 9.1 the perspectives we have discussed are summarized in terms of six general dimensions. For each perspective we have listed the basic metaphor underlying the perspective, related subordinate concepts, presumed causal factors, the terms used to describe abnormal behavior, the type of therapeutic intervention implied by the perspective and the major proponents of the perspective.

In the introduction to this book we argued that the current state of conflict among perspectives on abnormal behavior represents a distinct stage in the development of the field of abnormal psychology. Kuhn (1962) and other historians and philosophers of science (Hanson, 1965) have pointed out that this stage in growth is characteristic of the early stages of most sciences. It is therefore appropriate to review Kuhn's account and to examine its implications for the future of the field of abnormal psychology.

Kuhn argues that science is not the mere accumulation of facts, as the popular view suggests. Instead the history of science consists of periods of "normal science" where one or perhaps two views are dominant and direct the way in which we see the world. During periods of normal science nearly all practitioners of the science engage in research, which is a "strenuous and devoted attempt to force nature into the conceptual boxes supplied by professional education." (p. 5)

Normal science will, because a single view is dominant, often suppress

TABLE 9.1

	Psychoanalytic	Illness	Learning	Moral	Humanistic	Social
Basic metaphor	Intrapsychic conflict	Disease	Learning	Morality; religion	Actualization; growth	Deviance; norm violation
Subordinate concepts	Id, ego, superego, anxiety, defense	Nosology, etiology, symptom, syndrome, prognosis	Stimulus, response, reinforcement, classical and operant conditioning	Sin, guilt, confession, expiation, symptom	Experience, self-concept, incongruity, conditions of worth	Norms, rule breaking, career, stigma
Causal factors	Intrapsychic conflict	Organic, biochemical, genetic	Reinforcement; classical and operant conditioning	Sinful behavior	Conditions of worth, deficiency needs	Diverse factors: organic, psychological, social. Labeling
How abnormal behavior is described	Defense and anxiety	Symptoms, syndromes, disorders	Maladaptive behavior	Symptoms that deal with anxiety and guilt	Defensive and disorganized behavior	Behavior is deviant; audience reaction emphasized
Means of therapeutic intervention	Psychoanalysis	Medical treatment; drugs, shock treatment, surgical procedures	Behavior therapy, desensitization, shaping	Integrity, therapy via confession and expiation	Client centered therapy; sensitivity training	Institutional reform
Major proponents	Freud	Meehl, Ausubel, Kraepelin	Skinner, Eysenck, Bandura, Ullmann, Krasner, Wolpe	Mowrer	Rogers, Maslow, May	Goffman, Becker, Scheff, Sarbin

novel observations because such observations may subvert a basic conceptual commitment. During these periods, the scientific community shares the belief that it knows what the world is like. At times this view may be defended at considerable cost.

This description of normal science is not meant to imply that a period of normal science is unproductive. On the contrary, the very rigidity and strength of commitment to a single conceptual scheme is one of its most redeeming features. It means that a number of problems will be solved because a set of basic assumptions and a particular methodology will be fully exploited.

But even the conceptual commitments of normal science are in some ways arbitrary, and novel observations cannot be permanently suppressed. Sooner or later a normal problem may resist solution if the accepted conceptual and methodological approach is used. Or perhaps a particular method of observation may yield unexpected results. The few practitioners of normal science who choose to follow such leads may then perform experiments which are considered "extraordinary" from the point of view of the prevailing normal science. Kuhn argues that this is the beginning of a "scientific revolution."

New paradigms or conceptual schemes will then emerge to account for the novel observations and the result is what Kuhn has called a "paradigm clash." Almost invariably the paradigm clash is between the prevailing view of normal science and the new conceptual scheme that emerges. Often the new paradigm will produce a shift in the problems available for scientific investigation. More important, it will transform the way in which the scientist sees his world.

Periods of paradigm clash are periods of controversy. But the controversy is not over minor issues of fact or method but over basic metaphysical assumptions. As Kuhn (1962) remarks, in periods of paradigm clash and scientific revolutions "Neither side will grant all the non-empirical assumptions that the other needs to make its case." (p. 147)

We would like to argue that the field of abnormal psychology is currently in the midst of such a scientific revolution. The basic conceptual commitments are not over questions of the nature of physical reality, as has been the case in physics. Instead the fundamental controversy is over *the nature of man*.

The period of normal science from which we are emerging is not characterized by a single dominant view but is one in which both the illness perspective and the psychoanalytic perspective have been dominant if not always comfortable companions. These perspectives will certainly continue to make substantive contributions to our understanding. New developments in the biological sciences suggest that the illness perspective will continue to be vigorous for some time to come. Nevertheless, the other perspectives we have discussed—moral, humanistic, learning, and social—are all emerging with their own fundamental assumptions about the nature of man and, by extension, about the way we should view abnormal behavior.

In the section that follows we will take a closer look at the current state of "the paradigm clash" now underway.

Some Dimensions of the Conflict

The conflict among perspectives on abnormal behavior is not simple and has a number of dimensions. Three of them are: first, that advocates of different perspectives have difficulty communicating with each other; second, that perspectives operate at different levels of analysis; and third, that perspectives are pretheoretical in nature.

The communication problem

Kuhn argues that communication difficulties exist among advocates of different perspectives for at least three reasons. The first is that the proponents of competing perspectives will often disagree about the list of problems that any perspective must resolve. That is, their standards or definitions of science are not the same. For example, the illness perspective may suggest that the fundamental problem to be resolved is the discovery of an organic etiology. On the other hand, the learning perspective asks the question of how abnormal behavior is shaped by reinforcement contingencies; and the social perspective is most concerned not with abnormal behavior itself but how others may react to it.

A second reason for the communication problem has to do with a confusion that arises in the use of scientific vocabulary. Since new perspectives are many times derived from old ones, they often incorporate much of the vocabulary and conceptual apparatus that the traditional paradigm had previously employed. But the difficulty is that the new perspective seldom uses these borrowed elements in the traditional way. Consequently, advocates of different perspectives, even when using the same words, may be talking at cross purposes. For example, the term "symptom" may be used very differently by advocates of the illness, behavioral, and psychoanalytic perspectives. For advocates of the illness perspective it is part of a syndrome and a behavioral manifestation of a *disease*. From the learning perspective the symptom may be simply a single behavior that is subject to the principles of *reinforcement*. The psychoanalytic perspective may view a symptom as a defense mechanism indicating *intrapsychic conflict*.

The third reason for the communication difficulty is that the proponents of competing perspectives "practice their trade in different worlds." As Kuhn puts it,

Practicing in different worlds . . . groups of scientists see different things when they look from the same point in the same direction. Again, that is not to say that they can see anything they please. Both are looking at the world, and what they look at has not changed. But in some areas they see different things, and they see them in different relations one to the other. That is why a law that cannot even be demonstrated to one group of scientists may occasionally seem intuitively obvious to another. (p. 149)

Kuhn's description bears some striking similarities to our account of the nature of perspectives in Chapter 2. And as we suggested there, it is a potent reason for the difficulty in communication between advocates of different perspectives.

Levels of analysis

There is perhaps another reason for the conflict between perspectives which is related to the remarks we have just made. It is that the perspectives we have discussed do not all describe the phenomenon of abnormal behavior at the same level of analysis.

The scientific disciplines may be ordered on a rough continuum from molecular to molar levels of analysis, ranging from physics through chemistry, biology, psychology, and social analysis. For our purposes we may consider four general levels: biological, intrapersonal, interpersonal, and social. The biological level refers to physiological and genetic events occurring in a single individual. The intrapersonal level refers to intrapsychic events within a single person. The interpersonal level refers to events that occur between individuals, and the social level refers to events that occur between the individual and social institutions. Each of the perspectives we have discussed may be placed at some point or range of points along this continuum.

Of course, in most cases it is more accurate to suggest that a particular perspective occupies some range along this continuum since it is seldom the case that a particular perspective is described in terms of only a single level of analysis. Figure 9.1 shows the four levels of analysis that we have described and the general placement of the perspectives with respect to the levels of analysis.

In general, the fact that a perspective treats the phenomenon of abnormal behavior at a particular level of analysis implies at least two things. First, the basic metaphor or concept of the perspective will reflect the level of analysis occupied by the perspective. In addition, inferences about the causal factors in abnormal behavior are likely to be closely related to the level of analysis of the perspective. Thus, for example, the illness perspective takes as its basic metaphor the concept of disease, a biological concept.

Perspectives

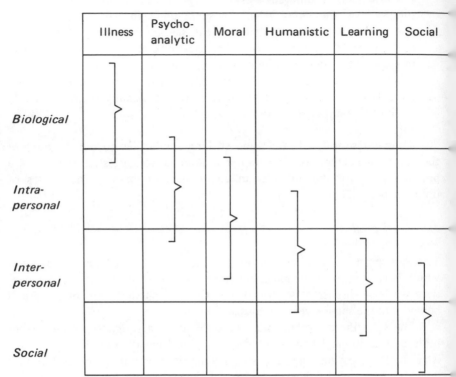

Figure 9.1   Levels of analysis of the perspectives

Furthermore, the causal factors in the illness perspective tend to be genetic, biochemical, or physiological.

Placing perspectives at a particular level of analysis suggests the fact that the advocate of that perspective has made his "bet" as to how the phenomenon of abnormal behavior can best be understood. But we will argue here and later that a complete account of the phenomenon of abnormal behavior will not be derived from a single level of analysis. Instead, a more complete account of the phenomenon of abnormal behavior will be one which can encompass observations from a wide range of levels of analysis.

Perspectives are pretheoretical

It is conventional to refer to what we have called perspectives as theories, and we have resisted that temptation throughout our discussion. There are several reasons for this. First, we argued in the second chapter that perspectives were products of a particular process of thought which we described as metaphorical. They are preliminary formulations despite the fact that they often powerfully shape the way in which we see and organize the phenomenon of abnormal behavior.

Furthermore, the perspectives we have discussed do not meet the criteria for a scientific theory as advanced by Nagel (1959). Nagel suggested at least three criteria which might be used in deciding whether a particular conceptual approach can be considered a scientific theory. First, it must be possible to identify explicit consequences that will arise from the assumptions made by the perspective. This is necessary in order to judge the meaning of any empirical data for whatever assumption we are examining. Second, at least some of the theoretical assumptions and concepts of the theory must be given definite and unambiguous specifications in terms of some rules of procedure. These rules of procedure are often called operational definitions. Third, the propositions of the theory must be capable of being disconfirmed. Thus the theory cannot be formulated in such a way that it can be manipulated to fit whatever the evidence at hand may be.

Certainly it is true that the perspectives we have described are not all pretheoretical to the same degree. Perspectives differ in the degree to which the basic metaphor has been spelled out in terms of formal description, operationalization, and the statement of propositions.

Some perspectives have developed in the direction of formal theory only to a small degree. The psychoanalytic and the humanistic perspectives are examples. Other perspectives (or at least aspects of them) are somewhat more advanced. In particular, the illness perspective, the learning perspective, and the social perspective display a higher degree of formalization. But, in general, no perspective has reached the stage of rigor implied by the criteria for a theory that Nagel has described.

If the current state of the field is as we suggest, then advocates of different perspectives have difficulty communicating with one another. Furthermore, the perspectives themselves reflect differing levels of analysis, and are pretheoretical. We may then ask, what are the possible solutions to this state of affairs? How will the field develop? It is to that question that we now turn.

Scientific Progress as Evolution

At the outset of this chapter we suggested that scientific progress is characterized by periods of normal science followed by periods when several alternative perspectives compete for dominance. We also suggested that the field of abnormal psychology may now be entering one of the latter periods. But what then is the nature of scientific progress? Toward what goal, if any, does it move? Kuhn (1962) uses the analogy of biological evolution to describe the course of scientific progress.

The analogy that relates the evolution of organisms to the evolution of scientific ideas can easily be pushed too far. But [for the present purposes] it is very nearly perfect. The process described . . . as the resolution of revolutions is the selection by conflict within the scientific community of the fittest way to practice future science. The net result of a sequence of such revolutionary selections, separated by periods of normal research, is the wonderfully adapted set of instruments we call modern scientific knowledge. Successive stages in that developmental process are marked by an increase in articulation and specialization and the entire process may have occurred, as we now suppose biological evolution did, without benefit of a set goal, a permanent fixed scientific truth, of which each stage in the development of scientific knowledge is a better exemplar (pp. 171–172).

This is an extraordinary statement. It asserts that science has no goal toward which it progresses. Instead, science is a process from primitive beginnings and is characterized by increasingly detailed and refined understanding; but it moves toward no specific goal. If we accept this evolutionary analogy even tentatively we can then ask what will give a particular perspective its "survival value"? What are the characteristics of particular perspectives that will lead them to survive while others will die out? Both Kuhn (1962) and Toulmin (1961) have suggested characteristics that may give perspectives survival value. To these we have added some of our own.

A new perspective is more likely to be adopted if it can solve the problems that led older perspectives into crisis. For example, the failure of psychoanalysis to form propositions and assumptions which were disconfirmable has had much to do with its current loss of appeal. Similarly, the failure of the illness perspective to deal with the social impact of abnormal behavior has stimulated a great deal of the recent criticism of that perspective. Perspectives that survive will certainly have to be responsive to these and still other problems.

A new perspective is also more likely to have survival value if it is capable of predicting phenomena that were unexpected while the older perspective prevailed. To take but one example, the humanistic perspective suggests that abnormal behavior may in some cases present the possibility of positive personality growth.

The degree to which a perspective is capable of moving from a primitive metaphorical formulation to formalized theory will certainly be important for its survival. Thus, perspectives must develop operationalized concepts and disconfirmable propositions. In the arena of science, perspectives that are not capable of such development will ultimately become historical curiosities.

A related consideration is that perspectives must be capable of describing abnormal behavior over a broad range of levels of analysis. Man is not merely a biological animal nor is he merely psychological or merely social in nature. He functions at all of these descriptive levels, and his behavior, both normal and abnormal, can be described at each level.

It is likely that perspectives will survive also for esthetic reasons. They may be retained because the scientist finds them more "suitable" or more "appropriate" or more "elegant."

Finally, a particular perspective may survive because it appeals to the scientist's basic prejudices about the nature of man. Of course, scientists are not above such concerns. These concerns often play a powerful if tacit role in the choice of a perspective.

We cannot predict with certainty which perspective on abnormal behavior will survive any more than we can predict the precise form that a species will ultimately take in the process of natural selection. But we can point to some of the characteristics it must possess in order to survive and perhaps to become the normal science of the future.

References

HANSON, N. R.   *Patterns of discovery*. New York: Cambridge University Press, 1965.

KUHN, T. S.   *The structure of scientific revolutions*. Chicago: University of Chicago Press, 1962.

NAGEL, E.   Methodological issues in psychoanalytic theory. In S. Hook (Ed.), *Psychoanalysis, scientific method, and philosophy*. New York: New York University Press, 1959.

TOULMIN, S.   *Foresight and understanding*. Bloomington: Indiana University Press, 1961.

CHAPTER 10

APPLICATION OF THE PERSPECTIVES

In Chapter 2 it was suggested that the perspectives we have discussed affect the "raw data" of abnormal psychology, the case history. In this chapter a generalized case history is presented, which has then been rewritten from the point of view of each perspective.

Perspectives shape not only what we "see" but also what we *look for* in formulating a case. As a result, the case histories may at times omit information—for example, earlier life events—that would have seemed crucial to the advocate of a particular perspective in reconstructing the case.

The six versions that result are in some ways caricatures. That is, they systematically distort the generalized case history to conform with the basic assumptions and point of view of the perspective. But a caricature can be instructive. It points up the distinguishing features of the perspective by exaggeration. Thus, while these case histories are in some ways distortions, they also demonstrate how the basic metaphor of each perspective selects from and shapes the raw data of abnormal behavior to produce six different yet coherent views.

A Generalized Case History: Amy J.

Mrs. Amy J. is a 34-year-old married woman. She is from a large midwestern town of approximately one half million people. Amy left school to work when she was 16, even though she had two years of high school to complete before graduation. She is an only child and both of her parents are still living. They live in the same neighborhood as does Amy and her husband. Amy's husband works in a factory at a semiskilled job that involves shift work. Although the family cannot be described as poor, their income seems not to be sufficient to allow substantial savings after all the bills are paid. Amy works as a part time waitress in a coffee shop to supplement the family income.

The first discernible indications of Amy's difficulties were noticed by her husband. Over a period of several months, he reported, she began to pay less attention to her housework; at times he would come home and no meal would have been prepared. He reported that "It was almost as if she forgot to make dinner, but I didn't say much about it . . . you know how it is when you're tired from work . . . you don't want to talk."

At about this time Amy's parents also reported noting signs of changes in Amy's behavior. Her mother reported that Amy "looked nervous" and that she "didn't seem to be herself." Amy's mother was particularly concerned because, as she put it, "We have always known our Amy well and if something was wrong she would let us know."

Both Amy's husband and her parents mentioned to Amy that they noticed a change in her behavior and inquired about her health on several occasions. As her father put it, "We figured she wasn't getting enough sleep or something. You know, if you don't get enough sleep that can really make you feel bad."

A few weeks after these first signs of difficulty were noted by her husband and parents, Amy began to have crying fits. She would often burst into tears when her husband asked her if she had remembered to do something for him or if he appeared irritated with her. At this time, Amy began to fail to report to work as often as once a week. She had had an excellent record of attendance before this, and although her employer was concerned he decided not to say anything in hopes that things would work themselves out.

As Amy's crying episodes became more frequent, her husband grew genuinely worried and irritated. At this point the husband consulted with her parents. As he described it later, "I figured I should talk to them about Amy since she was an only child. They always seemed to know what she was thinking, even when she didn't herself. They are the kind of parents who really care."

Amy's husband and parents agreed that "she wasn't acting like herself" and that the crying episodes were getting worse. They decided that they would "keep an eye on her" and that if things did not improve, they would encourage her to see a physician. Approximately two more weeks passed during which her mother and father visited more frequently in the afternoon and evening. Repeated inquiries concerning her health were met with silence or disclaimers such as "I'm OK, don't worry."

Amy's husband and parents again discussed her behavior. They agreed that Amy was getting not better but worse, and that recently she had been giving all of them "funny looks" when they asked how she felt. As a result of their discussion, it was decided to have Amy see a physician.

Amy's parents and husband decided to tell her together so that she would know that they were all concerned.

Amy greeted the decision of the husband and parents quietly but repeated her denial that anything was wrong. They made an appointment for her to see a physician on the following Wednesday.

When Amy's husband returned home after work on Tuesday evening, Amy was not there. After several hours he became concerned and went out looking for her. After another several hours of fruitless search, he called the police department and reported her missing.

She was found in the early morning hours by a police patrol. The following is an excerpt from their report:

> Subject was found wandering in a vacant lot at the corner of Green and Elm Streets. She was not wearing a coat and had on bedroom slippers. Subject was crying and we had difficulty getting her to identify herself. Subject kept repeating, "They're working on my mind." Since subject would not identify herself she was taken into custody.

Amy spent the evening in jail before she was identified and returned to her husband. Repeated questioning by the husband failed to reveal Amy's reasons for running away. At this point, her husband again called her parents and reported the incident. They came over immediately but their questions yielded no more information than her husband's had concerning the reason for her behavior.

It was decided to drive her to the doctor's office to keep the appointment previously made. Amy strongly resisted going but was finally convinced to go along. On arriving in the doctor's waiting room she burst into tears, repeating over and over, "I don't want to see him . . . I don't want to see any doctors." She could not be calmed and finally the physician gave her a sedative and recommended that she be put under observation at the state psychiatric hospital. As he described it later, "This woman was quite agitated and seemed somewhat irrational. I thought under the circumstances the best thing was to put her under observation."

When Amy learned that she was to spend two weeks in the state psychiatric hospital, she glared at her husband and ceased talking altogether. Repeated explanations that she "was just going for a rest and a checkup" seemed only to drive her into deeper withdrawal. She refused to speak to her husband or parents but muttered at several points that "they are trying to get rid of me."

Amy was placed on the admissions ward of the state psychiatric hospital. She was given a grey smock to replace her own clothing and her personal effects were taken away and kept in safekeeping for her. She was placed under intensive observation; the following is taken from the nurses' notes in Amy's folder.

Patient is quiet and withdrawn. She will not socialize with other patients and ignores them when they approach her. Her manner appears very suspicious and she replies to questions by asking, "Why do you want to know?" Patient goes to meals with the rest of the ward but eats very little. Patient is not cooperative about ward routine and seems somewhat disoriented. She tries the doors frequently during the day even though she knows they arc locked.

After two weeks of observation, Amy was interviewed at a psychiatric staff conference which included a social worker, the nurses on her ward, the ward physician, and a psychologist. What follows is the physician's report of that staff conference.

Patient is a 34-year-old, white, married female. At the time of admission she appeared withdrawn and depressed. Prior to admission she had been found wandering in a field by the police.

Her behavior on the ward had been withdrawn and generally uncooperative. Nurses' report indicates some suspiciousness and the report of the referring physician suggests some ideas of influence. Affect is somewhat flattened. Memory for remote and immediate events is not markedly impaired but she is unable to report with accuracy the events surrounding her arrest. Judgment is somewhat faulty and she insists she is just here for a rest, although she admits that she is in a psychiatric hospital. Orientation for place is intact but she is somewhat disoriented for person. She does not know the name of the ward personnel or the ward physician. Orientation for time is fair. She does know the month and the year, but is vague about the exact date and day of the week. Insight appears somewhat impaired. She does not know exactly why she is here but reports that she feels she is being watched by ward personnel. She appeared quite guarded in my interview with her but did admit that she was afraid that her relatives might be trying to get rid of her. She also said she felt as if people were "trying to read my mind and to work on it."

Current diagnostic impression is: *Schizophrenic reaction, acute undifferentiated type with depressive features and paranoid trends.*

It is recommended that hospitalization be continued and that the case be reviewed again in one month.

A conference with Amy's husband and parents, the ward physician, and the social worker followed, and the recommendations of the staff were communicated to the relatives. It was explained that the staff felt a brief stay in the hospital would be beneficial for her and that it was hoped she could be sent home in the husband's custody in about a month. Amy was then brought in and informed of the staff decision in the presence of her mother, father, and husband. She was told that everyone felt it was the best thing for her and that she would be "back to normal in no time." Amy greeted this news with a flash of anger and resentment, shouted, "You want to get rid of me!" and then burst into tears. Following this outburst she was returned to the ward and given an extra dose of medication.

Amy was discharged the following month as "much improved." She no longer had the fits of uncontrollable crying, but she had become quite taciturn. In his discharge report the ward physician stated that "no schiz-ophrenic ideation could be elicited." When Amy learned of her imminent discharge, she showed a great deal of apprehension. The social worker reported that Amy was quite concerned with "what people will think." Attempts to reassure her seemed to help to allay her fears somewhat.

Upon her return home, Amy found that everyone she met who knew about her hospitalization was quite concerned about her welfare. Her husband had arranged to work the day shift so that he could be with her at night. She discovered that her mother and father would visit her at frequent intervals during the day, saying that they "were just driving by and wondered how things were going." Amy found it difficult to accomplish household duties, and occasionally when her husband would return home she would still be in her bathrobe. He said little about this but it seemed to her that at times he looked at her peculiarly when this would happen.

After several weeks her husband suggested that perhaps she would enjoy going back to her job as a waitress on a part time basis and she agreed. Amy returned to the coffee shop and asked the manager if she could have her old part time job back. The manager replied that he was sorry but that someone had been hired in her absence. He suggested that perhaps she should look for a job where she "wouldn't have to deal with people so much" and offered to help her find such a job. Amy reacted to this remark with considerable emotion. She ran out of the shop in tears. The manager was distressed by her reaction and called her husband to inform him of what had happened. The husband immediately left work and began to look for her. He also called the police because, as he noted later, "I didn't know what she might do because of her condition."

Amy was found by the police standing on a bridge staring vacantly into the water below. Her clothes were disheveled and she was unresponsive when asked what she was doing there. Amy was returned home and after her parents and husband had a hurried conference, they decided to hospi-talize her for her own protection. The husband called the psychiatric hospital and reported what had happened to the staff physician. He agreed that she should be hospitalized immediately.

This time, when Amy was informed of their decision, the parents and husband noted that she did not seem surprised or particularly disturbed.

She agreed to hospitalization quite passively and remarked, "I must be sick; I don't know what's wrong."

The Psychoanalytic Perspective

Amy J. is a 34-year-old married woman and an only child. Her early difficulties included severe anxiety and extreme defensiveness. When asked about her difficulties by her concerned parents and husband, she responded with defensive denial. She denied any problems by stating, "I'm OK, don't worry."

At the same time, Amy began to regress. Her regression was reflected in her failure to perform routine household chores and her failure to appear for work as a waitress. The regressive behavior continued, and in addition Amy began to have uncontrollable fits of crying.

The denial and regression may be interpreted as attempts to deal with the intense anxiety resulting from a deep-rooted id–ego conflict. Id impulses reflecting a need for dependence had come into conflict with ego motives to cope with the demands of reality in the form of her household and job obligations. Since the dependency needs appeared to be intense, it is likely that they reflect fixated needs at the oral stage of development. Fixation at the oral stage often manifests itself in an infantile need to be cared for.

When Amy's husband and parents suggested that she visit a physician, the id–ego conflict was intensified and resulted in intense anxiety and projection. She accused her parents of "trying to get rid of her." Thus, her own need to escape from the reality demands and responsibilities of her own life was projected upon her parents and husband. The intensity of her emotional reactions and her irrationality prompted the examining physician to recommend hospitalization.

Once in the hospital, she remained suspicious and distrustful. At the same time, the supportive hospital setting served the purpose of meeting Amy's dependency needs and the severity of the id–ego conflict lessened to some degree. However, the conflict remained unresolved. Her anxiety increased again briefly when she learned of her imminent discharge from the hospital. For Amy, discharge symbolized the potential loss of support for her dependency needs and thus reactivated the basic conflict.

Nevertheless, she was discharged and soon the unresolved conflict began to reassert itself. Regression reappeared in the form of a continued inability to cope with household chores. At times her husband would find her still in her bathrobe at the end of the day.

The struggle between the ego demands to function effectively and the infantile needs of the id continued and after several weeks she reapplied for her old job as a waitress. Naturally, she was deeply conflicted about this venture and when she learned that her employer had no intention of rehiring her, her ego was overwhelmed and she ran out of the shop in tears. She was later found standing on a bridge in a disheveled condition.

Her remarks when found reflected the fact that her basic conflict was still repressed and completely out of awareness. Amy remarked in a bewildered tone, "I don't know what's wrong." She was subsequently rehospitalized.

Unless the basis of the fixated oral needs and resulting id–ego conflict are explored in intensive psychoanalysis, it is likely that Amy will continue to experience episodes of regression and need periodic hospitalization.

The Illness Perspective

PATIENT   Amy J.   MALE____   FEMALE X

AGE   34   SINGLE____   MARRIED X

DIAGNOSIS: 1. Schizophrenic Reaction, acute undifferentiated type
             2. Depression
MEDICATION: Thorazine, 20 mg. t.i.d.

Amy J. is a 34-year-old, well-nourished, white married female. The onset of her illness was marked by symptoms of anxiety, fear, depression, and emotional turmoil including episodic crying. Ideas of reference also became apparent early in the patient's illness. She is reported to have believed that people were "working on her mind" and that her relatives were "trying to get rid" of her.

The precipitating event associated with the acute onset of her illness was observed by the family physician. He reported her to be agitated and irrational and recommended hospitalization.

The symptoms displayed by the patient are characteristic of acute undifferentiated schizophrenia, distinguishable from simple schizophrenia by the acute onset. This diagnostic impression is confirmed by the staff physician's mental status examination report, which follows.

Patient is a 34-year-old, white, married female. At the time of admission she appeared withdrawn and depressed. Prior to admission she had been found wandering in a field by the police.

Her behavior on the ward has been withdrawn and generally uncooperative. Nurses' report indicates some suspiciousness and the report of the referring physician suggests some ideas of influence. Affect is somewhat flattened. Memory for remote and immediate events is not markedly impaired but she is unable to report with accuracy the events surrounding her arrest. Judgment is somewhat faulty and she insists she is just here for a rest, although she admits that she is in a psychiatric hospital. Orientation for place is intact but she is somewhat disoriented for person. She does not know the names of the ward personnel or the ward physician. Orientation for time is fair. She does know the month and the year, but is vague about the exact date and day of the week. Insight appears somewhat impaired. She does not know exactly why she is here but reports that she feels she is being watched by ward personnel. She appeared quite guarded in my interview with her but did admit that she was afraid that her relatives might be trying to get rid of her. She also said she felt as if people were "trying to read my mind and to work on it."

Current diagnostic impression is: *Schizophrenic reaction, acute undifferentiated type with depressive features and paranoid trends.*

The patient was discharged approximately one month after admission. At that time there was a marked remission of her presenting symptoms.

Patient was readmitted as a result of a recurrence of her schizophrenic symptomatology. It was reported that she displayed some suicidal behavior at that time.

In the light of the recurring schizophrenic episodes, a change of diagnosis to *Chronic undifferentiated schizophrenic* should be considered.

The Learning Perspective

Amy J. is a 34-year-old married woman who works part time as a waitress. Little is known about her reinforcement history. However, the fact that she was an only child suggests that she had previously received a relatively high level of positive reinforcement in the form of attention from her parents.

Amy's principal pattern of maladaptive behavior is characterized by a general decrease in the frequency of emitted behavior. Examples of responses in her behavioral repertoire that had decreased in frequency include performing household chores, preparing meals, and reporting to work. These behaviors had previously been maintained by their effect on stimulus persons in her environment who controlled reinforcement, particularly her husband. When Amy's husband failed to praise her or to pay attention to her, the reduction in positive reinforcement resulted in a lowered level of emitted behavior or "depression."

The stimulus properties of Amy's maladaptive behavior elicited attention, a generalized reinforcer, from her husband and her parents. The increased attention is reflected in their concern about her health and their decision to "keep an eye on her." Since much of their attention was contingent upon her episodes of crying and lowered level of responsiveness, the frequency of the maladaptive behavior increased as a result of this systematic positive reinforcement.

When it was suggested that she see a physician, Amy's response was also maladaptive. The stimulus situation involving physicians may have been associated in the past with aversive consequences or negative unconditioned stimuli. Her response suggests that this is the case, since she avoided this threatening situation by running away the night before the scheduled visit. As with most maladaptive avoidance responses, this behavior had additional aversive consequences, including arrest and incarceration. The "vicious cycle" quality of this pattern of behavior is evident in the sequence of avoidance responses followed by further negative reinforcement.

The anxiety-provoking power of the situation involving the visit to the physician remained quite strong since Amy's previous avoidance responses had provided no opportunity for extinction to occur. As a result, when she was forced to confront this stimulus situation by her husband and parents, her anxiety response and attempts to escape were intense. The resulting behavior was seen as sufficiently maladaptive by those controlling reinforcers in her life to warrant hospitalization.

It should be noted that hospitalization constituted a reinforcing event for Amy's parents and husband since it marked the termination of her aversive behavior for them.

Once hospitalized, Amy's behavior came under the control of a different set of reinforcement contingencies, those of the institution and staff. Attempts to affect her environment through emotional behavior were met with a variety of aversive consequences, including withdrawal of positive reinforcement and sedation. Amy soon learned the "patient role" and became quiet and unobtrusive.

When released from the hospital, Amy re-entered her home situation where her low level of instrumental behavior again received considerable attention as well as other forms of contingent social reinforcement from her parents and husband. Predictably, her "depressed" behavior again increased in frequency.

At this point she lost her job, and the behavior by her employer constituted yet another aversive stimulus situation. Her husband and her parents again saw her escape from the situation as maladaptive. Their decision to rehospitalize her was immediate, since this response had resulted in the termination of the aversive consequences of Amy's behavior for the parents and husband on a previous occasion.

The Moral Perspective

Our knowledge of Amy begins only after her abnormal behavior has already taken place. Although we have little direct information about what she has done, we do know that she had recently failed to report for work. It is possible that she feels her conduct and perhaps even her honesty in her job has been questionable. In any case this is an area which definitely requires further exploration. Thus we have little information concerning what she has actually done; however, this is not surprising if one considers that very often our abnormal acts are concealed from others.

Amy's guilty knowledge of her past abnormal behavior naturally resulted in a number of quite normal but intense emotional reactions. Her reactions were marked enough to be noticed by her husband and parents, who later remarked that she "looked nervous" to them on a number of occasions. As Amy's guilt and anxiety intensified she began to grow depressed and to have what her husband described as "crying fits." These emotional outbursts are understandable once we realize that Amy's crying and depression are normal emotional reactions to her knowledge of her own past abnormal behavior.

At this early stage in Amy's difficulties a number of symptoms— actually misdirected attempts at self-cure—began to emerge. These symptoms took several different forms but they also showed an essential similarity. Each symptom was an attempt to deal with Amy's feelings of very real guilt, anxiety, and depression; these feelings were intensified when she apparently began to suspect that her past abnormal behavior might be discovered.

Amy's actions revealed several examples of this sort of symptomatic behavior. She began to miss work and to avoid others, apparently because of her fear of discovery. When her husband began to ask Amy about her general welfare he reported that she began to give him "funny looks." It seems that she had begun to fear that her husband too might discover her past sins and she was unable to conceal her suspicion that this had happened. Another symptomatic attempt to cure herself was Amy's repeated and vehement denial that anything was wrong—as if her denial could somehow correct the situation.

At this point, Amy's husband and parents became concerned about her emotional outbursts and took several well-meaning but misdirected actions. They incorrectly assumed, as so often happens, that Amy's basic problem was with her "nerves" rather than her concealed abnormal behavior. As a result, they decided to have her seek professional medical help for what they believed to be her abnormal emotional reactions.

At this point the pattern of guilt and anxiety, followed by symptomatic attempts at relief and misdirected attempts by others to relieve the emotional discomfort, began to repeat itself. When she learned that she was to be seen by a physician, Amy became overwhelmed by guilt and fear of being discovered and tried to run away; this is clearly a symptomatic attempt to relieve her emotional pain. A second attempt to get her to see a doctor by the parents led to such an emotional outburst that she was hospitalized because of her "agitation." Since the hospital's therapeutic attempts were also directed at emotional relief, no real change took place, although Amy was subsequently released.

Although she returned to her home and family, Amy re-entered a situation that was essentially the same as before. The hospital experience did not provide her with an emotional re-education. It only drove her deeper into a pattern of duplicity and concealment.

An episode with her employer led to her rehospitalization. When she returned to ask for her job back on a part time basis, her employer refused her. Overwhelmed by feelings of guilt and unworthiness, which were apparently confirmed by her former employer's rejection, Amy fled from the shop in tears and was soon rehospitalized.

As long as her relatives and Amy herself continue to attempt to eliminate her emotional discomfort directly instead of allowing it to motivate her to change her abnormal behavior, her difficulties will continue as they have in the past. Only when Amy confesses her past sinful behavior and begins to make restitution for her actions will a lasting and effective self-cure be possible.

The Humanistic Perspective

Amy J. is a married woman in her early thirties. She is the only child of her parents who live in the same neighborhood as does Amy and her husband. As an only child, she grew up in an atmosphere in which she was the center of attention in the family. Like most parents, Amy's father and mother always "wanted the best" for her. So when she dropped out of high school at 16, they said very little about this although it was a bitter disappointment for them. They had always told her that she was "good" when she performed competently at school, but failures were greeted with disappointed silence. Thus, conditions of worth came to develop in Amy and she began to value herself for what others felt she should be rather than for what she was.

Amy was eager to please others, and when she married she made a special effort to do things which would please her husband. At first, the house was always immaculate and dinner was on the table when he arrived home at night. To supplement the family income she took a job as a part time waitress.

From time to time she was unable to meet the demands of her job and those of housewife. Although her husband said little about these lapses, Amy knew he noticed them and seemed to her to be disappointed. Slowly an incongruence developed between her concept of her self as an effective working housewife and the experience of her failures. The incongruence became even more severe when her husband and parents began to ask about her health. She knew this was their way of pointing out her failures to her.

At this point Amy's vulnerability to anxiety greatly increased and she began to react defensively to inquiries about her well-being. She denied that anything was wrong. At times, Amy herself was almost convinced by her denial. But at other times she couldn't convince herself that she was meeting the expectations of her husband and parents and would burst into tears.

When Amy's parents and husband suggested that she see a physician she interpreted the suggestion as a further indication of their belief that she was a helpless, ineffective person. She could no longer deny her difficulties, and the incongruence between her idea of the person she should be and the person that others saw greatly increased. This was an overwhelming experience for Amy and her behavior became disorganized. The night before her appointment she ran away from home rather than face the physician, who, it seemed to Amy, would also be critical of her for her failures. When she finally did see the physician her defenses were no longer adequate to deal with the incongruity and an intense emotional scene ensued. Seeing how irrational Amy seemed, the physician recommended that she be hospitalized. Naturally, this only seemed to confirm to Amy what she had feared all along—that she was seen by others as a worthless person.

In the hospital her concept of her self began to change. Everyone seemed to be treating her as someone who couldn't manage herself and she began to suspect that it was true. Nevertheless, she did not appear to be upset and after a time was released from the hospital. Back at home, her feelings of inadequacy did not make it any easier to deal with even routine household chores. Her parents also did a number of things to confirm her feelings of worthlessness. Although they said they were only "dropping by" she knew that they didn't trust her to get through the day.

It was in this state of vulnerability to threat that she finally summoned the courage to get back her old job as waitress. Perhaps her husband and parents would value her more if she were working again. But her employer only confirmed her worst fears about what people thought of her. He said there was no opening and suggested that she find a job where "she wouldn't have to work with people."

Overwhelmed by his rejection, she ran from the shop in tears. She wandered around in a disorganized state not knowing where she was going. Her husband finally found her standing on a bridge in a disheveled condition. Her remark at that time suggests that her self-concept had now changed and that she too now saw herself as an incompetent sick individual. She agreed to be rehospitalized and said, "I must be sick; I don't know what's wrong."

The Social Perspective

Amy's difficulties began when her husband and parents started to notice some puzzling changes in her behavior. Her husband reported that Amy had failed to make dinner for him on several occasions and had begun to neglect her housework. Her parents reported other changes in Amy's behavior. To them she didn't seem to be herself and appeared more nervous than usual. Like much residual rule-breaking, these initial norm violations on Amy's part were viewed by her husband and her parents with a minimum of concern. In fact, Amy's husband stated that it seemed to him that she had merely "forgotten" to make dinner. Her parents also minimized these early signs. From their point of view her peculiar behavior could have been the result of "not enough sleep." In any case, Amy's residual rule-breaking was initially minimized, rationalized, or denied.

Despite the attempts of Amy's husband and parents to minimize her rule-breaking behavior, her behavior persisted and in fact became more and more difficult to ignore. Amy began to have crying fits and failed to report to work. At this point, Amy's husband talked over the problem with her parents. They agreed to become more vigilant toward Amy's behavior but continued to refrain from mentioning their concern to Amy herself. It is likely that their vigilance provided cues to Amy that something was "wrong" with her.

Amy's husband and parents were beginning to suspect that she was suffering from "mental problems." This made them decide that they had to do something about her peculiar behavior. They decided to begin by having her examined by a physician.

Shortly afterward, Amy's actions precipitated a public crisis which made it virtually impossible for her husband and parents to deny any longer that her difficulties were more serious than they had thought at first. The evening before her appointment with the physician, Amy ran away from home and was subsequently picked up by the police. She refused to identify herself and broke a number of additional residual rules. She was wearing bedroom slippers when the police arrested her and was unable to give any coherent explanation for her behavior. The public crisis which Amy set in motion by running away from home reached its climax in the doctor's office. She burst into tears and repeated over and over again that she refused to see the doctor. At this point the physician decided that her behavior was "irrational" and that she should be sent to a psychiatric hospital for observation. Amy's husband and parents offered no objection; apparently they too were convinced that there was something mentally wrong with Amy.

The physician, as well as Amy's husband and parents, was apparently quite willing to interpret her behavior as mental illness. She behaved in ways that could be interpreted as consistent with the general stereotype of "craziness." She was agitated, extremely emotional, did not appear to be making sense, and could not be calmed down. Thus the compatibility of Amy's behavior with the deviant stereotype made it easy to label her problem as mental illness.

Amy did not share her husband's, her parents', and the physician's view of her behavior. She said she felt that "they are trying to get rid of me," which, in a sense, they were. Thus, at this point in the case, Amy resisted defining her own problems as "mental" and continued to resist being "type-cast" as a mental patient.

But in the hospital a number of events occurred that made it more difficult for Amy to resist thinking of herself as a mental patient. Her own clothes and personal belongings were taken away from her and she was given institutional clothing to replace it. She was placed in a locked ward under constant observation and was thus considered to be not responsible for her own behavior. The staff saw Amy's efforts against being identified as a mental patient simply as troublesome behavior, typical of mental patients. Finally, the staff conference that concluded with Amy's being diagnosed as "schizophrenic" officially labeled her as someone mentally ill.

As Amy's hospitalization continued, a variety of rewards and punishments in the psychiatric hospital setting offered additional inducements for her to accept her role as just another mental patient. When she displayed anger and resentment at being held in the hospital for an additional period of time she received heavy sedation. Similarly, when Amy's relatives had been informed of the staff's decision to keep her in the hospital, she was told that everyone felt that it was the best thing for her and that she "would be back to normal in no time"; this made it quite explicit that other people viewed her as not normal.

Eventually, the rewards and punishments operating in the institutional setting had their effect; rather than showing a variety of strong emotional reactions to her situation, Amy became quiet and withdrawn. However, when she learned that she was about to be discharged, she expressed considerable apprehension and concern with "what people will think." It is clear from this that Amy knew that mental patients were not considered ordinary persons and that once on the "outside" she would carry with her the stigma of the mentally ill.

Amy's concerns about her stigmatized identity apparently were well justified. Although a number of people expressed concern about her welfare, she couldn't help but realize that she was treated as someone who was "different."

Her transformed social identity and stigmatized status created yet another public crisis for Amy. When she attempted to regain her old job, her ex-boss said that the job had been filled. Furthermore, he suggested that she look for a job where "she wouldn't have to deal with people so much." The implication of his statement was clear to Amy: that as an ex-mental patient she was different, somehow not quite "right," and that she now possessed a spoiled identity.

Not surprisingly, Amy reacted to her ex-boss's remark with a great deal of emotion and ran out of the shop in tears. Amy's capabilities of self-control had been impaired as she had slowly incorporated the deviant role definition. She was found on a bridge, her clothes disheveled; she looked very much the mental patient. Her outburst, of course, was viewed by others as yet another instance of her mental problem, and she reentered the vicious circle: residual rule-breaking followed by the response of others to her rule-breaking and deviant status, and yet another hospitalization.

At this point, Amy has settled into a career of chronic "mental illness." Despite her effort to resist her new role definition as someone with mental problems, her bewilderment and dismay at others' rejection of her led her to accept the deviant role definition as the only alternative. As she agreed to be hospitalized a second time, Amy was heard to remark, "I must be sick; I don't know what's wrong."

INDEX